I0816326

ÉMILE ZOLA

ÉMILE ZOLA

A Determined Life

ROBERT LETHBRIDGE

REAKTION BOOKS

For Jonathan and Tamsin

Published by
Reaktion Books Ltd
Unit 32, Waterside
44–48 Wharf Road
London N1 7UX, UK
www.reaktionbooks.co.uk

First published 2025
Copyright © Robert Lethbridge 2025

All rights reserved

EU GPSR Authorised Representative
LOGOS EUROPE, 9 rue Nicolas Poussin, 17000, LA ROCHELLE, France
email: contact@logoseurope.eu

No part of this publication may be reproduced, stored in a retrieval system, or transmitted, in any form or by any means, electronic, mechanical, photocopying, recording or otherwise, without the prior permission of the publishers. No part of this publication may be used or reproduced in any manner for the purpose of training artificial intelligence technologies or systems.

Printed and bound in Great Britain by Bell & Bain, Glasgow

A catalogue record for this book is available from the British Library

ISBN 978 1 83639 017 6

CONTENTS

ABBREVIATIONS

References to Zola's writing have been included in the text using the following abbreviated forms:

Corr.	*Correspondance*, ed. Bard Bakker and others, 10 vols (Montreal: Presses de l'Université de Montréal/Paris: CNRS, 1978–95); vol. XI of this same edition was published as a supplement (*Lettres retrouvées*) in 2010, ed. Owen Morgan and Dorothy E. Spiers
EsA	*Écrits sur l'art*, ed. Robert Lethbridge (Paris: Classiques Garnier, 2021)
LA	*Lettres à Alexandrine, 1876–1901*, ed. Brigitte Émile-Zola and Alain Pagès (Paris: Gallimard, 2014)
LR	*Lettres à Jeanne Rozerot, 1892–1902*, ed. Brigitte Émile-Zola and Alain Pagès (Paris: Gallimard, 2004)
Ms	References to *Ms* and folio numbers are to Zola's handwritten preparatory work-notes for his novels, conserved (in the Nouvelles acquisitions françaises) in the Bibliothèque nationale de France
OC	*Œuvres complètes*, ed. Henri Mitterand, 15 vols (Paris: Cercle du livre précieux, 1966–70)
RM	*Les Rougon-Macquart*, ed. Henri Mitterand, 5 vols (Paris: Gallimard, 1960–67)

All translations are my own.

Zola and his box camera. Photograph by Jeanne Rozerot in the Tuileries Gardens, *c.* 1900.

Introduction

The nineteenth century was, it is generally agreed, the high point of realist fiction. Émile Zola (1840–1902) enjoys today a reputation as one of the greatest European novelists of the period. But it was not always thus, for his sheer popularity (supposedly reflecting, it was patronizingly assumed, the leisure habits of undemanding readers) seemed to exclude him from serious critical attention. That popularity is certainly not in doubt. The sales figures for Zola's major literary legacy, the twenty novels of his *Rougon-Macquart* series (1871–93), are astonishing: during his lifetime, nearly 2 million copies of individual novels were sold; by the millennium, ten times as many had been bought in France alone, with his best known, *L'Assommoir* (1877) and *Germinal* (1885), accounting for 7 million of them. And such figures can be multiplied several times over by translations of his work which Zola himself negotiated in the first instance, subsequently expanded by foreign publishers keenly aware, as they are still, of his similar appeal to an international reading public.

Only in 1952–3, around the fiftieth anniversary of his death, did things start to change. At that point, encouraged by national exhibitions and other celebrations of his prolific career, scholars began to investigate Zola's life and work in greater depth. This process was given its impetus by scrutiny of the manuscripts and work-notes carefully preserved for posterity by the novelist, almost all of which had been gifted to the national library in Paris by his widow in 1904. The result was a radically more detailed understanding of his habits of composition and how his fiction achieves its distinctive qualities.

This revaluation of Zola's literary work had for long been constrained, especially in France, by his intervention in the Dreyfus Affair.

The historic role he played in it is well known: his 'J'accuse', an open letter to the president of the Republic, published in *L'Aurore* on 13 January 1898, had a seismic impact. So devastating was Zola's indictment of the French army's collusion and cover-up that it reinvigorated the extended campaign to rehabilitate Alfred Dreyfus (1859–1935), the Jewish officer wrongly convicted – towards the end of 1894 – of spying for Germany. The 'Dreyfusards', those like Zola convinced of his innocence, were opposed by an alliance of Church and State. The 'anti-Dreyfusards', both nationalist and often rabidly antisemitic, denied the allegations in 'J'accuse', committed as they were to the defence of the honour of the military authorities, themselves perceived as representative of patriotic France. Dreyfus was finally rehabilitated in 1906. The Affair indelibly associated with his name, however, has never been forgotten. It is still frequently referenced as emblematic of irreconcilable ideological conflicts tearing a nation apart. Zola's posthumous reputation is inseparable from this most traumatic episode in modern French history, for the divisiveness engendered by the Affair was so long-lasting that it took the best part of half a century to be able to explore Zola's work without falling foul of political controversy.

Anglophone critics, in particular, exploited this newfound liberation from prejudice to illuminating effect. Angus Wilson's pioneering *Emile Zola: An Introductory Study of His Novels* (1952) benefitted from the insights of a fellow writer. But it was F.W.J. Hemmings's *Émile Zola*, originally published in 1953, that has been described as 'arguably the most influential book on Zola ever written'.[1] In the preface to the extensively revised edition of this study (1966), Hemmings justified the latter by pointing out that more work had been devoted to Zola in the intervening years than over the whole of the previous half-century. The corresponding growth of the body of relevant knowledge since that date has been of a different order of magnitude. For the decade 1970–80, for example, exhaustive Zola bibliographies list no less than almost 1,000 items. This proliferation of factual information and interpretative perspectives has continued apace, averaging around seventy publications each year and leaving aside innumerable reprintings of Zola's novels, often buttressed by the most recent research.

The most significant advance was the appearance of the fifteen-volume edition of his *Œuvres complètes* (1966–70), its 20,000 pages including texts never before accessible. This was followed by the publication of his long-anticipated correspondence (1978–95), without which, as generations of specialists had lamented, no comprehensive biography of Zola could be constructed. Some 5,000 letters, in addition to roughly double the same number he received (largely unpublished but also mostly conserved in the Bibliothèque nationale de France), are an indispensable source for tracking the chronology of Zola's working life and his relations with his contemporaries. They tell us relatively little, however, about his private self. When he was told in June 1884 that, for the first time, two of his letters were to be auctioned, Zola claimed to be relaxed about it: 'I don't have any secrets, the keys are in the cabinet; if my letters are published one day, they will neither disown any of my friendships nor contradict any of my declarations' (*Corr.*, V, 125). But, in practice, such apparent openness is limited to the public dimension of his life and work. A much more intimate view of the man has since been revealed by the publication of two sets of private letters: in 2004, those to his mistress, Jeanne Rozerot (1867–1914), by whom Zola had two children, Denise (1889–1942) and Jacques (1891–1963); and, in 2014, those to his wife Alexandrine (1839–1925). Many of these long letters to the two women in his life were written on the same day, thereby bringing us up close to the vicissitudes of a double life at several removes from Zola's public persona.

The present book takes as its premise that the time is ripe to engage in a reappraisal of Zola's achievements in the light of what we now know about his life and work.[2] For the increased availability of all the above source material enables us to largely overcome the challenges posed to would-be biographers by Zola himself. The story of his life both resists and invites scrutiny. Consistent with his refusal, after his earliest texts, to indulge in the confessional mode characteristic of Romanticism, he left no introspective memoirs or autobiography as such. The nearest he came to keeping a proper diary was the journals in which he recorded his impressions during his few visits abroad or when researching the far-flung locations of three or four of his novels.

Given his apparent determination to keep his private and public lives separate, it is all the more curious, at first sight, that Zola agreed to respond to a psychological experiment in 1895 designed to tease out his fears and fantasies. Over a whole year, he was subjected to a range of physiological and psychological tests by a young Dr Édouard Toulouse (1865–1947). On one occasion when he came to talk to Zola, one of the latter's servants benefitted from his medical training, but Toulouse's real project was devoted to exploring the then accepted relation between artistic genius and creative neurosis. If Zola's agreement to put himself through this invasive process was ostensibly justified by his own commitment to scientific progress, he may also have been flattered to be the subject of such a study. It tended to focus on aspects of Zola's personality largely hidden from view: his superstitions and phobias; his anxieties about impotence, and of not being able to complete a book or a speech; his arithmomania – counting steps, carriages, street lights and doors, and the significance for him of certain numbers, bringing either good or bad luck; and a morbid disposition responsible for frequently waking during the night to check whether he was still alive.[3]

Zola's letter of thanks to Dr Toulouse, dated 15 October 1896, would also serve as a preface to the published study. It gives expression to something approaching relief: that the study would act as a corrective to those who believed he had something to hide, and that his public image as a 'thick-skinned beast of burden' shackled to his writing labours could be dispensed with by critics now having access to the complexities of a 'brain as transparent as glass' (*Corr.*, VIII, 258). He added that the thousands of pages he had written were equally open to those inspecting his personality.

Zola himself seems to have been aware that Dr Toulouse's investigations had confirmed, in retrospect, much of what can be inferred from his novels and short stories or detected in non-fictional texts over his own signature: his many prefaces, including to the work of other writers; hundreds of newspaper articles; some of his letters. These allow us insights into his beliefs and values, political and cultural sympathies, and mood swings from contentment and euphoria to depression and self-doubt. In addition, of course, many of Zola's friends, colleagues and family have provided testimony, whether objective or not, of his temperament and concerns. Reading his fiction with a view to illuminating these remains problematic. Zola largely subscribes to the imperative of 'impersonality' often rehearsed by Gustave Flaubert (1821–1880): that, in the interests of sustaining for the reader the illusion of an unmediated representation of external reality, the author should be 'present everywhere but visible nowhere'. There are notable exceptions: John Lapp has shown that, prior to embarking on the *Rougon-Macquart* and while still in thrall to Romantic subjectivism, some of Zola's first novels are 'deliberately and unabashedly autobiographical'.[4] Almost four decades after these appeared, Zola himself felt able to admit as much: asked by an interviewer about his early life, he responded that he really had nothing to add beyond what he had already included in his books. But in his mature work, Zola was at pains to frustrate critics tempted by the uncanny resemblance between himself and fictional artists or writers.

To this end, his techniques included the deliberate distortion and displacement of dates. The protagonists of *L'Œuvre* (1886) and *Le Docteur Pascal* (1893) nevertheless provide the most unmistakeable, if partial, mirrors of their creator. But even in the most transparent cases, this is not entirely straightforward. *L'Œuvre*, for example, has complementary self-portraits in the juxtaposed antitheses of Sandoz, the writer, and Claude Lantier, the painter – as Edmond de Goncourt (1822–1896) uncharitably recognized: 'I like coming across Zola in his novels . . . but, honestly, to find him constructing from his personality, in a single book, two individuals . . . that's just too much.'[5] Nor are such amalgams to be found only in the *Rougon-Macquart*: they are also an intermittent feature of Zola's subsequent novel cycles, *Les Trois Villes* (1894–8) and *Les Quatre Évangiles* (1899–1902). In the case of these three major series we have the work-notes, which provide firm evidence of their autobiographical dimensions. Unlike the disembodied narrative voice of the novels themselves, these handwritten preparatory notes take the form of an interior monologue. They allow us an uncommon proximity to the travails of the novelistic imagination, and, cast in the first person, these notes are often punctuated by allusions to Zola's own experience.

Equally potentially revealing is the obsessive return to fictional scenarios which clearly have their origin in episodes from that personal experience. Exemplary in this respect is the case of typhoid contracted by him in Paris in the autumn of 1858 – so severe, he confided to writer and Zola biographer Paul Alexis (1847–1901), that at one stage it seemed he would not survive it.[6] A decade later, Zola put together a text recalling in detail his slow return to health, unfinished and not intended for publication but subsequently exploited almost word-for-word in the description of Serge Mouret's convalescence (also from a delirious bout of typhoid) in *La Faute de l'Abbé Mouret* (1875), during which the character recounts his symptoms.

The illness itself, with its sensation of limbs being crushed by an immoveable weight, is likened to being buried alive. In one of Zola's earliest novels, *Le Vœu d'une morte* (1866), the terminally stricken Daniel has 'the impression that he was already dead, finding himself buried in the earth' (*OC*, I, 213). This nightmare is periodically revisited: in the short story 'La Mort d'Olivier Bécaille' (1879); in *Germinal*'s minefield dramas of imprisonment underground; and in the episode in *La Bête humaine*

(1890) in which a locomotive is trapped within a collapsed tunnel. Another variant, although more pleasurable and psychologically intriguing, is identifiable in a short piece he first published in 1872 and subsequently incorporated in his *Nouveaux Contes à Ninon* two years later as one of a sequence of 'memories' whose reliability is left unclear: the narrator imagines himself locked in a lady's trunk, among her 'silky skirts, delicate underwear and all sorts of warm and perfumed things' (*OC*, IX, 406). Curiously, that same image of a trunk is used by Edmond de Goncourt in a journal entry of 17 April 1882: in a nasty swipe at what he considered Zola's self-enclosed abstraction from sexual realities, he extrapolated an unspeakably vulgar interpretation of the authorial fantasies being played out in Zola's fiction.[7]

There are other recurrent scenarios not adequately accounted for by reference simply to novelistic habit or technique, such as the voyeuristic organization of dramas of jealousy. In Zola's very first novel, *La Confession de Claude* (1865), the eponymous hero is alerted to his lover's infidelity by observing in a window the outline of her and his rival. For *La Curée* (1872), Zola originally planned that the betrayed Maxime should learn of his stepmother's renewed physical relationship with his father, thus finally establishing a quasi-incestuous sexual triangle, in a 'conjugal scene secretly witnessed by the son'. Although ultimately not exploited in the definitive text, this idea resurfaces in Maxime's earlier 'smutty story' of 'a cuckolded husband who had spotted, behind a curtain, the shadow of his wife in flagrante and that of her lover' (*RM*, I, 407). The most developed such catalyst of suffering occurs in *Nana* (1880), in which Count Muffat spends an entire night in the street watching the lighted window of his wife's lover's apartment, with his recognition of her silhouette marking his despair. That this should amplify almost exactly the emotional trauma of the scene in *La Confession de Claude* is particularly interesting, given that text's acknowledged autobiographical dimensions: 'Claude' being the pseudonym Zola used in his early journalism; the narrator's experience precisely reflecting, in both tone and substance, what he was writing to his friends in years immediately prior to the publication of the novel; and the modelling of the figure of Laurence on a certain Berthe, with whom, in February 1861 (as he confided in letters that month), Zola had his first sexual relationship.

We know little about this young woman except that she apparently transferred her affections to one of his close friends at the time, Georges Pajot (1842–1904), whose letter to Zola on the appearance of *La Confession de Claude* underlined the accuracy of the transposed portrait of Berthe while evoking, in decidedly ambiguous terms, his giving her a temporary roof over her head. Colette Becker, the scholar who documented this anecdote, concluded that the two men never saw each other again after 1870.[8] By chance, however, Zola bumped into Pajot at the October 1897 wedding of the daughter of his friend, the painter Antoine Guillemet (1841–1918). He was not best pleased, for reasons of which Alexandrine was obviously aware, to be reminded by a tiresome Pajot of this episode in the past: 'you can imagine', Zola wrote to his wife, 'how this filled me with sadness' (*LA*, 202).

A further layer of interpretative possibility is offered by another early novel, *Madeleine Férat* (1868), with its stress, inspired by Zola's enthusiastic reading of Jules Michelet's bestseller *L'Amour* (1858) (as he explained in an article in *La Tribune* of 29 November 1868), that a first lover possesses a woman for her entire life, to the distress of his successors. Laurence, in *La Confession de Claude*, is 'soiled for ever' (*OC*, I, 43). In *Madeleine Férat*, Guillaume is haunted by his wife's sexual history: confronted by portraits of his friend Jacques, to whom she had given her virginity in the very room in which he himself becomes her lover, it destroys his marriage. The extent to which Zola subscribed to this eccentric theory also underlies the plotting of Gervaise's return to Lantier's bed in *L'Assommoir* and the murderous rage of Roubaud, in *La Bête humaine*, when he belatedly discovers that his wife had been seduced during her adolescence.

What prevents us from dismissing all the above parallels as either derivative or arbitrary is a set of intimate facts only brought to light the best part of a century after Zola's death.[9] There has long been a legend that Zola's future wife – Alexandrine Meley, but at the time known as Gabrielle – may have been introduced to him by a former lover of hers. Its only substance is provided by the unpublished notes of the writer Henry Céard (1851–1924), perhaps the most privileged of the Zola couple's confidants for many years. These notes record that when Zola first met Alexandrine in March 1864, she was then the mistress of a medical student, Louis Barbelet, and that during one of his holiday absences from Paris she became close to Zola, but not definitively so, before, like Madeleine in relation to Jacques in *Madeleine Férat*, returning temporarily to her lover. But there is also a documented fact with implications beyond analogies between art and life or the theme of sexual jealousy so prevalent in Zola's fiction: for before he consummated his relationship with Alexandrine later in 1864 (on 24 or 28 December, according to, respectively, an inscribed copy of *La Confession de Claude* or the couple's subsequent 'anniversary' reminders), she had in 1859 given birth to an illegitimate child, of father unknown or not declared, which was neither the first nor the last of Zola's family secrets.

Related to a principled masking of the private self were Zola's efforts to project a public persona invulnerable to the kind of attacks to which his 'scandalous' novels were often subject. In the preface to *L'Assommoir*, for example, he countered accusations of having a political agenda (in alerting readers to proletariat misery) by stressing his own credentials as 'a respectable bourgeois'. He refuses there to confront 'the lies about me'. It is clear, however, that this was precisely the motivation behind the first biography devoted to him, Alexis' *Émile Zola*: *notes d'un ami* (1882). Its very title underlines the sympathetic perspective adopted by Zola's best friend, and it is so 'authorized' a version that Zola even dictated to him some of its passages as well as correcting the proofs of the book. It remains a mostly reliable, if compressed and sanitized, account of the writer's life up until its date of publication, as well as functioning as advance publicity for the novels of the *Rougon-Macquart* not yet written. When the book appeared, it was subject to a devastatingly parodic review by Albert Woolf, spread across the front page of *Le Figaro* of 17 February 1882, mocking Alexis' affording Zola the status of a 'genius for the ages'. With the wisdom of hindsight, its lacunae might have problematized a heroic narrative. That, unsurprisingly, was not its subject's view. In correspondence with Ferdinand Chastenet (1858–1902), an administrator at the Théâtre Antoine who had already published a guide to the characters of the *Rougon-Macquart* and who now wanted to provide an updated sequel to Alexis' volume, Zola was still insisting in 1901 that it was 'the most exact' account of his early life and work (*Corr*., x, 264).

Nothing is perhaps more symptomatic of Zola's curation of his public profile than his nineteen failed attempts (for which he was much mocked), in the 1890s, to be elected to the Académie Française. Being awarded the Légion d'honneur in July 1888 was clearly not sufficient official recognition of his intellectual stature. Nor was this assured simply by worldwide fame, exemplified by an enquiry from abroad seeking his address which elicited the reply, as early as 1883, that it would suffice to put on the envelope 'Émile Zola, France' to ensure it reached him (*Corr*., iv, 448). By then, Zola was regularly interviewed by journalists who were given access to his homes, on condition that their texts would be subject to his approval before being published. The various portraits of him, whether verbal or pictorial, are as consciously controlled by Zola as the one penned by Alexis: that of a committed, successful, psychologically well-adjusted and socially distinguished writer, untrammelled by self-doubt.

Integral to such a self-projection was his seriousness. There have been a few recent attempts, notably by Marie-Ange Voisin-Fougère, to qualify posterity's perception of Zola that he was serious to the point of dullness.[10] There are indeed in his work comic moments and instances of black humour, often inspired by irony. But his was a far cry from the uninhibited mirth of a Maupassant or a Flaubert. None of Zola's contemporaries reported of his personality that he was witty or jocular, although he was often more cheerful than is suggested by any photographic portrait of him, in which he adhered to its unsmiling protocols. But above all, and whether or not he occasionally comes across as a slightly dour character, Zola wanted to be taken seriously as a writer. Writing, for him, was a profession which allowed him to address a vast public. Its motivation was quasi-pedagogic, as is made virtually explicit in his very last novel – published posthumously – *Vérité* (1903), the hero of which is a teacher with whom Zola identifies. His perspective is to reveal to his readers worlds

Zola aged 35. Photograph by Étienne Carjat.

TROISIÈME ANNÉE. — N° 17. Un numéro hebdomadaire : 10 centimes DIMANCHE 23 AVRIL 1882.

ADMINISTRATION
et Rédaction
167, rue Montmartre
DIRECTEUR
S. HEYMANN
ABONNEMENTS
Un an . . . 8 francs
Six mois . . 4 —
Les Annonces commerciales sont reçues chez M. de Lagrange, 28, rue St-Lazare.

LA NOUVELLE LUNE

ADMINISTRATION
et Rédaction
167, rue Montmartre
DIRECTEUR
S. HEYMANN
ABONNEMENTS
Un an . . . 8 francs
Six mois . . 4 —
Les Annonces commerciales sont reçues chez M. de Lagrange, 28, rue St-Lazare.

Le POT-BOUILLE à ZOLA, par André GILL

André Gill

Ce que ça sent bon ! ! !

André Gill, *La Nouvelle Lune*, 23 April 1882.

out of sight (Parisian slums in *L'Assommoir*, the mining community in *Germinal*, the grim realities of rural life in *La Terre* (1887)), the hidden cogs behind political machinations, base appetites behind respectable facades. This investigating stance was recognized at the time, as is clear from a Robida caricature associated with the publication of *Pot-Bouille* (1882): Zola is represented here as an 'Asmodeus-like voyeur', peeking under the roof of the novel's apartment building to reveal its bourgeois inhabitants' hypocrisy and concupiscence.[11] André Gill's caricature of 'Zola lifting the lid' on their 'goings-on' is as pertinent. A major theme of his fiction is such a disjunction between the private and the public. It is also central to any account of Zola's life.

The writer Henry James (1843–1916) had first met Zola in Paris in 1875 and on a number of occasions thereafter. When he saw him again in London in 1893, he famously recorded his impression of Zola, albeit before the Dreyfus Affair, as 'fairly bristling with the betrayal that nothing whatever had happened to him in life but to write *Les Rougon-Macquart*'.[12] It will be one of the central arguments of this book that there is in fact an indissociable link between his writing and a life with more imbricated dimensions than James knew or could possibly have guessed. Behind the public mask, there intermittently emerges a personality of unsuspected complexity. Hemmings, commenting on James's perception, argued that the fact that Zola's life history was a 'very simple one' explained why, in order to make it more interesting, 'he had received more than his fair share of *biographies romancés*.'[13]

One might add that, almost by definition, *literary* biography often struggles to dramatize those long periods of a writer's life when he or she, isolated in their study, is simply engaged in the business of writing, from planning to correcting page proofs. Even Zola's accounts of these compositional stages are as carefully managed as his public persona, to the extent of destroying aborted drafts and revised manuscript pages in the interests of leaving the impression of an uninterrupted creative process. That is deceptive. Occasionally in his correspondence, and more visibly in his work-notes, Zola reveals the struggles he faced as his series and their individual components assumed their definitive shape. Given the size of the corpus, it is manifestly beyond the scope of this book to engage in a detailed critical analysis of each of his novels in turn. My reading of them is instead designed to position Zola's prolific creativity within the narrative of a life not limited (*pace* Henry James) to the writing of fiction. Contextualized by personal difficulties overcome, what this story underlines is a single-minded determination responsible for his successive achievements.

Another of my emphases indexed by the subtitle of this book will be the extent to which Zola's vision of the modern world, as it is elaborated in his novels, is determined by the history of the period in which he lived. Fortuitously or not, this shaping influence on his own career exemplifies the epistemological underpinning of his fiction: that of Positivism, as formalized by his intellectual mentor Hippolyte Taine (1828–1893). Its philosophical premise was that human behaviour is determined not by innate qualities or divine programming, but rather by the combined agencies of racial specificity, social context and historical circumstance. In relation to the last, the context of Zola's life and work was so dramatic that it could hardly be ignored, however much part of his self-image was derived from the residual Romantic myth of the 'poet in his garret'.

He was certainly not averse to subscribing to this myth: in Rome, in the late autumn of 1894, his awed contemplation of the ceiling and frescoes of the Sistine Chapel shades into an identification with Michelangelo's labours, working on 'an enormous page' (Zola's own metaphor) of white plaster, 'in solitary confinement with his gigantic project . . . for four and a half years of stubborn effort spent on the daily task of creating his colossal masterpiece' (*OC*, VII, 664–9). Zola thereby figuratively assimilated Michelangelo's work with the relentless progression of the *Rougon-Macquart* novel cycle over more than two decades. This corresponds to an *idea* of his writing life, projected in the preface to the *Nouveaux Contes à Ninon*, in which the narrator claims to have 'shut myself away in order to devote my whole life to my work' (*OC*, IX, 350), and it is sustained in the working habits of Sandoz, the authorial surrogate of *L'Œuvre*, which amount to an isolated martyrdom, divested of domestic and social distractions: 'I locked the door to the outside world and threw the key out the window . . . leaving me in my bolt-hole with just my work' (*RM*, IV, 263). Zola himself did sometimes disappear from view for months at a time, discouraging visitors who might interrupt his work and complaining about those who did. Even on holiday, he would sustain his writing. For the most part, however, nothing could be further from the truth in Zola's case than such images of an author ensconced in his private study (a more professional version of a 'garret', one might say), signalled by the imperative of the *nulla dies sine linea* (no day without a line) inscribed on its mantelpiece. It is entirely misleading to assert that, prior to the Dreyfus Affair, Zola's presence in the public domain was minimal at best. In refuting that legend, indeed, the Affair can be viewed instead as the culmination of a lifelong engagement with the political and cultural issues of his times.

Through his reading as well as his close attention to current affairs, Zola was acutely aware of the vicissitudes of France's history. Born on 2 April 1840, in the reign of Louis-Philippe, he was only seven when the riots of February 1848 finished off the French monarchy once and for all, the conservative counter-revolution in June of that same year putting the Second Republic, at least temporarily, on a constitutional footing acceptable to its self-interested middle-class progenitors. Living at that moment in the then sleepy backwater of Aix-en-Provence, Zola was probably oblivious of bloody events on mainly Parisian streets. But those upheavals, representative of abortive attempts to resurrect the ideals of the French Revolution of 1789, leave their mark not only on his fiction but on his thinking about the whole of a post-1848 period, coinciding with his adult life, characterized by national turmoil intermittently exploding into crises. The most significant of these was Louis-Napoleon's *coup d'état* of 2 December 1851, the precise anniversary of his uncle Napoleon Bonaparte's great victory at Austerlitz in 1805 and of the latter's coronation the year before. Coming towards the end of his four-year term as president of the Republic since 1848, Louis-Napoleon's seizure of personal power was confirmed exactly twelve months after his coup in the proclamation of the Second Empire (1852–70), simultaneously styling himself as Napoleon III.

The imperial regime's suppression of democratic freedoms, starting with draconian legislation muzzling that of expression, would be a major theme of Zola's polemical journalism in his twenties and beyond. And this hostility towards an authoritarian dictatorship is either satirically overt or never far from the surface of the historical panorama his *Rougon-Macquart* novels were designed to be, the 'Rougon' and 'Macquart' being the conjoined families whose destinies Zola tracks. The subtitle of the series explicitly defines its time frame in referring to 'the natural and social history of a family under the Second Empire', with the French *sous* (rather than *pendant*, or 'during') more determining than simply indicating a temporal span. The opening novel of the series, *La Fortune des Rougon* (1871), allegorizes Louis-Napoleon's *coup d'état* in the plotting of the fictional Rougon family's own ruthless ascendancy in the social and political microcosm of the provincial city of Plassans (the name given to a barely disguised Aix-en-Provence throughout Zola's novel cycle). It also dramatizes the failed political opposition to the coup, notably in the Var, the *département* adjacent to the Bouches-du-Rhône (and to Aix). We know that Zola, in preparing this novel almost twenty years later, consulted various historical sources to fill out his memorable evocation of this particular insurrection, with its marching crowds flowing across the Provençal countryside and singing the revolutionary anthem of 'La Marseillaise'. It remains entirely plausible that, even during his schooldays, he knew of it at one remove, retailed through the regional press at the time and the recycled memories of fellow Aixois young and old.

It is hardly by chance, however, that his family saga conjures up a picture of France not limited to that of the Second Empire. At a pragmatic level, the fictional biographies of his characters are rarely constrained by the exact dates of the regime's beginning and ending. To his prospective publisher, he had categorically declared that his historical ambitions precluded depicting contemporary society, consistent with his corrected first draft of the subtitle of his novel cycle which had originally, and over-ambitiously, referred to 'the story of a family in the nineteenth century'. But he was forced to admit, during the preparation of the novels, that his focus on more general trends occasionally involved taking anachronistic liberties with the facts. In a more important sense, however, his 'history' of the Second Empire, written in retrospect between 1871 and 1893, has superimposed upon it a palimpsest of concerns which are those of the century itself. My account of the writing of the *Rougon-Macquart* will explore the ways in which events determine the novel cycle's enlarging focus, both historical and thematic.

Zola's preliminary notes for the series stress that his literary project would have been inconceivable before the French Revolution. This had brought to a cataclysmic end eight hundred years of monarchy. Zola's novels are grounded in a post-1789 reflection on the fundamentally altered world replacing that of the Ancien Régime: one characterized by disorder and confusion faced with the instability of institutional structures and the disintegration of traditional certainties and hierarchies. This is less a background to Zola's career than its properly informing context.

The patterns of French history between the French Revolution and the watershed of 1848 are dislocating: the Napoleonic dictatorship (1804–14) definitively ended by Waterloo; the double restoration of kingship bringing the interrupted reign of Louis XVIII (1814–24), followed by that of Charles X (1824–30); the 1830 revolution leading to the constitutional monarchy of Louis-Philippe (1830–48), but itself periodically disrupted by protests eventually forcing his abdication. By the time Zola was thirty, the Second Empire too had been swept away, as a result of France's defeat in the Franco-Prussian War (1870–71). Many of the *Rougon-Macquart* novels are haunted by this catastrophe. But it is insufficient to locate in them simply the wisdom of hindsight. If the 1851 *coup d'état* had shaped Zola's politics, the fall of the Second Empire had more far-reaching consequences: it not only modified the scope of his *Rougon-Macquart* series, it also left a permanent mark on an understanding of contemporary history to which Zola gave expression in all three of his novel cycles.

That understanding was by no means unique to himself. It is inseparable from the fact that the *Rougon-Macquart* novels were written during the long period of national introspection following the Franco-Prussian War. This generated a virulent xenophobia fuelled by the chauvinistic rage to avenge the country's military humiliation. The 25 years after the Second Empire's demise in September 1870 intensified a collective sense of indirection and crisis, starting with its destructive epilogue in the civil war of the Commune: the brutal suppression of this Parisian uprising, during the infamous 'Bloody Week' in May 1871, would cast a long shadow over the next decade. So far-reaching were these events that they prompted question marks being placed over how the country (with the Republic now in its third incarnation) should be governed. The political climate would remain exceptionally febrile and occasionally as violent, alternating between the electoral reinforcement of republican principles and the recurring threat of conservative reaction: notably in the 1873–9 law-and-order presidency (its initial phase known as 'l'Ordre moral') of Marshal MacMahon (1808–1893) and the revived monarchist claims championed by General Georges Boulanger (1837–1891) between 1886 and 1889, with barely thwarted ambitions to install himself as dictator.

Zola was also witness to the advent of a militant socialism in response to the exploitation of the working class in the service of the capitalist boom unleashed by the liberal economic policies of Napoleon III and sustained during the Third Republic. Murderous anarchist attacks (bombs hurled into the Chamber of Deputies in 1892; President Carnot assassinated two years later) were further evidence of the irreconcilable fractures in the fabric of French life which would culminate in the Dreyfus Affair. And those are only some of the most visible historical markers of what Zola calls the 'contemporary anxiety' he intended to depict (imperfectly translating his 'Le moment est trouble. C'est le trouble du moment que je peins' (*RM*, V, 1739)), complicated by science, medicine, secularization and their philosophical and ideological ramifications. Zola may have first identified that 'anxiety' during the closing years of the Second Empire. Its intensification in the ensuing decades is not in doubt.

These conflictual cross-currents of the age are integral to Zola's writing. The imaginative response to them is, at first sight, paradoxical, for the formal qualities (architectural solidity, legibility, a satisfying coherence of plot and theme) of his finest novels testify to a residual, but not absolute, confidence in the mimetic mastering of the dissolution they register. Dr Toulouse noted in Zola a compulsive need for order, manifest, at a prosaic level, in the organization of his desk and unvarying daily routine, starting with exactly three hours of drafting. This is equally visible in his seeking to overcome the intermittently threatening turbulence of his private and creative self. In relation to both his own deep-seated anxieties and those of the modern world, that ordering propensity, whether entirely realized or not, is one of the keys to Zola's life and work.

1
Origins

'I can picture myself, just before my seventh birthday, walking behind my father's body on its way to the cemetery, surrounded by the respectful mourners of an entire city.' Many biographies of Zola start with this poignant recollection of Tuesday, 30 March 1847. Few mention what triggered it, or the fact that it dates from as late as 1898. It appears in an article Zola published in *L'Aurore* on 28 May, headed 'My Father' (*OC*, XIV, 1005–10), as a direct response to that of Ernest Judet in *Le Petit Journal* five days earlier. The latter, entitled 'Zola Father and Son', was subsequently described by the great socialist politician Jean Jaurès (born in 1859, assassinated in 1914) as the most 'odious' of all the personal attacks on Zola during the Dreyfus Affair.[1] Long before this, however, the premature death of his father, while he was still a little boy, had major consequences for Zola's life and work.

The Paternal Shadow

Having, with the connivance of one of the main protagonists in the Affair, secured access to the military record of François Zola (1795–1847), Judet had accused the novelist of being driven by a vendetta to avenge his father's treatment by the French army. He alleged that, instead of a dishonourable discharge following François' arrest in 1832 for having purloined a considerable sum from military funds, the mutually agreed reimbursement and resignation, in lieu of prosecution, amounted to a cover-up. Filling in the details of the Italian origins of Zola's father ('the Venetian adventurer') allowed Judet to claim that the writer's intervention in the Affair made him as guilty as Dreyfus himself of 'criminal' disloyalty towards France.

Although Zola had the satisfaction of successfully suing the journalist for libel, it transpired that, however distorted, the facts of the matter were broadly true. As he discovered when, overcoming the bureaucratic obstruction of the Ministry of Defence, he engaged in a forensic reading of the documents in his father's file. In seeking to refute Judet's defamatory claims, Zola published three further articles in *L'Aurore* (23, 24 and 31 January 1900), which he at one point intended would form the basis of a book devoted to his father's 'glorious career' (*Corr.*, x, 133). Such a project was never realized. But his archival research, together with family papers and press reports consulted to corroborate his findings, remains a key source of information about François Zola, revealing, to his son's amazement, the details of a life story so 'surreal' (as Judet had only slightly exaggerated) that its 'dramatic intensity was stranger than fiction'.

Zola already knew that Francesco Zolla [*sic*], as he was christened, had changed his name on joining the Foreign Legion in 1831, giving him

Zola aged four or five.

(as it still does to recruits today) the rights of a French citizen. Zola himself was naturalized on 31 October 1862. But he readily acknowledged his provenance. Legend has it that the future author of *La Terre* was pleased that *zolla*, in Italian, could be translated as 'a clod of earth'. When exploring, in 1868–9, the possibilities offered by his reading of tracts on heredity, Zola played with the idea of a war novel which would stage a 'racial mix (Italian and French)' (*RM*, V, 1741). On a brief first visit to Italy in 1892, as part of a French delegation to celebrate in Genoa yet another centenary of the exploits of Christopher Columbus, he was overcome by the fervour of his reception: in public ovations and the press, his setting foot on Italian soil was hyperbolically equated with a homecoming. During a more extended stay in the country two years later, he wrote from Rome to the mayor of Venice to explain that his imminent detour on his way back to France was 'a sort of long-promised pilgrimage . . . to the superb ancient city where my father was born' (*Corr.*, VIII, 180). He spent four nights there (8–12 December), where he met his cousin, Carlo Zolla, then aged 67 and formerly attached to the appeal court of Brescia. A banquet in the writer's honour ended with a toast to the Zola family, which may have prompted the idea of writing a book about his father.

The latter was indeed of Venetian origin, as Judet had maliciously reminded readers of *Le Petit Journal* on the very morning the writer was to appear in court at Versailles to face charges related to the Dreyfus Affair. Francesco Zolla was descended from a long line of military men who had fought on the city-state's behalf. On that side, Zola's grandfather, also called Carlo (1752–1810) and an army engineer, had died when Francesco was only fifteen, while his grandmother Nicoletta (née Bondioli (1780–1832)) was herself Venetian and the daughter of a sergeant major in the artillery corps. Zola's father would follow in these martial footsteps. Having graduated from the Padua military academy, his precocious advance through the ranks saw him, by the age of seventeen, as an artillery officer in the regiment initially raised by Napoleon Bonaparte's stepson, Prince Eugène de Beauharnais (1781–1824), in defence of the Empire's Italian conquests (Napoleon III's 1859–60 campaigns to restore them were to be the subject of the war novel, mentioned above, which Zola originally had in mind); however, it is indicative of the flux of the times that the regiment was then assigned to its former enemies – following France's ceding of Venice to Austria in 1814. That Zola rehearsed these episodes merely added to the heroic gloss of a career he was at pains to underline, characterized by brilliance, courage and, above all, a loyalty uncompromised by shifting international allegiances.

While many of the specific details of his father's life, long before he was even born, were gleaned from his research, Zola was also adamant that an outline of it had been passed down to him by his mother, Émilie (née Aubert (1819–1880)), after whom he was named (he always dispensed with the supplementary 'Édouard-Charles-Antoine', the last two of which gestured towards Italian ancestors). She was a native of the Beauce, the region around Chartres in which, coincidentally or not, *La Terre*, the novelist's epic portrayal of rural life, would be set. In response to a journalist enquiring about its sources, Zola recalled conversations with his maternal grandfather which had taught him much about village life there.

Émilie married Zola's father in a civil ceremony in Paris on 16 March 1839, subsequently confirmed in church, consistent with French practice, a month before Zola's birth. The 1845 formal collective portrait of Zola as their only child, with his parents, still has its permanent place in the study of his country house at Médan, 28 kilometres (17 mi.) to the north-west of Paris, which he purchased in 1878. It is not a very good painting in its own right, but is nevertheless interesting for what it tells us about the affective structures of the family. Mother and son, almost bound together and with their impassive gaze, sit slightly apart from the dominant presence of a much more animated father figure. Some 25 years younger than her husband, Émilie retained throughout her life, according to Zola, a reverence for his swashbuckling charisma, inventive flair, irrepressible determination and manifold achievements. Although it was, of the few memories of his early childhood, only the funeral of his 'adored' father which Zola could evoke, he stressed that his widowed mother was the source of his own love and respect for him: 'her unqualified adoration of him for his divine goodness and sensitivity'. She had never said anything, he added, about François being accused of theft, 'knowing only the noble and admirable things about the life of a man she so dearly loved' (*OC*, XIV, 1005). It seems pretty unlikely that she knew what Zola discovered some fifty years after his death: that the circumstances surrounding his leaving the Foreign Legion in 1832 included faking his suicide by leaving his clothes on a beach near the capital of Algeria, where he was serving in the interests of France's brutal 'pacification' of its colonial territory, and that most of the money he had taken was given to help the escape of a fellow officer and his wife (who both

Zola and his parents, *c.* 1845 (artist unknown).

ended up in prison) with whom he had been involved in an indiscreet *ménage à trois*. What an extraordinary story, Zola admitted, which, 'had I not been so emotionally involved, would be a good subject, I have to say, for a tearful melodrama' (*OC*, XIV, 1028).

More germane to any assessment of the influence his father might have had on the writer are the less novelistic dimensions of François Zola's career. Simultaneously to his military training, he had specialized in mathematics at the University of Padua, producing a doctoral thesis, published in 1818, devoted to overcoming the technical difficulties posed by levelling terrain (*Trattato di livellazione topografica*) and so widely praised as to earn him the status as one of the leading civil engineers of the day. Zola's proudly referencing its authorship as *Dottore matematica Francesco Zola, luogotentente* (OC, XIV, 1006) is less evidence that his father had already dropped the double 'l', as has been claimed,[2] than consistent with 'Frenchifying' his own origins. Between leaving the Austro-Italian army in 1820 and joining the Foreign Legion eleven years later, François' pan-European profile was enhanced by visits to Holland, Germany and England while working on infrastructure challenges inseparable from the early development of railway networks across the continent. He played a crucial advisory role in the very first, in what was then Bohemia, but, foreshadowing the recurrent pattern of his professional life, he was the victim of conflicts between contractors and shareholders, leaving him out of work and out of pocket. In 1830–31 he was in Paris making contacts in the hope of securing gainful employment consistent with his expertise, before setting off for Algeria.

In *L'Argent* (1891), the character of Georges Hamelin, his mind brimming with engineering projects and ideas about how they might be financed, falls out with his bosses and thus returns to Paris after nine years abroad, only for his 'naivety' to become responsible for none of his hopes being fulfilled. François Zola's dreams were similarly dashed. On returning definitively to France in January 1833, he set up a civil engineering practice in Marseilles. His experience there, however, was the beginning of more than a decade of unremitting frustration and disappointment which his son would never forget. Among the projects conceived by his restlessly fertile mind were new dockyards for Marseilles (the detailed drawings for which Zola had at hand in 1898) and a design for the reinforcement of the fortifications around the French capital. For all the time and energy expended on drafting updated reports, organizing press support, dealing with objectors, soliciting local politicians and civic authorities, and even an audience with King Louis-Philippe in May 1836 during one of his frequent visits to Paris, none of these perfectly viable plans came to fruition. Xenophobia may have played its part in the successive rejections of his big ideas; his somewhat curious decision to enlist in the French Foreign Legion was perhaps intended to mitigate it. What is certain is that his failures can be accounted for by better-connected competitors, official procrastination and insecure financial backing. More mundane work had just about allowed his business to stay afloat, but not without him taking out various loans. By the beginning of 1839, François Zola was heavily in debt.

What turned out to be his last throw of the dice was the 'Canal Zola', immediately given this designation less in his honour (such an official naming was only implemented as late as 17 September 1871) than by virtue of the more prosaic fact that the company he established to build it was the 'Société du Canal Zola'. This was a complex scheme designed to alleviate Aix-en-Provence's chronic shortage of fresh water. It involved constructing dams in the hills above the city in order to redirect downwards tributaries of the principal rivers in the region.

A partial view of one those dams behind Mont Sainte-Victoire is Paul Cézanne's (1839–1906) *Montagnes en Provence* (National Museum of Wales, Cardiff), whose alternative title is, significantly, *Le Barrage de François Zola* (The François Zola Dam). Although this one is dated around 1879, it is clear from the correspondence between Zola and Cézanne that the painter was working on a similar composition in September 1862, intending to give it to the writer, clearly impatient to see it. In his private collection, Zola retained a painting, dated that same year of 1862, by his friend Numa Coste (1843–1907), *Le Barrage de Jaumegarde* (current location unknown), described in 1880 as 'poorly executed' by a visiting journalist who nevertheless drew attention to its caption, 'Canal

Paul Cézanne, *Le Barrage de François Zola*, *c.* 1879, oil on canvas.

Zola', thereby eliciting from Zola the explanation of Coste's title.[3] And in a letter to Zola of 2 November 1866, Guillemet sensitively addressing filial pride with his own painterly eye, stressed that, having often made excursions to that particular dam, it was 'wonderful to behold'.[4]

On a visit to Aix in September 1892, Zola went to the dam to refamiliarize himself with the setting of *Le Docteur Pascal*, in a preparatory note for which he wondered whether he might include in the novel a complete description of it, coinciding with what he termed an 'idyllic episode'. In the event, he contented himself with positioning the invented Les Tulettes below the dam, while alluding to the dusty village's revival as a result of the new aqueduct. It was the paternal project about which Zola was most informed. It was also the one which would have the most direct and indirect consequences for his life and work – and indelibly so, judging by his late novel, *Travail* (1901). For here, with memories perhaps stirred by countering Judet's slander, Zola imagines the messianic engineering figure of Luc Froment, stoned by the inhabitants of the city for which he has a utopian vision of endlessly flowing clean water, bringing to its citizens 'health and happiness' (*OC*, VIII, 682).

François Zola had set his scheme in motion in 1838–9. Progressing it was given added urgency by having to provide for his recently acquired wife and child. After endless false starts, a contract with the municipality was finally signed off over five years later. He moved Zola and his mother to Aix in June 1843 when it seemed likely that being on the spot might bring a more promising outcome than commuting back and forth from Marseilles to Paris. Further convoluted obstacles resulted in a temporary return, with his family in tow, to the capital in the second half of 1845. By June 1846 the project seemed to have overcome countless legal and topographical hurdles, only for two recalcitrant landowners affected by the proposed engineering works to lodge an appeal against planning permission. In January 1847, however, the rocky terrain behind Aix was at last being reshaped by pickaxes and explosives.

But two months later François Zola was dead. Supervising outdoors the progress of the work, he caught a chill and died from either pleurisy or pneumonia in the Hôtel de la Méditerranée in Marseilles on 27 March 1847. He was only 51. Zola himself remained in Aix, three hours distant at the time, in the care of his maternal grandparents, Louis-Étienne Aubert (1783–1861) and his wife Henriette (1787–1857), who were part of the family household. His distraught mother, on the other hand, was by François' side as he lay dying. Although Zola was not a witness to his father's agonizing final hours, thirty years later the novelist would reimagine this distressing scene, transposed to Paris, in the second chapter of *Une page d'amour* (1878), in which the sudden death of Hélène Mouret's husband in the hotel room of an unfamiliar city leaves her as frighteningly isolated as Zola's mother frequently recalled about herself.[5]

Almost as catastrophic was the financial disaster which François Zola left behind. He had no assets, not even owning the family furniture, with his will itemizing just a few personal effects. Although the 'Canal Zola' (initially rebaptized simply 'le Canal d'Aix') would be completed by other companies over the decade following his death, his own was wound up in 1852. Before that, its shareholders had launched in the courts multiple claims on his debts, amounting to 80,000 francs. To put this sum in perspective, his widow would retain, until the final liquidation of her husband's company, a monthly pension of 150 francs, enough to survive on, at a time when the average skilled worker's wage was half as much, but dwarfed by François' debts. Clearly aware of his deteriorating financial situation, he had had the foresight in November 1846 to legally protect (under the French provision of *la séparation des biens*) the little his wife had brought to the marriage as a dowry. In theory, this also meant that she was absolved from trying to satisfy his creditors after his death. In practice, the latter would continue to seek redress from her for years to come. Even before and after her own death in 1880, Zola himself was subject to such claims for compensation, many of which he settled once the commercial success of *L'Assommoir* allowed him to do so.

Such was the oblique or overt denigration in Aix of François Zola's achievements in the light of his bankruptcy that his son's memory of a funeral marked by the collective mourning of an 'entire city' is as idealized as much of the rest of his retrospective portrait. Its substance was derived from the graveside oratory of local dignitaries, whose moving speeches were reprinted in the contemporary newspapers Zola retrieved. Bracketed out of these tributes, of course, was any hint that, for all his undoubted qualities, François Zola was a bit of a chancer. Left unsaid, such a reputation was not irrelevant to proposals in 1847 to erect a statue to commemorate his contribution to the future well-being of the city being deemed by the conservative press to be premature, given the provisional state of his untested project and the disenchantment of those who had lost a great deal of money by investing in it. A public subscription initiative by *La Provence* to place, in the interim, a memorial stone on his tomb raised a pitiful sum. But it did allow the newspaper to claim that even the 50 francs its offices had received were sufficient to put paid to the rumour that Zola's mother had drawn from the fund money owed to others.

Zola was aware that Aixois admiration for his father was less unequivocal than he would later claim. In correspondence dating from 1860, after he had moved to Paris, he was still lamenting to friends that nobody had seen fit to inscribe François' name on the imposing Rotonde fountain visible from the far end of the cours Mirabeau, the grandest avenue at the centre of Aix-en-Provence. And, in the summer of 1868, alluding to that omission, Zola would engage in a vigorous polemical campaign to counter what he saw as the disrespect in which his father was held by the citizens of Aix: published in the local *Le Mémorial d'Aix*, his letters to its editor-in-chief accused the city of refusing to pay homage to what François Zola had achieved to the extent of either suppressing his name altogether or subordinating it to murky anecdotes surrounding his 'disgrace'. On 14 September, he wrote directly to the mayor and municipal council arguing that civic 'gratitude' towards his father could be repaid by at least renaming a street in his memory (*Corr*., II, 153); thereby the former boulevard du Chemin-Neuf

The Rotonde fountain, cours Mirabeau, Aix-en-Provence.

does indeed bear his name. The lengths to which Zola went, some twenty years after his death and beyond, to rehabilitate his late father's reputation are telling. It seems somewhat unfair to suggest, as Hemmings puts it, that Zola was primarily engaged in self-defence, his father being thought of 'as simply an extension of his own self',[6] though the catalyst for his correspondence with *Le Mémorial d'Aix* was his declared outrage at the paper's suggestion that he was invoking his father's name merely to raise the profile of his own. What is certain is that, for Zola and his family, François Zola assumed an almost mythical stature in the stories about him passed down through the generations. Writing in 1931, Zola's daughter still insisted that her grandfather was 'a magnificent hero worthy of a novel, comparable to the great captains of the Napoleonic army'.[7]

The naming of a street in his honour did not assuage, however, his son's feelings about the city, as distinct from the surrounding region, in which he grew up. *L'Œuvre* evokes the Collège Bourbon, where Zola and Cézanne, only a year ahead of him, had both been pupils between 1852 and 1856. Its second chapter is pervaded by memories of the 'three inseparables' (referenced as such both in their correspondence and in the work-notes for the novel): the two of them plus their fellow schoolmate Jean-Baptistin Baille (1841–1918). These nostalgic pages evoke their adolescent escapades in the Provençal countryside, reading poetry, fishing and swimming in rock pools under the summer sun. And a preparatory note is heartfelt: 'which allowed them to escape' from the monotony and 'stupidity' of provincial life (*Ms* 10316, fol. 26).

However creatively indifferent a picture it might be, Zola would retain, until his death some four decades later, Baille's early 1860s watercolour of Mont Sainte-Victoire. A sun-drenched landscape is also atmospherically evoked in his *Rougon-Macquart* novels wholly set in Provence (*La Fortune des Rougon*, *La Conquête de Plassans* (1874), *La Faute de l'Abbé Mouret* and *Le Docteur Pascal*). After moving to Paris in February 1858, Zola's self-pitying letters from Paris to his friends contrast the rain and cold to permanently azure skies. He returned to them regularly, at least until 1867, by which time his career-enhancing commitments in the capital no longer made this possible. In 1877, exceptionally, he spent five months at L'Estaque, the small fishing village outside Marseilles where Cézanne was often at work. In a letter from there in June, he waxed lyrical about the surrounding countryside: 'I was brought up in the midst of these bare rocks and the uneven scrub, and

I feel tears come to my eyes when I see them again. Just the scent of the pines is enough to conjure up my whole childhood' (*Corr.*, III, 74).

Such nostalgia is not extended to Aix-en-Provence itself, for the fictional transposition of the city throughout his work is stained by the resentment Zola felt about its treatment of his father. He blamed it too for the physical and mental exhaustion which had corroded François' health. Already, by 1843, his energy was at a low ebb: yet another four-day journey to Paris, to plead the cause of his great project, had resulted in him being laid low there for two months, his chest infection and bronchitis being sufficiently grave for doctors to warn that his life was in danger. But apart from the implication that this also made him fatally vulnerable to pulmonary affliction in the winter of 1846–7, Zola's sense of Aix's culpability for his father's tragically early demise was also grounded in a perception of the city as innately hostile to outsiders of talent.

In sketching the origins of the fictional novelist of *L'Œuvre*, Zola included a version of his own. As he wrote in its work-notes, 'my self-portrait, but slightly altered' (*Ms* 10316, fol. 226). Sandoz's father is referred to as a foreigner settled in Plassans, having tried to earn a living through the exploitation of his innovatory technical processes, but dying 'hollowed out by bitterness, undermined by local malice, and leaving his widow in such a complicated situation and embroiled in such unfathomable court cases that their entire fortune had been swallowed up in the disaster' (*RM*, IV, 35). As her husband is Spanish rather than Italian, in a characteristic displacement of potential autobiographical recuperation, so Zola gives the bereaved wife's provenance as Burgundy rather than the Beauce. She bears such a grudge towards the city's inhabitants for this family destiny that she also holds them responsible for the creeping paralysis wearing her away. Zola initially imagined that she would be 'completely paralysed' (*Ms* 10316, fol. 94).

Almost a decade earlier, in an April 1878 article in *Le Messager de l'Europe*, Zola had penned a hardly more dispassionate assessment of his 'philistine' native city with its population of 24,000 disproportionally peopled by lawyers, and with its 'stultifying arrogance', its 'bourgeois complacency', its 'avarice', its urban decay and vestiges of an aristocracy unable to come to terms with the modern world (*OC*, XIV, 308–12). Three of his novels, in particular, develop this analysis. *La Fortune des Rougon* describes the segmented class-defined *quartiers* in which his cast of self-interested characters operate, while its virtual sequel, *La Conquête de Plassans*, as its title suggests, thematically explores the literal and metaphorical spatial distinctions overcome by the underhand electoral strategies of its fanatically religious protagonist. In *Le Docteur Pascal*, in which Plassans is revisited as the context of the epilogue-like final novel of the *Rougon-Macquart* series, the city's traditional reactionary ideology threatens, but ultimately accepts, the heralds of progress living outside its walls, with the more recently developed parts of it representing the 'final conquest', populated as it is by 'middle-class civil servants and the newly enriched' (*RM*, V, 1077).

Such a view of Aix-en-Provence was shaped by the experience of mother and son after François Zola's death. So increasingly desperate were their circumstances, ever more so after Émilie lost her pension, that Zola's maternal grandfather had to go back to work at the age of 72. The precarity of their situation can be tracked through their five successive moves as the extended family sought cheaper rents in order to make ends meet. Each move to more modest accommodation, in the end to two rooms overlooking an alleyway, was also a precise geographical marker of social decline. While their original address at 6 rue Silvicanne, with a garden and a well, was on the edge of the city, subsequent homes placed them firmly outside its walls and the equally impenetrable hierarchies delineated by the city's history and traditions. They were not poverty-stricken as such but, with neighbours such as minor municipal employees, jobbing gardeners and day workers, their status was indeterminate – they belonged to none of the three recognizable categories of the city's inhabitants to which Zola's provincial novels testify: the nobility, those in commerce and the poor.

In 1999, in his sympathetic commentary on François Zola's travails, Henri Mitterand concluded that, for Zola, his father remained a haunting presence, a figure of immense stature whose tragic destiny he was subconsciously determined to avenge. Later, in 2021, in what proved to be the very last book by a scholar who did more than any other to illuminate Zola's life and work, Mitterand's extended reflections are more nuanced and far-reaching.[8] Zola's poem 'Le Canal Zola', published in *La Provence* on 17 February 1859 in support of his mother's application for a grant from the city council in recognition of her husband's services to Aix-en-Provence, reads like an unproblematic confirmation of François' heroic image in the eyes of his son (*OC*, XV, 861–6). He was also, however, an absent father in more ways than one, constantly away from home during Zola's childhood and never recalled by him as displaying even a modicum of paternal affection.

Troubling at first sight, moreover, is the fact that fathers, in his fiction, seem to be generally weak and ineffectual. Even the dictatorial M de Viargue, in *Madeleine Férat*, ignores and neglects his son. On the other hand, the episodic figure of Mignon in *Nana* (1880) is a model of paternal integrity, committed to the education of his two boys, ensuring that they know their La Fontaine as specifically as Paul Alexis writes of Zola learning to read through that author's *Fables*.[9] And Mignon's intelligent disregard for contemporary decadence is highlighted in a curious little digression in the novel's penultimate chapter, entirely disconnected from its plot and not mentioned in its preparatory notes, in which Zola evokes hundreds of men sweating under the summer sun, moving rocks aided by 'the inventions of engineers', to build Cherbourg's new port, and recalls, 'near Marseilles . . . an aqueduct, with its stone arches spanning an abyss, a colossal work which had cost millions and a decade of struggles' (*RM*, II, 1466–7).

In relation to his own father, such contradictions throughout Zola's work are worth exploring. His readers have not failed to notice his fascination with power, incarnated in many of his male characters. Zola's closest friends made the same point, contrasting his innate timidity with his creation of figures, even antipathetic ones, admired for their strength of purpose. The case of Aristide Saccard, the mover and shaker of both *La Curée* (1872) and *L'Argent*, provides us with critical purchase on his fictional father figures. In the first of those novels, it is Saccard's lack of patriarchal authority which is deemed responsible for the moral capitulation of his wife and son, to the extent that Zola initially outlined to his publisher a denouement to the novel's plot as 'the father being punished by his son' (*Ms* 10303, fol. 53). In the process of writing of *La Curée*, however, Zola lends to the character positive qualities which relativize his turpitude. This is most discernible in the scene during which he contemplates Paris from the heights of Montmartre and imagines, Haussmann-like, an urban topography remodelled by his forceful hand. Jean Borie argued that it is 'impossible' not to recognize here a coincidence with the François Zola depicted overlooking the Aix landscape in the stanzas of 'Le Canal Zola'.[10]

In the preface to the text of the theatrical adaptation of *La Curée* in 1887 (given the title of *Renée* – the name of the novel's tragic heroine), Zola confessed that he was attracted, almost in spite of himself, to Saccard's determination and strategic intelligence. This would be reinforced in the conception of the character's role in *L'Argent*. It is debatable whether one can ascribe such ambiguities directly to Zola's view of his father. At one level, they may simply undermine the simplistic equations of real-life and fictional figures. At another, however, it is precisely the gaps between paternal presence and absence, whether lived or imagined, that bring into focus alternative versions of the truth. Mitterand argues that only in *Le Docteur Pascal*, in a therapeutic fantasy inspired by the creation of a real family of the writer's own, are these contradictions resolved. Hemmings engaged in a more intensely psychoanalytical interpretation of the relationship between Zola and his father, arguing that an 'infantile jealousy' in respect of his mother's affections was responsible for the 'guilt' provoked by François' 'convenient' disappearance.[11] But, as Angus Wilson cautioned, it remains 'difficult to estimate the significance of his father's memory on Zola's life', suggesting that the novelist's 'will to power' was 'derived not from rivalry of his father's achievements but from determination to avoid his lack of success'.[12] On the other hand, we now have the testimony of a series of daguerreotypes which Zola put together around 1900, turning sixty and perhaps with intimations of mortality, akin to the *vanitas* of the Renaissance: in one of these anticipatory *in memoriam* compositions, a monumental stack of Zola's novels

Adolphe Thiers.

Foreign editions of *Les Trois Villes* and *Les Quatre Évangiles* framing a daguerreotype of François Zola and his son, *c.* 1900.

in translation has affixed to it a photograph of him as a six-year-old with his father's arm around his shoulder, eloquently offering to himself and posterity a spectral reminder of a debt repaid.

That the writer's massive achievement had by then rehabilitated the family name is beyond question. What is also not in doubt is that Zola justifiably believed that, during his whole career, François was often the victim of unscrupulous behaviour: corruption, mendacity and elbowed out by supposed partners as much as by greedy rivals and rapacious speculators. His mother's protracted confrontations with shareholders in her late husband's company, refusing to honour their legal and financial obligations, merely added to Zola's awareness of the savage ramifications of the unbridled capitalism of the time. That formative experience is integral to a vision of the period given its fullest expression in his mature novels.

From his memories of his father, however, there are a number of other consequences. The most surprising, perhaps (and discomfiting for those too certain of the writer's radical credentials), is the extent to which even Zola's political perspective is inflected by his father's experience, notably in his assessment of the conservative Adolphe Thiers (1797–1877). In his 1898 defence of the credibility of François' plans for Aix, Zola stressed that his father had had the support of Thiers as one of the dominant politicians of the age, even before becoming president of France (1871–3). That he had been born in Marseilles and was the elected representative of Aix-en-Provence in the Chamber of Deputies encouraged François in his repeated efforts to secure a decisive intervention on his behalf, particularly given that Thiers had been Minister of Public Works between 1832 and 1834. In Zola's journalism, Thiers does not entirely escape the irony directed at virtually all contemporary politicians. But, in a long September 1877 article devoted to the recently deceased Thiers (*OC*, XIV, 282–307), there is no mistaking his admiration for the man who had, on a visit to his constituency four months after the death of Zola's father, personally congratulated both his son and his widow on the progress of the 'Canal Zola'. In an 1861 letter to Cézanne, Zola drew attention to the fact that he had once lived at Thiers' address in Aix, while leaving it unclear whether he was being serious about such a residential 'destiny' (*Corr.*, I, 258). His daughter later added that, after Thiers assumed power in 1871, the writer was advised by his mother to approach him to further his own prospects.[13]

No less important is that the qualities Zola ascribes to Thiers come close to effecting a double identification, with both his father and himself. He writes of Thiers' sudden illness and unexpected death as being the object of collective mourning, led by his dignified widow, not unlike the memory of his father's funeral. He describes Thiers as a paternal figure, an 'honest *père de famille*', much-travelled, intellectually brilliant, with an energy and imagination qualifying him to undertake the 'colossal work' so long dreamed of; it is notable that Zola refers specifically to the politician's own involvement in reinforcing the fortifications around Paris, proposed by him in 1840 as by François Zola a decade earlier, if only implemented as the 'Thiers Wall' by his successors between 1841 and 1846.

As a 'conqueror' Thiers assumes the status, as a fellow southerner made good in spite of the stifling constraints of Aix, of what Zola's father might have been. This compensatory version, however, is inseparable from a virtual *self*-portrait, inscribed in Zola's account of Thiers' multifaceted career: as polemical journalist, as 'naturalist historian' (in his 'scientific' reliance on documentation) and as a perceptive art critic (his early recognition of Eugène Delacroix's genius implicitly referencing Zola's pioneering championing of Édouard Manet (1832–1883)). With his 'encyclopedic ambitions' (couched in the very terms of the writer's own, 'tout voir, tout connaître' (to see and understand everything)) and work ethic, his career mirrors that of Zola himself. The protagonist of his great novel of political life, *Son Excellence Eugène Rougon* (1876), published only the year before this posthumous eulogy, is largely modelled on the most prominent and devious politicians of Napoleon III's regime. But the ambivalence undercutting Zola's satirical intentions can be accounted for by his respect for Thiers' acumen and achievements, both before and after the Second Empire to which, like Zola, he was opposed. And that also explains how the fictional politician, yet another of his characters distinguished by their power to shape events, was viewed by the novelist's closest friends. As Alexis put it, without his biographical subject demurring, 'for me, Eugène Rougon is Émile Zola as a minister, in other words what he might have dreamed of being if he had focused his ambition on politics.'[14]

Inseparable from such a superimposition of portraits, there is between Zola and his father a similar cast of mind – one enthused by what have been perennially known in France as *grands projets*: merely adumbrated in the writer's 1860 dream of producing 'La Chaîne des êtres' (the Great Chain of Being), a three-part versified history of humanity, described by himself as 'grandiose' (*Corr.*, I, 179–83); realized in the gigantic *Rougon-Macquart* series, as well as in the imposing trilogy of *Les Trois Villes* and, equally ambitious in conception, the unfinished *Les Quatre Évangiles*. Zola's writing also depends on a planning process possibly more systematic than in the case of any other novelist before or since. That planning is analogous to that of his father: Zola's own preparatory notes (in dossiers ranging in size from a hundred or so pages to over 1,200 for *La Débâcle* (1892)) proceed from the kernel of an imaginative idea to the mechanics of plotting, with proleptic alternatives and belated about-turns conceived in the interests of a narrative dynamic, thematic coherence and verisimilitude. Given his father's distinction in the discipline, it is interesting that a key term in these notes, whether in relation to logic or causality, is 'mathematically'. They contain outlines and revisions, synopses, paginated cross-references and memoranda. Awareness of potential difficulties generates possible solutions. There are notes from a variety of sources: background reading, specialist documentation, meetings with experts, site visits. They are punctuated by figures and calculations (prices, distances, measurements, timetables). They do not lose sight of practical issues such as the equilibrium of chapter lengths and, for the *Rougon-Macquart* as a whole, alternating modes and settings. They include engravings, postcards, photographs and, in his own hand, scale drawings of fictional locations (buildings, rooms, towns, villages, streets, crossroads), thereby helping him visualize settings and intersections.[15]

It may be that these aspects of the writer's compositional methods are purely fortuitous approximations of his father's. But one is almost tempted to say that his novels are *engineered*. In conversation with the Goncourt brothers in 1868, Zola envisaged his works as 'grandes machines'.[16] In the preliminary notes for the *Rougon-Macquart* cycle, Zola himself (literally) underlines the necessity of constructing successive chapters like integrated 'building blocks'; he assured his prospective publisher, using the same metaphor, that the solid proportions of individual novels would add up to 'a single vast entity' (*RM*, V, 1743–5). These metaphors are rehearsed in the preface to the *Nouveaux Contes à Ninon*, where he writes of his dream to produce a cosmic work which would be an all-embracing 'arch' (*OC*, IX, 351), in the sense of a monumental triumphal structure; he twice repeats that image in *L'Œuvre*: 'Ah! Wouldn't it be a fine thing to be able to devote one's whole life to a work of art in which we could include everything, every animal and human being, an enormous arch' (*RM*, IV, 46, 162). Sandoz, in *L'Œuvre*, is characterized as a 'constructeur', a 'builder' of fictions (*Ms* 10316, fol. 33) architectural in design, reflecting Zola's conception of his own art – compensating for his father's unrealized ambitions. And, unlike his father and through hard-nosed contractual negotiations with publishers and newspaper editors (for the pre-publication serial rights), Zola ensured that his own 'constructions' were properly rewarded.

The Maternal Embrace

We know far less about Zola's mother. In his 1898 refutation of Judet's allegations, he refers to her marriage to his father being 'a love match'; he also records, somewhat improbably (given that François was a lapsed Catholic turned Freemason) but testimony of course to his probity, that their first meeting took place on the steps of a church after Mass. As further evidence that he was not ashamed of his origins, Zola also includes the fact that his mother kept in contact with François' Italian relatives. The perspective from which he looked back at Émilie's life is consistent with the fact that so many of his female characters are victims of their circumstances, mostly orchestrated by men. Zola held to the view that his mother was so ill-equipped to deal with the fallout from the demise of the 'Société du Canal Zola' that the court cases she either delusionally initiated or to which she was subject simply left the family worse off. In continuing these legal battles, however, she in fact displayed an exceptional resilience, aided by a number of François' former colleagues. It may be that she became particularly close to one of them. An unresolved mystery is that Zola was sent as a boarder to elementary school between his father's death and 1852, even though it was only a few dozen metres from his home. In an 1877 essay (*OC*, XIV, 239–57), he recalled in some detail its just-about-tolerable dormitories. He never referred to what could be seen as a period when his being conveniently out of the way allowed his widowed mother, not even yet thirty, the freedom to try to rebuild her life.

In this respect, the fine line between speculation and supposition is blurred by Zola's elaboration of the plot of *Une page d'amour*: after the death of her husband so clearly based on Émilie's devastating experience, the fictional Hélène emerges from two years of widowhood to the recognition that she now has the 'absolute freedom' to put her solitude behind her by falling in love with the man who has helped her in times of crisis. The fact that he is married is not at issue. Indeed, Zola's reconfiguring of a conventional love triangle provides a variant on the recurrent theme of sexual jealousy mentioned earlier, for the definitive obstacles to a renewed future are the jealousy not of a rival but of Hélène's daughter Jeanne and the guilt the mother feels in the conflict between her personal happiness and her only child's chronic ill health. The latter is resolutely opposed in principle to Hélène's remarriage. Hidden behind curtains or trees, Jeanne spies on scenes of desire barely held in check. It is her gaze which aggressively interposes itself in moments of possible intimacy between her mother and her suitor; when the child finds material evidence, in 'noises off' and discarded clothes, of that relationship finally having been consummated, her despairing solitude anticipates her death. In the light of the novel's other autobiographical transpositions, it is interesting that the fictional child's feelings for her widowed mother (with her 'passionate love' for her daughter) are those of 'a tyrannical adoration' (*RM*, II, 816). And it is not beside the point that Zola's own medical fragility during his childhood and adolescence was, like the fictional Jeanne's, a cause for maternal concern: at the age of two, for example, he was bedridden for weeks with an undiagnosed condition severe enough for his survival to be considered to be in the balance, as it would be again during his bout of typhoid in 1858.

Whatever the reason, Zola's mother was unable to make any kind of fresh start. Partly because she had loathed Aix itself long before her husband's creditors made her life a misery, she moved (and thereby, in effect, belatedly returned) to Paris at the end of 1857, shortly after her own mother's death on 11 November; she was joined there in February 1858 by her father and a seventeen-year-old Zola. The former died in 1861, and for the next six years mother and son led a peripatetic existence, occupying a dozen different addresses on the Left Bank. In 1867 Zola and his future wife moved across the Seine, setting up home in the Batignolles district but still accompanied by his mother. Between June 1860 and the end of 1862, there had been a short break from living with her in a couple of tiny rooms or in adjacent apartments. This may have coincided with Zola's sexual involvement with the Berthe mentioned in the Introduction, and there was another interlude of a few months early in 1866 when he had first moved in with Alexandrine.

Living permanently with his mother was hardly an ideal arrangement, and it may be significant that Zola waited until 31 May 1870 to get married to Alexandrine, just after reaching the age of thirty and thereby

Alexandrine Zola (née Meley), *c.* 1870.

no longer subject to the legally required parental approval. Hitherto unremarked is that, in a barely legible 1869 draft of the genealogical tree ultimately published with *Une page d'amour* in 1878, Zola noted in relation to the partial self-portrait of Claude Lantier: 'a domestic drama between him and his mother' (*Ms* 10345, fol. 130). There is no trace of this in either of the two novels in which he appears: first in *Le Ventre de Paris* (1873) and then in *L'Œuvre*. But the tension between a possessive mother and her daughter-in-law resulted in Émilie deciding in 1877 to move next door when the married couple, after a further five temporary homes, moved to 23 rue de Boulogne, which they would retain as their Parisian address until 1889. Zola's daughter later recounted that the physical distancing on this occasion was not unrelated to Alexandrine objecting to two of Émilie's four surviving brothers endlessly borrowing money from the Zola household and never paying it back.[17] But this anecdotal explanation seems primarily designed to sustain for posterity the image of a mostly harmonious extended family.

Such ructions were certainly trivial compared to the circumstances surrounding Émilie's death on 17 October 1880 (17 would be one of those sinister numbers for the writer from then on), by which time she was as often at Médan as Zola and his wife. Alexis, writing shortly afterwards, in the spring of 1881, and dedicating his biography to her memory, provided the soothingly authorized version that Zola's mother had 'quietly slipped away'.[18] In reality, she died in agony, from complications of heart failure and oedema, accusing Alexandrine of poisoning her each time she tried to give her medicine to relieve her suffering. And Zola would recall her extended death throes, including such unfounded accusations, in those of Mme Chanteau in *La Joie de vivre* (1884), a novel first conceived in the very year that his mother's death had so affected him. As he wrote to Edmond de Goncourt, in a letter of 15 December 1883, he had postponed progressing it 'because I wanted to put much of myself and my family into the novel, but the recent pain of my mother's death meant that I couldn't summon up the courage to write it' (*Corr.*, IV, 443).

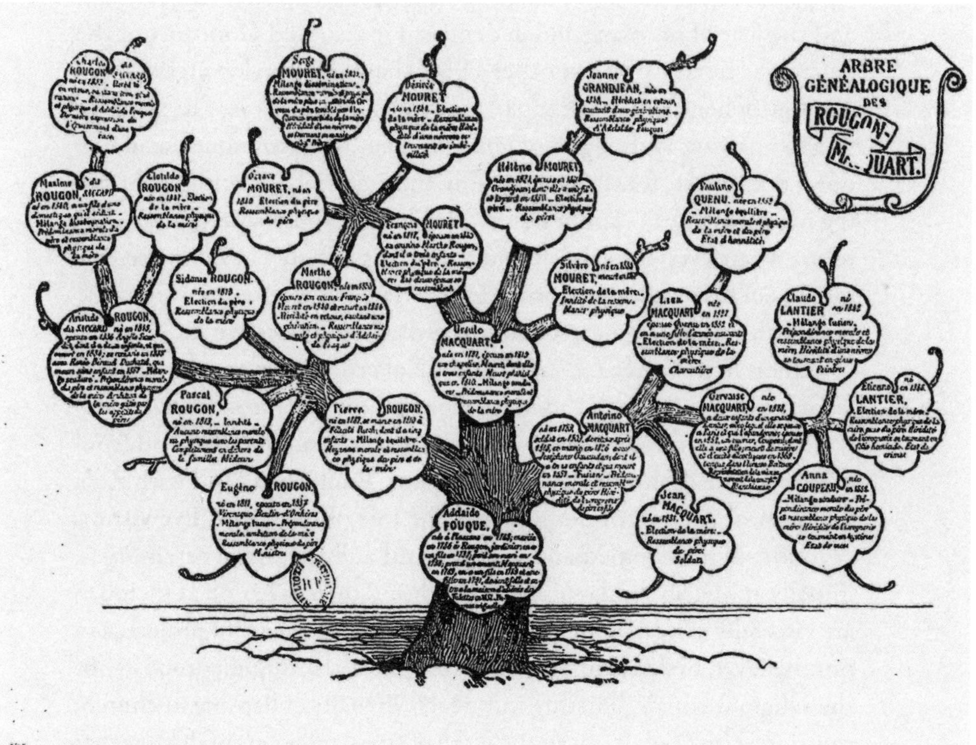

Frédéric Régamey, genealogical tree of the Rougon-Macquart family, *Une page d'amour*, 1878.

The death of Zola's maternal grandfather back in 1861 had affected him badly, as is clear from letters to his friends itemizing his related physical ailments. But, occurring in the same year as the shockingly premature deaths of friends and colleagues such as Flaubert (b. 1821), on 8 May 1880, following that of Edmond Duranty (b. 1833) on 9 April, and for both of whose funerals Zola had acted as a pall-bearer, that of his mother changed his outlook on life for ever. In response to expressions of condolence, he wrote of his determination to get back to his writing in order to counter his miserable introspection. But even eighteen months after Émilie's death, he confided to Goncourt that he and his wife now had a night light to ward off unbearable thoughts in the dark and that 'some nights I suddenly leap out of my bed, standing at the foot of it for a moment in a state of unspeakable terror.'[19] While the verbatim recollections in the Goncourt *Journal* are sometimes unreliable, this is exactly the behaviour of Lazare, the bereaved son in *La Joie de vivre*; Dr Toulouse, some fifteen years after Zola's mother's death, would confirm this idiosyncratic habit, symptomatic of Zola's increasingly morbid preoccupation with his health and the fear of his own sudden demise. He also told Goncourt of the particular horror of his mother's body having to be lowered from a window of her room at the top of his Médan house because its staircase was too narrow. Although not going as far as that grotesque detail, the novel does evoke, for the same reason, the practical difficulties of bringing Mme Chanteau's coffin down. And Lazare's obsessive return to her room, where everything is left undisturbed, is reflected in Zola's preserving that of his mother as a shrine. Even as late as 1901, the anniversary of her death was still being marked by flowers being placed in it.

In his fiction after *La Joie de vivre*, Zola continued to acknowledge what his mother's death had meant for him: in *L'Œuvre*, Sandoz's similar bereavement is described as 'an irreparable fracture, a wound from which his life drained away' (*RM*, IV, 308). Émilie had lived with Zola for most of the rest of her life after the loss of his father. Eyewitness accounts of him immediately before, and at, her funeral ceremonies, initially at Médan the day after her death and then in Aix on 21 October, are viscerally at odds with the persona he took such care to project: as a non-believer, beside himself with irritation at the turgid pomposity of the religious rituals, bursting into tears, virtually collapsing in church, prostrate with grief. It was in the wake of those moments of distress that he described his mother's life as a long martyrdom, associating it with François Zola's own and arranging for her to be interred beside him in the vault he had commissioned in 1877 in the cemetery of Aix-en-Provence, one of the sites he would visit with emotion during his 1892 research for *Le Docteur Pascal*. From the vantage point of public success, in his 1898 article devoted to his father, he concluded by honouring their joint memory:

> As the future is mine, rest in peace, father, in the tomb in which my mother went to join you. Sleep in peace beside each other. Your son watches over you and will be responsible for keeping the memories of you alive. (*OC*, XIV, 1009)

There is a distinct echo here of the interchange about their deceased parents (the father having died in an explosion), published only a few months earlier, in *Paris* (1898), between Guillaume Froment and his younger brother Pierre (another of Zola's surrogates), which spells out the latter's destiny: 'our poor mother and our poor father will sustain their painful struggles through you' (*OC*, VII, 1325). But the symbolic end of that late novel also includes the fantasy of resurrection, as Guillaume himself, feared dead ('the father in danger, the father who will die', as the repeated chorus-like invocation puts it, while his family await news of his fate), miraculously emerges from a world blown apart by an anarchist attack. Memories related to Zola's father are, as I have suggested above, more ambivalent than is sometimes claimed, grounded in a reconstruction of the whole span of François' abbreviated life. In the case of his mother, nothing had a greater impact on Zola than her death, sweeping away the first forty years of his own life and leaving him to negotiate, in his writing, the far-reaching implications of mortality.

Sex and Procreation

Judet's poisonous 1898 article introduces another dimension of this chapter's concerns. It offers a seamless transition between a preoccupation with parental origins and the vexed question of the importance of the theories of heredity commonly associated with, and elaborated within, Zola's writing. While pouring scorn on those theories, Judet exploited the genealogical tree inserted within the concluding novel of the *Rougon-Macquart*, *Le Docteur Pascal*, as an earlier version of it had been offered to buyers of *Une page d'amour*, to arrive at an invidiously slanted cliché: 'like father, like son'.

The most intensive of Zola's own reflections on those theories are transferred to Pascal Rougon in the novel which bears his name. *Le Docteur Pascal* thematically accommodates both a reaffirmed commitment to, and a questioning of, their credibility. In synoptic form, the novel returns us to the voluminous notes Zola took from his reading in 1868–9, prior to embarking on the *Rougon-Macquart*: notably the *Traité philosophique et physiologique de l'hérédité naturelle* (1847–50) by Prosper Lucas (1805–1885). By the standards of modern research, Lucas' classificatory analysis of inherited physical traits and psychological tendencies reveals a limited understanding of genetic filiations, with its conclusions vitiated by exceptions and counter-examples.

Zola found in Lucas' permutations, however, a veritable treasure trove of character types and potential plots. Whether or not he wholly subscribed to his theories has, by contrast, occupied a disproportionate amount of critical attention. In the work-notes for *La Curée*, Zola's 'don't forget heredity' (*Ms* 10282, fol. 240) has often been cited as evidence that his recourse to it is superficial at best (this marginal comment is in fact simply a reminder to himself, cross-referencing another section of his preparatory notes). Nor does his awareness, during his reading of Lucas, that the notion of Fate needed scientifically updating necessarily problematize Zola's engagement with contemporary theories of heredity. More significant is his admission that while these might not be entirely valid, they offered him a narrative logic which could hold together the sprawling extensions of his fictional family and the component parts of his series. The 1871 preface to the *Rougon-Macquart*'s opening novel, *La Fortune des Rougon*, serves in this respect as a form of pre-emptive defence against both his own doubts and critical scepticism, declaring that 'heredity has its laws, like those of gravity', and that his intention was to track the 'thread which mathematically connects one human being to another' (*RM*, I, 3). At numerous points, in the writing of individual novels, Zola exploits that linearity to reinforce verisimilitude. In preparing *Nana*, for example, faced with accounting for Muffat's virtuous wife turning to vice, he explains (to himself, in the first instance) the hereditary fault lines justifying the inevitability of the character's moral decline. But the novelist was far from being constrained by his 'mathematical' principles: realizing that none of the existing fictional offspring could plausibly be the homicidal protagonist of *La Bête humaine*, Zola belatedly invented in Jacques another son of the Lantier and Gervaise Macquart of *L'Assommoir* – without worrying too much about the retrospective enlargement of his genealogical tree. In any case, the latter can be seen less as an index of Zola's commitment to contemporary theories of heredity than as a superimposed fictional structure, with its scaffolding of authenticating dates, further encouraging his readers to suspend their disbelief.

What is most striking about his annotation of Lucas' treatise on hereditary origins is Zola's transparent fascination with its detailed correlation of sexuality and procreation. This would remain fundamental to his personal life and artistic vision. In the work-notes for *L'Œuvre*, in relation to the premise of his fictional writer's novels, he spells out what is 'most important': 'the sexual act as the origin and continuation of the world' (*Ms* 10316, fol. 277). That formulation brings to the mind's eye Gustave Courbet's *L'Origine du monde* (1866, Musée d'Orsay, Paris), with its sprawled female exposing the vulva synonymous with the work's title. Without approaching the notoriety of this painting, Zola's fearless representation of sexual realities was another of the reasons why, in addition to critical condescension, his work was for so long considered beyond the pale.

Contemporary accusations of the pornographic nature of some of Zola's novels look ludicrous in the light of modern concerns. Only once did Zola draft a description of sexual congress which might be considered graphic, and that remained unpublished.[20] In Lucas' inventory of the habits and circumstances of sexual intercourse, obviously central to his study's scientific pretensions, erotic suggestibility is corseted by quasi-medical terminology only occasionally transcribed by Zola in a more vulgar idiom: 'Too much fucking results in a husband's children resembling his wife' (*RM*, V, 1716). Zola focused on even the most fantastic of Lucas' reproductive equations, such as loveless coupling resulting in ugly children; the preponderance of illegitimate girls; gender and physical characteristics determined by whether conception coincided with the loss of virginity, as well as by age and paternal vigour; and so on. Zola's notes faithfully rehearse Lucas' topics, more or less couched in clinical terms: ovulation, menstruation, embryonic development, puberty, testicular particularities and seminal fluid, but also miscegenation, rape and the transmission of hypersexuality from generation to generation.

No less instructive is the fact that Lucas' hypotheses, however absurd, as well as Zola's annotations, are replete with analogies between the human and animal kingdoms. At one level, such comparisons simply substantiated Zola's despairing view of human behaviour, which would receive its fullest expression in *La Bête humaine*, the title of which (The Beast in Man), as he explained to a correspondent in 1889, highlighted the extent to which atavistic origins were barely disguised by modern civilization. Lucas devoted much space to primitive carnal appetites. So too did Charles Letourneau (1831–1902) in another book which Zola perused at this time – initially for a review in *Le Globe* of 23 January 1868 and subsequently annotated at length – his *Physiologie des passions* (1868). The principal thesis of the latter is that rationality is invariably subordinate to elemental need, whether for food or sex, thereby establishing an irreconcilable opposition between cerebral qualities such as willpower and moral sense, on the one hand, and, on the other, instinctual desires pleasurably satisfied. Zola's narratives and fictional characters dramatize such internal conflicts. But they are also reflected in his life. On being apprised of François Zola's scandalous affair in Algeria, and unlike in response to other calumnies to which he objected in the 1898 text cited earlier, his son was sanguine:

> My father, like so many other men, had his moment of madness . . . and would not have succumbed to a woman he had come across unless subject to the unassailable insanity which passion often brings in its wake. (*OC*, XIV, 1028)

The same terms characterize an affair Cézanne had in 1885, involving Zola in its logistic complications while begging forgiveness for his 'folly'. But Zola's own adulterous life after 1888 could not but have brought home to him that the imperatives of sexual desire were neither a theoretical abstraction nor an age-old catalyst integral to the plotting of stories.

To measure the transformation of Zola's ideas about sexuality, confirmed by his more systematic focus on genetic legacies prior to embarking on the *Rougon-Macquart*, one has to return to his thinking a decade earlier. That is marked by an idealism which testifies to the influence of his reading of Jules Michelet (1798–1874). The latter's *L'Amour*, to which passing reference has already been made, was complemented the following year by his bestseller *La Femme* (55,000 copies in 1859 alone), both of which Zola enthusiastically recommended to his friends. Partly written as a reaction to the Romantic advocacy of love freed from social or moral constraints, Michelet's enormously popular studies argued that marriage was the precondition of female emotional and physical satisfaction, consecrated in motherhood. So convinced was Zola of these 'insights' that, to Cézanne, in a letter of 30 December 1859, the callow nineteen-year-old felt able to declare that marriage was the only source of happiness and that 'in every woman, there's the potential of a good wife, it being the husband's duty to realize that promise' (*Corr.*, I, 143). And, in an earlier letter to the painter, he wrote of his hope to distinguish himself from Michelet, whose starting point was a woman's marriage, by describing the courtship preceding it. He was, he almost admitted, totally unqualified to do so. Although the nubile objects of Zola's worship from afar can be identified, his claims of reciprocated passion were a figment of his imagination. He was not totally deluded about matrimony itself, acknowledging the force of the opposition, most actively propounded by George Sand (1804–1876), to a transactional institution dictated by financial and familial pressures. But his letters from this period reveal Zola to be uncritically immersed in Michelet's celebration of purity and fidelity. His juvenile poetry is saturated by fantasies of beautiful virgins. And even as late as May 1860, a long narrative poem such as 'Paolo' has as its central theme the repudiation of carnality (*OC*, XV, 898–911).

Set against these ideals, Zola's transient relationship with Berthe was a rude awakening. As he confided to Cézanne, in his letter of 5 February 1861, he was 'crushed' by his first experience of the sordid 'reality' of sex (*Corr.*, I, 259). And to Jean-Baptistin Baille, five days later, he wrote at length of his abortive attempts to set such a woman on the path of redemption (*Corr.*, I, 261). His disillusion takes the form of a review of the possibilities of love frustrated by missed opportunities, misunderstandings and incompatibility, culminating in a lament for his lost innocence. In both letters, we can discern a residual confusion in Zola, torn between lust and love, available bodies and platonic female friendships deliciously on the verge of physicality, troubled by his own sexual appetites, compared to greedily eating, and now acutely aware of post-coital disenchantment.

Many of Zola's novels thematize a secular version of the biblical Fall: *La Faute de l'Abbé Mouret* takes place in the garden of 'Le Paradou'. Zola made this association explicit: 'I will base my plot on the Bible' (*Ms* 10294, fol. 3). To surrender to sexual temptation is Paradise Lost: in *Une page d'amour*, Hélène, with her legs suggestively in the air, tumbles prophetically from a garden swing. And it might appear otherwise strange, at first sight, that a man on the cusp of middle age should include prolonged reflections on virginity in the preparatory notes for *Le Rêve* (1888). But the consequences of his apparently sordid experience with

Berthe were far-reaching. In either confirming or defining Zola's puritanical and moralistic attitude towards unregulated sexuality, it also reveals a fear: of the Fatal Woman figured in so many of his texts.

At the same time, there is an underlying ambiguity in Zola's attitude. On the one hand, promiscuity revolts the moralist in him: whether behind the bourgeois hypocrisy of *Pot-Bouille*, within *L'Assommoir*'s working-class slums or in the ubiquity of prostitution in *Nana*. On the other, there is the fascination with sexual relations evident in his reading of Lucas and so extended that the fictional biographies of the characters of the *Rougon-Macquart* almost necessarily include a curriculum vitae of male conquests and female sexual histories; in novels like *Germinal* and *La Terre*, descriptions of unselfconscious couplings in natural settings are liberated from authorial opprobrium. This is not always consistent with Zola's oft-repeated belief that sexual relations were ultimately meaningless if devoid of the purpose of procreation. In *Le Docteur Pascal*, making love simply for pleasure, without such an explicit intention, is described as 'dirty and stupid' (*RM*, V, 1087). The most sustained such perspective is in Zola's aptly titled *Fécondité* (1899), occasioning his response to Leo Tolstoy's (1828–1910) view that self-imposed chastity was the marker differentiating civilized men and women from other species. This response can be paraphrased as: sexual desire makes the world go round; the sole *raison d'être* of human beings is to procreate; the ideal woman is embodied in the figure of the Mother.[21] Such an inversion of female hierarchies, promoting the maternal over the virginal, is inseparable, of course, from Zola's own belated accession to paternity in 1889.

The biological imperative informing Zola's representation of human sexuality makes it unsurprising that both his personal views and his texts consign alternative forms of erotic desire to the margin. The lesbian relationships discreetly signalled in his novels are mostly inscribed within a polemical discourse equating the decadence of the Second Empire and the legendary perversions of Nero's imperial Rome. Such is the case of Adeline d'Espanet and Suzanne Haffner in *La Curée*, much indebted to Adolphe Belot's (1829–1890) mildly scabrous *Mademoiselle Giraud, ma femme* (1870). Zola's unpublished review of it, which served as a preface to later editions of this *succès de scandale*, referred to 'the monstrous liaison of two former convent friends' (*OC*, X, 941). The character of Satin, in *Nana*, is not treated quite so pejoratively: the portrayal of her same-sex interludes with Nana herself, it has been asserted, is voyeuristic as well as gesturing towards a threat to patriarchy; however, that her tendencies are explained not just by her disgust for the base desires of men but also by her amoral taste for every kind of vice hardly suggests, on Zola's part, a sympathetic understanding of her initiating sapphic embraces.

More directly linked to his biography is Zola's attitude towards male homosexuality. That might be invoked in relation to a number of his characters, ranging from the abbé Surin in *La Conquête de Plassans* to Hyacinthe Duvillard in *Paris* (1898), the last of the *Trois Villes* trilogy. Quite different are instances in his life and work of homoerotic feelings: his 'crush' on Cézanne, embarrassingly figured in some of the amorous poems Zola affixed to his earliest letters, substantiated by memories of their naked bathing and the anatomical ambiguities of the painter's *Femme piquant une tête dans l'eau* (Woman Diving Headfirst into the Water) (1867–70, National Museum of Wales, Cardiff), or the passionate male friendships in his more autobiographical texts, culminating in the intensity of Maurice and Jean's falling into each other's arms towards the end of *La Débâcle*, thereby symbolically reconciling their opposing roles in the civil war of the Commune.

Beyond such inconsequential affections is another question. The prevalence of gender fluidity in *La Curée*, for example, notably in the androgynous figure of Maxime, has served to promote Zola's apparently countercultural thinking about the inadequacy of binary categories. Against any such conclusion is the fact that, in an 1896 article (*EsA*, 401–9) on the latest developments in the visual arts, Zola expresses his outrage at the ways in which the gender of the pictured human body is increasingly indeterminate, blurring conventional differentiation. His most explicit commentary is to be found in a June 1895 letter to Dr Georges Saint-Paul (1870–1937), which has been misrepresented as yet another example, on a par with his defence of Dreyfus, of Zola's 'crusade for unpopular causes'.[22] Revisionism has its limits: unlike a few other writers or contemporary sexologists exploring the issue with a more enlightened approach, Zola's positioning is unreconstructed. His letter granted Saint-Paul permission to publish it as a preface to *Le Roman d'un inverti-né*, within a supposedly medical study of 'sexual deviance' (in 1896, under the anagrammatic pseudonym of 'Dr Laupts' – an inversion of his actual name – and with intermittent recourse to Latin translation of physiological details).

The 'brave confession', as Zola termed it (*Corr.*, VIII, 230), had been sent to him in 1889 by an Italian homosexual, then aged 23, who admitted that *La Curée* was his favourite novel because he recognized himself in the figure of Maxime. Dr Saint-Paul later explained that the context of his own interchanges with Zola since 1893 was the latter's continuing preoccupation with sexual origins. The topicality of his study was enhanced by the inclusion of a section devoted to the two criminal trials, in the spring of 1895, of Oscar Wilde (1854–1900), prosecuted for his 'gross indecency' with Lord Alfred Douglas. Saint-Paul's prejudices, however, were not in doubt, starting with the notion of 'perversion' embedded in his study's scientifically authorizing title and chapters devoted to prophylaxis and cure. More doubtful, in that light, is whether we can rely on his 1907 recollection of Zola telling him that, on shaking hands with homosexual men, he was barely able to suppress 'an instinctive revulsion'.[23]

If Zola's letter to Saint-Paul strikes a more humane tone ('the saddest expression of personal suffering I have ever known'), he appears to share the view that homosexuality was a genetic aberration or 'mistake' requiring both corrective measures and policing by the state. As far as that vigilance is concerned, it is as revealing that, in 1893, he first allowed Saint-Paul to include the confessional text in instalments of the pioneering journal *Archives d'anthropologie criminelle*, as it is that the opening chapter of *Vérité* refers to the homosexual rape and murder of a small boy, the 'abominable' crime having been motivated by 'uncontrollable urges' (*OC*, VIII, 1014). Zola's more general concerns emerge in the final paragraph of the 1895 letter used as a preface by Saint-Paul precisely because it seemed to validate his own views. Here Zola returns to the hereditary enigmas posed by his reading of Prosper Lucas more than a quarter of a century before. Now, however, he refers to the 'monstrosity' of the hermaphrodite, whether effeminate male or 'unnaturally' masculine female:

> everything related to sex has social consequences. An invert threatens the basis of the family, the nation and humanity. Man and Woman are surely here on earth only in order to create children, and human life will be extinguished if they no longer do what is necessary to sustain it. (*Corr.*, VIII, 231)

It has been argued that Zola's exclusively biological premise – and the extension of this in terms of moral degeneracy and social pathology – is contradicted, or at least qualified, by his oblique references to the equally determining influence of personal experience.[24] A case in point is Zola's lifelong and severely critical views on the schooling of girls. In his review of Belot's novel, mentioned above, it is clear that Zola too ascribes lesbian tendencies to the pernicious effects of a convent education. Boys, however, and as Zola knew, are no less subject to sexual corruption: at a private gathering in 1876, he confided that his own schooldays had been marked by disgustingly intimate episodes.[25] In an 1870 newspaper article in *La Cloche*, he had already hinted as much (*OC*, IX, 929), and, before that, the Daniel of *Le Vœu d'une morte* refers to those 'first lessons in vice which young men of fifteen teach each other' (*OC*, I, 48).

Maxime's androgyny, in *La Curée*, so the narrator tells us, has its origins and legacy in this same 'sordid' milieu of his school. The manuscript version of the relevant passage, eliminated from the serial proofs of the novel, had been more explicit in its reference to the 'infamous ill-lit room familiar to every little wretch in the city for what went on there' (*Ms* 10281, fol. 130). Also attenuated was the depiction in *La Curée* of Baptiste, the homosexual servant, and for much the same reason as he gave to Saint-Paul for not exploiting material in *Le Roman d'un inverti-né* in one of his own novels (*Corr.*, VIII, 229–31): it would be a brazen step too far, given the accusations of pornography which had clouded the reception of his work during his whole career. In his work-notes for *La Curée*, he had elaborated Baptiste's proclivities not only in his habitual withdrawal from the Saccard mansion to spend the night in the stables with the grooms, but in that he should at one stage seduce Maxime. In the novel itself, readers learn little more than can be inferred from the character's glacial contempt for the heterosexual dramas to which he is the silent witness.

It is debatable, in relation to the above, whether a disturbing incident in Zola's childhood cast such a long shadow. Discovered in 1929 in the municipal archives of Marseilles is the record that, on 3–4 April 1845, a certain Mustapha, aged twelve, a native of Algiers in the service of Zola's father, was indicted for sexually 'assaulting' François' young son. Henri Mitterand discounts the significance of this, dismissing it as a 'banal anecdote'. For Joanna Richardson, however, 'it may help to explain Zola's lifelong horror of homosexuality and his timid, often guilty attitude towards sex.'[26] Neither assessment seems quite right. Between these two extremes, it remains possible to situate this incident, its memory either repressed or sublimated, within the wider consideration of Zola's ambivalence towards human sexuality. It is difficult to ignore the fact, however, that the shocking episode in *Vérité* is only one of many instances of, or references to, sexual assaults on little boys as well as on underage girls.[27] Zola's oral account of corrupting schooldays, and the filtering of such memories through *La Curée*, are both overlaid by a claim that adulthood allowed a return to 'health'. In the case of Maxime, a manuscript draft reads that his move to Paris 'cured him of certain shameful weaknesses' (*Ms* 10281, fol. 131). But the novel itself nevertheless declares that the uncertainty, at the point at which he self-identified as a girl, would 'stay with him for ever, leaving an imprint on his virility from then on' (*RM*, I, 408). Much of Zola's writing and personal life has its deep-seated origin in such a preoccupation, both literal and metaphorical, uncertainly lodged between creative potency and sterility.

His marriage brought these tensions into the sharpest relief. The intimate questions it poses are possibly illuminated by his wife's background. That this, however, remains vague is partly a result of her own sustained efforts to draw a veil over her own origins. Symptomatic of this is her substitution of the 'Gabrielle', as she was familiarly known when she first met Zola, with 'Alexandrine', the middle name on her birth certificate. Cézanne could not resist a certain irony provoked by this newfound formality: in letters to Zola before 1870, he sends his regards to Gabrielle; after her marriage, at which he acted as one of the witnesses, he addresses them to 'Madame Zola'. She was the illegitimate daughter of a sixteen-year-old Caroline Wadoux, soon abandoned by her lover. Both her parents went on to marry others. When she was ten, shortly after the marriage of her mother, the latter died in the cholera epidemic of 1849. She was not to be forgotten: the name of the baby to which Alexandrine gave birth on 7 March 1859 was registered as Caroline Gabrielle Meley, and in her letters to Zola during his exile in England in 1898, 'Caroline Wadoux' was the pseudonym used by his wife to disguise their correspondence.

Alexandrine's mother's death, at the age of 27, had left her in a dire situation: taken in by a 'bereaved' stepfather who remarried within six months, she was treated as an unwelcome imposition by his new wife. She was minimally educated, as she found to her discomfort when Zola introduced her to cultured social circles in Paris once he started to move within them. Her sexual history before meeting him in 1864 is shrouded in the euphemisms of hand-to-mouth occupations associated with the *grisette*, the generic label given to young women in the Latin Quarter of reputed 'easy virtue'. All we know is that she became pregnant at the age of nineteen and was living with a lover at the point her relationship with Zola began. That she was not simply another Berthe may be reflected in a paean to a 'Gabrielle' in an article Zola published in *Le Petit Journal* of 13 March 1865, under the title of 'L'Amour sous les toits' (Love under the Rooftops) (*OC*, IX, 223–5). It was recognized by friends as joyously autobiographical, and it does read as a declaration of unselfish young love prefiguring a happy future.

In the novels written during this period, however, Zola remains haunted by less euphoric scenarios. And in organizing the first edition of Zola's correspondence, Alexandrine admitted to its publisher in a letter of 18 October 1906 that she had edited out a number of 'intimate' passages in early letters to friends of mutual acquaintance, and to Cézanne in particular, prior to their marriage. This was consistent with her commitment to Zola's posthumous reputation. Whether it was also related to ensuring that her own past remained invulnerable to malice is no more than a possibility. There is not a shred of evidence to lend credence to tittle-tattle that, during the five years fending for herself before moving in with Zola, she had worked as a part-time model and slept with Cézanne, who had first introduced her to her future husband. It is well known, as Zola's daughter testified, that she disliked both Cézanne's person and his pictures. But her refusal to also welcome to Médan his live-in companion, Hortense Fiquet – uncomfortably reminding Alexandrine of her own humble origins, and not only at that point unmarried (until 1886) but already with a secret family to boot – is explained by her adoption of a self-styled bourgeois respectability most fully portrayed in the figure of Sandoz's wife in *L'Œuvre*.

Equally subject to speculation is why Zola's marriage remained childless. In the light of his idealized inseparability of sex and procreation, one of the most painful episodes in his relationship with Alexandrine was certainly their joint search in 1877 to find out what had happened to her child after it was given up to the social services and conveyed to a state orphanage in the provinces. They discovered that her baby girl had survived barely three weeks. Alexandrine's residual guilt was seldom voiced but no less deeply felt. In the work-notes for *L'Œuvre*, Zola initially imagined Sandoz's first employment being in the Registry of Births; Claude's picture of his dead child in that novel is only one of a series of such deaths and miscarriages punctuating Zola's work as a whole. Another recurrent detail is that of unwanted baby girls being given away for adoption, such as that of Adèle in *Pot-Bouille* whose seducer is indifferent to her plight. In *Le Rêve*, however, and as its title (the dream) indicates, a more optimistic fantasy of lost and found is played out: Angélique, having been similarly given up by her unmarried mother, emerges from a series of foster homes to become the blessed heroine of the novel.

Just as prevalent as these kinds of variants on the absence of children is the fear of infertility: in his reading of Lucas' treatise on breeding, Zola noted instances of 'coercive intercourse resulting in sterility'; in the short story 'Les Quatre Journées de Jean Gourdon', published within his *Nouveaux Contes à Ninon*, the heroine's repeated failure to conceive underpins a narrative of suffering only resolved in a conclusion anticipating that of *Le Docteur Pascal*, the final image of which is that of a newborn child. In the real-life case of Alexandrine, it may be that some gynaecological consequence of her pregnancy prevented her having the children which she and Zola so desired. Or perhaps Zola was unable to liberate himself from Michelet's obsession which had made such an impression on him: that any child subsequently born to a woman would inevitably bear the mark of a first impregnation. For Joanna Richardson, as little constrained by the risk of overstatement as in her assessment of the Mustapha incident, it was much simpler than that: 'sexually the marriage was a failure.'[28] If it was, a number of factors played their part. Alexandrine's recurrent ill health was one: suffering from fatigue, asthma, aches and pains, nervous disorders and many doses of hypochondria, the only surprise is that she lived on until 1925, dying in her eighty-sixth year. Can we dismiss as merely gossip Alexis telling Edmond de Goncourt that while Zola appreciated his wife's excellent housekeeping, she gave him little physical 'warmth' (with the italicized 'choses *réfrigérantes*' suggesting more than coldness)?[29] Zola apparently told Henry Céard that he had decided to father a child with a woman of a less neurotic disposition.

On the other hand, in the self-portrait of Zola in *Le Docteur Pascal*, the protagonist is described as a 'timid lover' beset with doubts about his virility (the work-notes are more physiologically explicit, detailing loss of libido, premature ejaculation, and related 'weaknesses'). Those anxieties might be inferred from the compensatory boasting with which Zola unconvincingly competed with his misogynistic dining companions' accounts of sexual prowess; for example, in 1876: 'when I lost my virginity, I went down on the woman I was with before fucking her . . . I have absolutely no moral sense. I've slept with the wives of my best friends.'[30] The language is only shocking to those not familiar with the grossly unbuttoned table talk of the fellow members of the self-styled 'Société des Cinq': Flaubert, Ivan Turgenev (1818–1883), Alphonse Daudet (1840–1897) and Goncourt himself. Doubtless egged on by their alcohol-fuelled crudity, Zola's licentious claim, mild and abbreviated by comparison with theirs, is totally at odds with his habitually respectful attitude towards female chastity and marital rectitude, as novels like *Au bonheur des dames* (1883) underline. Nor does it fit with what he confided to closer friends after his first sexual experience with Berthe. This macho version is surely explained by the fact that this was the same evening occasion at which Zola had divulged his 'corrupted schooldays', immediately tempered by this attempt to allay suspicions that he might not have put these behind him.

In a work-note for *L'Œuvre* in relation to his complementary self-portraits, another angle on Zola's marriage is opened up, contextualized by his intention to tell the 'intimate story of my creative life' (*Ms* 10316, fol. 262). One dimension of it, figured in the childless Sandoz couple, allows uninterrupted productivity; however, the complementary relationship between Claude and Christine is more problematic. Zola's early elaboration of the fictional painter's wife's character hesitates between presumptions of sexual innocence and experience: 'obviously not a virgin, having slept around from a young age' (*Ms* 10316, fol. 283). Arriving at the compromise of a 'knowing virgin', Zola describes the physical rapture of the early stages of her cohabitation with Claude in much the same terms as his own 1865 evocation of his relationship with Alexandrine/Gabrielle. After Christine gives birth to their child, she and Claude marry; there is immediately a disjunction: 'irretrievably irreparable after their marriage . . . the lover diminished by the formal ceremony' (*Ms* 10316, fol. 127). Indeed, Claude only finally marries her out of 'pity', at the exact point he no longer loves her, and this is compounded by the authorial indication that, from then on, the couple no longer have sexual relations. While this rehearses the prevalent nineteenth-century myth that an artist's 'virility', or sexual energy, had to be directed exclusively towards his creative work, what gives it an arguably more personal dimension is the coincidence of abstinence and the transformation from mistress to wife, tracked in the development of the fictional character herself.

In Zola's case, the sense of 'all passion spent' is reinforced by the correspondence between him and Alexandrine between 1876 and 1901. That during these years we have no fewer than 318 letters from Zola to his wife suggests increasingly separate lives. The letters themselves are both affectionate and solicitous. But they are also banal and businesslike in their reach, often dominated by domestic trivia. The relationship with Alexandrine has something about it caught in the work-note for *L'Œuvre* in which Zola repeatedly refers to Claude as his wife's 'grown-up child' (*Ms* 10316, fols 135, 143, 170). No less revealing is the fact that Zola's dining companions were not taken in by his efforts to enter the braggadocio spirit of the 1876 occasion: in a concluding summary of their various libidinous propensities, in the same entry in the Goncourt *Journal*, it was agreed that Zola's sexual urges, by contrast, were entirely accommodated in his writing.

Zola's rejection of Tolstoy's views on sexuality, mentioned above, is unambiguous: 'Abstinence only results in erotic dreams.' That his own find expression in his novels is arguably confirmed by the note that Claude 'only copulates with his work . . . preferring to create a work of art rather than a child of flesh and blood' (*Ms* 10316, fol. 199). In a letter twenty years earlier, Zola was already referring to the manuscripts entrusted to his publisher as 'my two children' (*Corr.*, I, 524). Where Zola and his fictional artist part company may be in the 'preference' as opposed to a necessary displacement.

Unlike his alter ego, Zola found his salvation in a woman who would be, unlike the fictional Christine, both lover and mother: Jeanne Rozerot, Alexandrine's 21-year-old chambermaid. Hired in May 1888, she suddenly resigned her post after summer holidays spent with husband and wife in Royan (north of Bordeaux), at which point she was initially installed by Zola in an apartment not far from their Paris home; once their two children had been born, he set her up at a more permanent address. That alone distinguishes a genuine love affair from the predatory seduction of maids so often exploited by nineteenth-century novelists, as in, to take one example among many in his own work, *Pot-Bouille*. She and Zola became lovers on 11 December 1888. Once he had embarked on that sexual relationship, his reassessment of life's priorities is striking: 'what is a book worth', Zola mused in conversation with Edmond de Goncourt six weeks later, 'compared to the sight of a beautiful young woman?' It was during this January 1889 interchange about what a dedication to literary production had cost them in personal terms that Zola, approaching fifty, spoke of his renewed appetite for the pleasures of life.[31]

His remarks to Goncourt are not simply a rationalization of his behaviour. Almost uncannily, in the work-notes for *Le Rêve*, drafted six months before Jeanne came into his life, Zola's thoughts on that novel's direction are prefigurative: 'my literary work has consumed the whole of my life, and its upheavals, crises and the need to be loved all need to be the subject of a psychological study' (*Ms* 10323, fols 221–2). Its plot was accordingly intended to depict 'a man of 40 who, having never been in love and wholly immersed in science until that moment, falls for a sixteen-year-old girl'.

It has to be said, however, that it is difficult to correlate exactly the rhythms of his novel series, alternating between despair and optimism, with the ups and downs of Zola's biography. The positive mood of *Au bonheur des dames* (1883) is seemingly contradicted by the bleakness of that of *La Joie de vivre* the very next year. Most awkwardly of all, *La Bête humaine*, prepared at the same time as Zola was confiding to Goncourt his newfound happiness, is a nightmarish vision of criminal drives and sexual aberrations, which can only be explained either as a final liquidation of the 'erotic dreams' of the past or as a proleptic version of the dreaded conjugal 'violence' his affair with Jeanne Rozerot would in due course provoke.

Alexandrine only discovered it, as a result of an anonymous letter, on 10 November 1891, almost three years after the relationship had begun. Her understandable fury progressed over the next eighteen months from crisis to crisis: breaking into Jeanne's apartment at some stage and destroying Zola's letters to her; verbal assaults at such a pitch that Zola was forced at one point to hide in his study, equally terrified that his betrayed wife might murder his mistress and children. The exact date of this particular blow-up is unclear. It was only recorded in Edmond de Goncourt's diary entry for 10 February 1895. But testimony to its credibility is Zola's letter to Jeanne of 16 August 1892: it refers to 'the terrible crisis, after the events you know about' (*LR*, 54), having three days earlier expressed his relief that they had gone to the seaside for their own safety.

This series of personal crises coincided with a period of Zola's unprecedented public visibility: as the most interviewed man in France following the completion of the *Rougon-Macquart*, feted in celebratory banquets at home and during visits abroad. The complications of a double life would challenge as never before the desired separation of his private and public selves. In respect of the latter, as well as to reassure Alexandrine of her permanent place in his affections, Zola prefaced *Le Docteur Pascal* with an official dedication 'to the memory of MY MOTHER and to MY DEAR WIFE' (*RM*, V, 916) This, the most autobiographical of all the *Rougon-Macquart* novels, transposes in the figure of Clotilde, Pascal's niece, Zola's relationship with Jeanne. It received much adverse critical commentary: reservations about the proximity to incest and mockery of the glaring age discrepancy between Pascal and his very young mistress. But the former's sexual reawakening is detailed in terms which Alexandrine, as well as other readers, could hardly ignore. Unmistakeable is its lived erotic intensity. For Jeanne herself, Zola inscribed a personal copy of the novel on 20 June 1893 in terms which tell us a great deal about his emotional life, both before and after leaving behind the constraints of celibacy and the fear of sterility:

> To my beloved Jeanne, to my Clotilde, who has given me the royal feast of her youth and taken thirty years off my life by giving me the gift of my Denise and my Jacques, the two dear children for whom I wrote this book, so that they might learn, when they read it, how much I loved their mother and how tenderly they should repay her for the happiness with which she consoled me in my great sorrows. (*OC*, VI, 1402)

ORIGINS: family trees, blood relations, parental silhouettes, hereditary legacies, ancestral curses. The currents of Zola's imagination are inseparable from the cornucopia of stories, both intimate and cosmic, through which human beings have, from time immemorial, related the present to the past. These genealogies, both literal and metaphorical, are the subject of an intensified or revitalized focus in the age of Darwin. Although Zola probably never read *On the Origin of Species* (1859), translated into French in 1862, this was far from being the only marker of a contemporary intellectual climate in which interpretations of Darwin's conclusions were often more influential than what he had actually written. Nor were evolutionary narratives restricted to the biological sciences. Long before Darwin, Michelet's *Origines du droit français* (1837) was a marginal appendix to his monumental history of France (1833–67), of which Zola was an admirer. He also devoted long reviews to the succeeding volumes of Hippolyte Taine's *Origines de la France contemporaine* (1876–91). In the same way as he himself noted that his novel cycle was a product of a post-1789 world, nineteenth-century historians returned again and again to the 'birth' of the modern represented by the French Revolution. More generally, such work amplified Positivist thinking, in which historical determinism has pride of place.

Zola's shared preoccupation with origins extends beyond the personal. It feeds into his polemical journalism, with its recurrent signalling of the illegitimate origins of the Second Empire, not least in Louis-Napoleon's specious claim of direct imperial descent from his uncle. There is a continuity between Zola's planned 'La Chaîne des êtres', transposed in *L'Œuvre* a quarter of a century later as 'The Origins of the Universe', and that same novel's exploration of the genesis of a work of art. His understanding of cultural history is also genetic in conception. Both his literary and art criticism are teleological in design: in the visual arts, and in this order, Ingres, Delacroix, Courbet, Manet, as precursors of Impressionism, compared by Zola to Haydn and Mozart preparing the ground for Beethoven; in the novel, Balzac, Stendhal, Flaubert and, as the ultimate representative of this lineage, Naturalism itself. Recourse to patrilinear models is almost by default: the fictional sculptor of *L'Œuvre*, Courajod, is described as 'the father of us all' (*RM*, IV, 260). This status would in due course be conferred on Flaubert, especially after his sudden death in 1880, which left Zola again bereaved. But it is Honoré de Balzac (1799–1850) who inevitably casts the longest paternal shadow over his own ambitions: 'There is no French novelist today', he wrote in an 1875 essay, 'who does not have in his veins some drop of Balzac's blood' (*OC*, XI, 158). A statue of the author of *La Comédie humaine*, he insisted in 1891, would be 'to the glory of the father of the modern novel' (*Corr.*, VII, 153). But, as Naomi Schor has emphasized, Zola is, no less than Darwin, Nietzsche and Freud, subject to 'the *anxieties* of origin and difference'.[32] The tensions between origins and originality can be overlaid on many dimensions of Zola's personal life. In his work, there is no more explicit conjunction of these concerns than in the heading of a section of notes for the future *Rougon-Macquart*: 'Differences between Balzac and myself' (*RM*, V, 1736–7).

The conclusion to this chapter necessarily returns to Zola's 1871 preface to the opening frame of his series, *La Fortune des Rougon*, for he stresses here that the novel should be read in the light of its 'scientific title: the Origins'. At one level, it does just that: it details the origins of his fictional family and those of the Second Empire, and it looks forward to episodes inseparable from these beginnings. The family saga is correlated with historical events through his indication that the matriarchal Adelaïde Fouque, otherwise known as Tante Dide, had set in train its sexual degeneracy in, precisely, 1789, for the novel's political mythology is foundational in the sense of conjuring up the spectre of the French Revolution. But the supposed 'scientific' credentials of the text are impossible to reconcile with its admixture of documented historical reconstruction and poetic licence. It thereby substantiates Sandoz's lament in *L'Œuvre* of being 'born at the confluence of Hugo and Balzac' (*RM*, IV, 48), so visible is the debt, respectively, to Victor Hugo's *L'Homme qui rit* (1869) and Balzac's *Pierrette* (1840). But it also gives to the novel another dimension, allowing us to integrate the personal and thematic strands of Zola's writing.

La Fortune des Rougon is filled with recollections: of Aix and its topography; of the urban and rural sites of the writer's childhood; in the partial modelling of its adolescent sweethearts, Sylvère on his friend Philippe Solari (1840–1906) and Miette on that of his sister Louise, one of those girls adored from afar during Zola's own youth. Less recuperable are the novel's imagined scenarios, beginning, as the novel startingly does, with the courtship between the young couple under the stars. Their contact is mediated by a dividing wall, across which they can glimpse only their reflections in a well, on a piece of waste ground ominously littered with the fragments of tombstones. As the monstrous Tante Dide predicts, this ephemeral idyll (unconsummated by definition) anticipates their inevitable deaths, staged by Zola in overtly symbolic counterpoint. Their destinies are universalized by the invocation of a cultural heritage of star-crossed lovers down the ages: among them, Théophile de Viau's *Les Amours tragiques de Pyrame et Thisbé* (1621), illustrated engravings of which had hung in the room Zola and Alexandrine rented in 1868 during a stay at the riverside hamlet of Bennecourt, and which are also the prophetic, if sinister, images decorating the marital bedroom of *Madeleine Férat*.

The fertile profusion of the abandoned cemetery described in the opening pages of *La Fortune des Rougon* looks forward to the garden of *La Faute de l'Abbé Mouret*, but also to the metaphors of germination encoded in the very title of *Germinal*. It is to be reminded that the thematic matrix of Zola's writing is the myth of Eternal Return, inscribing singularity within repeated cycles: of the seasons, most obviously, but also of the repetitive patterns of history whereby the 'death' of the Republic only awaits the next *revolution* to be reborn. In his 1871 preface, the wisdom of hindsight allows him to confirm this circularity by referring to the Second Empire as 'a dead reign', its beginning and ending making of it 'a closed circle'. In *La Débâcle*, bringing the *Rougon-Macquart*'s historical panorama to such a close, the account of the regime's demise in 1870 ends with a confident assertion of France's inevitable rebirth. *La Fortune des Rougon*, the novel of the 1851 *coup d'état*, the necessary prologue to Zola's 'history' of the Second Empire, is simultaneously a fable, with its origins discernible in the recesses of Zola's inner life: in the oppositions between procreation and its negation, Eros and Thanatos.

Zola aged 22.

2
Apprenticeships

Zola's move to Paris in 1858, not quite aged eighteen, changed the coordinates of his life and work. The years between that February and the fall of the Second Empire in 1870 shaped his career as a writer: his intellectual development, his understanding of contemporary philosophical and cultural issues, his political stance and the major themes of both his journalism and fictional texts. In retrospect, his childhood and adolescence in the Midi were a prelude to his formative Parisian experience. 'I was born in Paris,' he insisted in the work-notes for *L'Œuvre* (*Ms* 10316, fol. 297), putting his Provençal friendships in their merely introductory place and thereby subverting in advance the coincidence retailed by tourist brochures ever since that both he and Cézanne were 'natives' of Aix-en-Provence. In the 1970s, the house where Zola was born in the rue Saint-Joseph (in Paris's 2nd arrondissement) was marked by what Hemmings described at that time as a 'grimy plaque' originally affixed to it in 1924.[1] It is a further measure of Zola's present stature that no. 10 in this narrow street, running between the rue du Sentier and the rue Montmartre, today bears a refurbished reminder of his birthplace. Zola's return to the capital would have many consequences, over and above those intimate dimensions of it highlighted in the previous chapter.

Paris

One of the most long-lasting of these consequences was the result of Zola's first experience of urban poverty. Neither the increasingly straitened circumstances of those in Aix nor the various Parisian addresses he shared with his mother quite prepared him for the hardship of 1861–2.

He later recalled the unheated attic room he rented in the rue Saint-Étienne-du-Mont (now the rue Rollin) in a bitterly cold February 1861, reduced to a single daily meal of a piece of bread, apples and a few roast chestnuts bought at a street corner. When Zola moved the following December to a boarding house in the rue Soufflot, so Alexis recounted, its porous walls offered him an uncomfortable proximity to the private lives of the students, prostitutes and pimps housed in a building so dilapidated that it was shortly to be demolished. The characters in *La Confession de Claude* reside in exactly this kind of furnished lodgings. And the sordid tenement in which Gervaise lives, in *L'Assommoir*, is characterized by a similar lack of privacy.

Zola's sympathy for working-class privation, throughout his work, is undoubtedly coloured by his own years in its midst. In *La Curée*, which brings its impoverished provincial protagonists to the ostentatious luxury of Napoleon III's capital, the remark that 'to be poor in Paris is to be poor twice over' (*RM*, I, 364) is from the heart. The novel contains a scene in which those excluded from enjoying the contemporary economic prosperity catch an envious glimpse, through a window, of material wealth. Alongside 'admiration and awe' is a certain resentment at the imperial extravagance so blatantly flaunted before the penniless onlookers. There is a similar sentiment in the more autobiographical *La Confession de Claude*: its hero, aware of his inability to accept 'the sacred penury of a poet', admits, 'I love heavy curtains, candelabra and highly polished marble. I love everything shiny, beautiful, sophisticated and rich' (*OC*, I, 13). As Zola wrote to Cézanne in January 1862, the pleasures of Paris were so far beyond his means that he had no choice but to stay in his room huddled under a blanket for warmth. But the poverty was perhaps not entirely abject. His fullest recollections of it, replete with hair-raising anecdotes, were published in 1901, by which time he was almost embarrassingly rich.[2] Alexis' account, appearing soon after the phenomenal commercial success of *Nana* and the phased enlargement of his substantial country residence at Médan, also served to burnish a successful life story rooted in humble beginnings.

It was in the 1901 text that Zola stressed his initial disillusion on first arriving back in Paris: his horse-drawn coach lumbering through 'sinister' streets of slums rather than opening up long-imagined vistas of palaces. 'One of the cruellest disappointments in my life', as Zola put it.[3] But this was soon mitigated by intermittent euphoria. While professing homesickness, he also reported to his friends in Provence on the marvels of the city. Even some of his dismal lodgings had their positive aspects. To Cézanne, he wrote of the room on the seventh floor he inhabited in the rue Saint-Victor between April 1860 and February 1861, made more 'delightful' by its vast terrace from which the whole of Paris could be contemplated. Alerting Cézanne of his next address, he stressed that it was equally 'charming': 'a real jewel of a place . . . admittedly tiny . . . but sunlit . . . reached by a winding staircase, with its two windows, one facing north and the other south, . . . and a horizon stretching across the great city' (*Corr.*, I, 258).

A recurrent description in Zola's novels is that panorama, plausibly justified by leading his characters up to privileged vantage points, whether the Tour St Jacques (in *L'Assommoir*), an elevated building (in *La Débâcle*) or that classically afforded by Montmartre. In *Une page d'amour*, each of its five parts begins with an extended description of the city, seen from the heights of Passy, at different seasons or times of day. They have been likened to the Impressionist series-paintings of Claude Monet (1840–1926) and Camille Pissarro (1830–1903). Faced with critical reservations about these prologues, Zola attached to the second edition of the text in 1884 an explanatory preface evoking his attic rooms two decades before:

> Paris framed in my window . . . was a source of consolation but also of my greatest moments of happiness. From the age of twenty onwards, I have dreamt of writing a novel in which Paris itself, with its sea of rooftops, would play a role akin to that of the ancient chorus. (*RM*, II, 1605)

Zola's reference in this preface to the great city being 'immobile and indifferent', as well as being habitually compared by him to an ocean, underlines the extent to which he ascribes to it an ahistorical permanence putting the affairs of its changing rulers and their subjects into a longer perspective. When he had arrived back in the city in 1858, it was in the midst of being radically rebuilt, as a result of which it largely remains the Paris with which we are now familiar. Nearly 5,000 private homes were flattened and 350,000 people displaced. Specific reminiscences of this, on Zola's part, are few, though in 1878 he recalled seeing the last buildings in the rue de la Harpe being demolished two decades earlier. But for a writer whose entire work bears witness to his fascination with the metropolis, it is clear that such spectacles were so ubiquitous that they even provided the metaphors of his critical vocabulary: as he wrote in the preface to *Mes haines*, a collection of his journalism which was published in 1866: 'we are living in an era of demolition, with the air filled with the dust of plaster and the ear-splitting noise of falling rubble' (*OC*, X, 27).

Baron Haussmann's urban planning during the Second Empire extended to giving the city new sewers, public gardens and cemeteries. Its most visible legacy involved driving boulevards through Paris's medieval labyrinths and expelling its working-class inhabitants from its central slums. Taking their place, new avenues were rapidly lined by imposingly expensive mansions. Compulsory purchases prior to such redevelopment unleashed property speculation on a gigantic scale. In *La Curée*, Zola mounts a devastating critique of that speculative excess; the greed on display was, he insisted, symptomatic of the opulent decadence of Napoleon III's imperial capital. Disengaged from his future novel's polemical slant, however, he admitted in the late 1860s that he could not entirely subscribe to the residual nostalgia, expressed by many Parisians, for the city's historic topography. In a number of articles across the years, Zola deprecates his own ritual lament for its filthy alleyways, granting that Haussmann, whatever his underhand methods and unscrupulous financing, had provided for its citizens the Paris of their dreams. Haussmann's critics deplored the uniformity of the 'new Paris', with its calculated architectural symmetries and streets angled to create vanishing points for the ambling spectator. Zola's later photographs of the city suggest that he, at least, was sympathetic to the optical order imposed on it. His lifelong love for Paris is inseparable from his immersion in its modern transformation witnessed at first hand.

From 1858 onwards, Paris was so firmly his centre of gravity that he seldom went anywhere else. His returns to Provence gradually petered out. The five months spent at L'Estaque in 1877, mentioned earlier, were primarily dictated by his wife's health. Between that summer and 1892, Zola never again set foot in Aix. Alexandrine's medical advisers also forced Zola to take occasional holidays on the Atlantic coast, as well as in Brittany or Normandy. In 1884 her doctors recommended a thermal spa in the Auvergne, in the hills within reach of Clermont-Ferrand. And to research the locations of some of his novels, Zola made brief visits elsewhere within France: in the north, the mining country around Valenciennes for *Germinal*; in the east, the battlefields of the Franco-Prussian War for *La Débâcle*; in 1889, Le Havre, the terminus of the trains of *La Bête humaine*. Such visits were always compressed to the minimum

Photographing Parisian streets: the place de Clichy (after 1894).

necessary, such as the merely six days in the Beauce in January 1884, while preparing *La Terre*, notwithstanding his intention, so he told Edmond de Goncourt, to spend a whole month there.

To venture a great deal further from Paris was even less appealing. As Zola wrote to a correspondent in 1891, politely declining an invitation to China, such a journey was not worth a second thought, given that a recent trip just to the Pyrenees had left him out of sorts: 'I am not a traveller' (*Corr.*, VII, 204). This was something of an understatement. At the end of that trip, he had crossed into Spain, staying in San Sebastián for a couple of days. Another couple were spent in Brussels in November of the same year to attend the premiere of the operatic adaptation of *Le Rêve*. To go abroad was neither a habit nor a pleasure. Such travels amounted to no more than his two visits to Italy, his 'celebrity' welcome to London in July 1893 and his enforced ten months there during the Dreyfus Affair. It is not by chance that the overseas experience of the few fictional characters Zola imagines beyond France is one of either exile or disenchantment.

It is also revealing how little attention Zola pays to the travels of others, either real or invented: all he could say about Chateaubriand's *Itinéraire de Paris à Jérusalem* (1811) is that it was very 'colourful'; there are cursory references in his literary criticism to Victor Hugo's *Les Orientales*

(1829) and Théophile Gautier's *Voyage en Russie* (1866); nothing on Lamartine's *Voyage en Orient* (1835); Maupassant's visits to Algeria in 1881 and 1887 are never mentioned – 'he travelled a great deal' (*OC*, XII, 685), his fascination with exotic sites seen by Zola as verging on the eccentric. Even Flaubert's journeys to Egypt in 1849–51 (and, by circuitous routes on return, places in between) are simply compared to Gautier's 'passion' for the Middle East, though Zola does balance his amused disgust at his fellow novelist's liking for its spicy cuisine with approval for a research trip to Carthage during Flaubert's preparation of *Salammbô* (1862). Zola's reservations are extended in his art criticism to the contemporary vogue for 'Orientalism': 'I prefer my modern Paris to the antiquities of foreign lands' (*OC*, XII, 392).

That preference, once Zola had established himself in the capital, would never vary. The large number of the novels of the *Rougon-Macquart* cycle set there add up to a multidimensional representation of the Paris of the second half of the nineteenth century. It accommodates the monumental and the hidden, bourgeois interiors and proletarian drinking dens, domestic rituals and public spectacles, the corridors of power and urban backstreets, railway stations and cab-choked thoroughfares, the stock exchange, department stores and central markets. Parisians are depicted at work and at play: in laundries, forges, theatres, museums, parks, ballrooms, restaurants and racecourses. Strict historical accuracy is sometimes subject to fictional imperatives. But both the texts and Zola's notebooks (with their descriptions in pencil drafted on the spot) are afforded a properly anthropological or ethnographical value by virtue of his acute sensitivity to the city's sights, sounds and smells.[4] What is also evident, however, is Zola's stress not only on the pulsating energy of Paris, but on its sheer physical beauty.

The move to the capital also provided Zola with an education of different kinds. For the pedagogical one, it was thanks to the good offices of his late father's lawyer, Alexandre Labot (1807–1870), that he was enrolled in March 1858 at the Lycée Saint-Louis, one of the great Parisian schools. He was one of fifty boys exempted by ministerial decree from the annual 200-franc fee. This embedded him in a milieu at a sanitized distance from the coarse and bullying environment of the years in Aix evoked by the Daniel of *Le Vœu d'une morte*, the equally victimized Guillaume of *Madeleine Férat* and the autobiographical protagonist of *La Confession de Claude* haunted by the jeering cruelty of schoolmates. Zola's longest overt reflections on his earlier school are included in an

1877 essay devoted to the state of French education: he remembered the Collège Bourbon as 'a lesson in life' in a cloistered social world characterized by the ignorance and 'malicious brutality' of many of the pupils recruited from the back country around Aix. He referred to his time there as 'an apprenticeship in vice' (*OC*, XIV, 242). By comparison with the provincial staff he had known, his teachers in Paris were open-minded and in touch with the issues of the day. In 1894 Zola acknowledged what he owed the Lycée Saint-Louis by making a donation to it through its alumni association. On the other hand, he was intimidated at the time by the precocious sophistication of the Saint-Louis pupils, flaunting their pretentions and regaling their peers with inflated tales of their familiarity with the attractions of Parisian streets. Zola was excluded: a year older than the rest of his class in the penultimate year of secondary education and thus considered backward, he was treated as an outsider, not least on account of a slight lisp melded with a Provençal accent he was at pains to disguise.

Zola's academic progress was undoubtedly disrupted by his severe illness, the attack of typhoid mentioned earlier, in the autumn of 1858, postponing his return to school until the following spring. But he would profess that he had simply been a mediocre student. That too served the projected image of the self-taught man of letters. It does not quite square with him having told Cézanne, in a letter of June 1858 (*Corr.*, I, 97), that he was aiming for an end-of-year prize – duly achieved for French composition. For the *baccalauréat* (the examination hurdle for university entrance, as it still is today), however, he was in the science stream with a view to entering either the École polytechnique or the École centrale (both institutions specializing in engineering). This was perhaps at the instigation of family and former colleagues of his father who hoped he might follow in the latter's footsteps. A curious and seldom-remarked jotting in the preliminary notes for the *Rougon-Macquart* reads: 'me and my uncles, Paul and his father' (*RM*, V, 1738). Ostensibly a reflection on the admixture of social classes, it also conjures up Cézanne's well-known transgression of the paternal intention that he should qualify as a lawyer, and the painter's father, according to Zola (*Corr.*, I, 213), partly blamed him for Cézanne abandoning his legal studies. The juxtaposition with his own situation may also refer to unwelcome career advice from his mother's brothers, particularly that of Lucien Aubert (1815–?), who had been employed by Zola's father; he was the uncle with whom Zola was in the closest contact at this moment, specifically in relation to money matters such as the cost of the family's journey to Paris or ensuring that his grandfather received his pension.

Unlike in Cézanne's case, Zola's determination to follow an artistic vocation was less a conscious decision than a rationalization of circumstances beyond his control. His letters of 1858–9 speak of confusion: enthusiasm for a potential career as an engineer countered by what he called 'an inner voice' questioning whether it would suit him; sharing algebraic complexities with Jean-Baptistin Baille (who would go on to a distinguished scientific career); and simultaneously toying with the idea of registering instead, or in addition, for the *baccalauréat ès lettres* (the humanities alternative) to gain admission to the Faculty of Law. In the event, he took his science exams twice, failing on both occasions: at the Sorbonne on 3 August 1859 and in Marseilles that November. With the possibility of higher education now closed off, his formal schooling had come to an end. Zola later explained that it was his time-consuming dedication to poetry and fiction which was responsible for his failures. Such implied martyrdom in the interests of a future devoted to literature hardly shines through the melancholy conveyed to Cézanne in his letter of 9 February 1860:

> I am absolutely crushed. I look to a future which seems so black, so black, that I dread it. No money, no job . . . nobody to give me support, no wife, not a single friend nearby. All around me, I sense nothing but indifference or contempt . . . I never finished my studies; I haven't even got good French; I know nothing. My time in school has been useless: a bit of theory, nothing practical. What should I do? (*Corr.*, I, 133)

The first thing he had to do was secure some sort of income. Such was Zola's depression that, as he exaggerated to Cézanne in that same letter, had he not been responsible for his mother, he would have been all too glad to live as a hermit with just enough money to be able to eat. Within a couple of months, by May, he had instead found a clerical job at the central office of the Paris Docks. And he was not quite as bereft of support as he claimed. It was thanks once again to the influence of Alexandre Labot that he obtained this position. Labot was so prominent in legal circles that he was a member of the Cour de cassation (the regulatory body charged with overseeing the implementation of judicial policy in accordance with the law) as well as being temporarily seconded to the administration of the Paris Docks. His successive interventions on Zola's behalf were motivated by loyalty: he had been involved in setting up the Société du Canal Zola; he had been François Zola's close friend as well as his legal adviser since 1841, the year after Zola was born; it was his eulogy at François' funeral, reprinted in local newspapers, from which Zola derived much of the information about his father's career; and he remained the staunchest of protectors of the family for the rest of his life. It may be that Zola's ephemeral ambition to pursue a career as a lawyer is related to the influence of Labot and the role he played, substituting that of an absent father, behind the scenes.

But Zola did not last long working for the Paris Docks. By the end of June 1860, he had quit. He reported to Baille and Cézanne that not only was his clerical job boring beyond belief, but that his monthly salary of 60 francs was so derisory that even unemployment was preferable. It was not, judging by the destitution of the next eighteen months of his life, as detailed earlier, plagued as it was by recurrent health problems and unsuccessful attempts to find gainful employment. Only on 1 March 1862 did this miserable period come to an end when he was taken on by the publishing firm of Hachette. Labot, for whom Zola had done some part-time editorial work the preceding April and whose constitutional responsibilities included engagement with some sections of the press, may well have facilitated the future writer's apparently fortuitous entry into the world of books. And this provided him with an 'education' far more instructive than his school curriculum.

The World of Books

Zola started at Hachette by working in distribution, packaging volumes to dispatch to retailers or individual buyers, in return for a monthly salary of 100 francs. After only a few weeks in this mundane job, he was assigned to the publicity department, rapidly becoming head of it and doubling his salary at a stroke. He would remain in the post for nearly four years. What he learnt there informed his own publishing strategies in the decades to come. Among other things, it was an apprenticeship in marketing. This involved amplifying entries in updated catalogues which he himself redesigned. Zola was responsible for a monthly bulletin, not merely listing forthcoming books but also, on his initiative, splicing bibliographical details with critical superlatives. Such tasks shaped his conception of literature as a commercial product, often repeated but most fully articulated in an article in *Le Figaro* of 25 April 1896 devoted to what we would now call 'intellectual property' (*OC*, XIV, 762–7). 'A writer', he had already stressed in 1880, 'is a worker like any other, earning his living from his work' (*OC*, X, 1269).

The experience at Hachette also taught him the importance of making direct contact with reviewers, drafting enticing blurbs and exploiting opportunities for controversy. When it came to his own earliest novels, Zola didn't hesitate to do likewise: he sent unsolicited copies of them to literary editors or penned effusive flyers for insertion in the press. Over the course of his later writing career, the launch of each and every one of his novels was conducted as a campaign, making it a literary 'event'. This was equally true of the publication of his shorter texts: for his *Contes à Ninon* (1864), he organized and had to pay for the publicity himself, reporting to his friend Antony Valabrègue (1844–1900) on 4 November 1864 that the result of such efforts had been 'splendid' (*Corr.*, I, 385). Zola was under no illusion about such strategies: in an 1866 tale (reprinted in 1868, 1869 and 1872) headed 'Une victime de la réclame' (A Victim of Advertising), he had fun at the expense of any reader organizing a private library 'according to the degree of lyricism in the flyers which publishing houses had sent to newspapers' (*OC*, IX, 260). This apprenticeship, however, goes some way to accounting for the extraordinary sales figures of the *Rougon-Macquart*. These were generated by advertising techniques, designed to intensify the anticipation of the public, such as plastering billboards around Paris with seductive images of what the next 'chapter' in the ongoing family saga might contain. Alexis' 1882 biography, as mentioned earlier, partly served a similar purpose by alerting readers to the episodes of the novel cycle yet to come.

His prefaces to many of the novels of the series respond to charges afforded by, and aimed at, their prior serialization in newspapers, itself so carefully scheduled to overlap with publication of the text in volume form that the impatience of subscribers could only be satisfied by buying the book. If the preface to *Une page d'amour*, cited earlier, was merely explanatory, others take the form of aggressive rebuttals. His first volume of art criticism, appearing in 1866 under the title of *Mon salon*, appended a sample of the vituperation he had encountered. Less than favourable readings of his work were immediately followed up by open letters to the newspaper in which they had appeared. For *Thérèse Raquin* (1867), Zola persuaded a complicit journalist to attack it sufficiently violently in *Le Figaro* of 23 January 1868, designating the novel as 'putrid', to merit an equally belligerent response by Zola in the same paper a week later. That then forms the basis of his very long preface to the second edition of the novel published in April.

Driven by an urgent need to make a name for himself, Zola would adopt contrarian critical positions provoking outraged responses which reinforced his sense that 'there is no such thing as bad publicity.' The more the better. As he wrote in a letter of 13 January 1865, 'I have an easily understandable mania for publicity' (*Corr.*, XI, 27). His review in *L'Événement* of the 1866 Salon (the annual Paris art exhibition), Zola told Numa Coste, had created a furore as satisfying as deliberate (*Corr.*, I, 451). The next year, he wrote to his publisher seeking to persuade him to bring out a new edition of the *Contes à Ninon*, this time illustrated by Manet; the latter's 'scandalous reputation' was such that a volume bearing both Zola's name and that of the painter could not fail: 'Aware as you are of my experience in matters of publicity, you can rely on my assurances' (*Corr.*, I, 496).

In Louis Hachette (1800–1864), who had, since buying out a bookshop in 1826, transformed his firm into a dynamic financial production line, Zola was also confronted by a model of capitalist enterprise. Notwithstanding modest beginnings, it was through his personal energy and imaginative recasting of the industry (notably in the development of technically modern printing processes) that, by the 1860s, Hachette had created the dominant publishing house of the era. As Colette Becker has suggested, here was another incarnation of what Zola's father might have been.[5] More obviously, many of Louis Hachette's talents are reconfigured in the Octave Mouret of the department store of *Au bonheur des dames*, starting with his advertising acumen and marketing innovations. There, however, the comparison stops: as opposed to the nakedly exploitative mechanisms invented by the fictional character at the expense (in every sense) of gullible women shoppers, the fortunes of Hachette were underpinned by a more enlightened ethos, perfectly attuned to developments in contemporary thinking. And this, for Zola, was intellectually formative.

Grounded in its traditional pedagogic mission (dictionaries, encyclopedias, manuals, etc.), and staffed by a disproportionate number of qualified teachers unable to obtain a post by virtue of refusing to swear allegiance to Napoleon III, the firm made available to an expanding educated public the latest scientific and philosophical works by writers whose ideas would definitively undermine the certainties of the past. It specialized in books and periodicals popularizing advances in knowledge: discoveries, for example, in geology, astrology and physics. The milieu in which Zola found himself was also politically liberal: Hachette's 'stable' of writers included Jules Simon (1814–1896), a future head of government during the Third Republic, the thrust of whose studies of the proletariat resurfaces in his concerns as a future Minister of Education.

Familiarity with the epistemological currents of the time would leave an indelible mark on Zola's writing: on the subtitle of the *Rougon-Macquart*, indexing its two branches of a family at a particular historical moment, and on the deterministic logic informing his narratives. There are no surprise endings in Zola's fiction. I previously referred to Hippolyte Taine as the leading exponent of Positivism and the relation between its deterministic premises and the shape of both Zola's career and work. During his years at Hachette, the firm published books by, among other luminaries, Émile Deschanel (1819–1904), Émile Littré (1801–1881), Charles Augustin Sainte-Beuve (1804–1869) and Taine himself. Zola wrote admiring articles on such writers, having met them all at Hachette. But it was Taine with whom he had the closest personal contact there and to whom he devoted the most detailed studies over the next fifteen years, having proudly admitted in 1866, 'I am the humble disciple of M. Taine' (OC, X, 563). In fact, he had reservations about some aspects of Taine's many books, which range from explorations of national cultures to French history. But Zola's debts to him were manifold: he adopted his critical methodology, while engaging in a dialogue with him about what he perceived as its limitations; he sent him copies of his early novels and received advice in return; and he even headed the first edition of *Thérèse Raquin*, in 1867, with an epigraph culled from Taine which pithily summed up principles they were deemed to share ('vice and virtue are as much products as sulphuric acid and sugar').

There are other reasons too for considering Zola's years at Hachette as a decisive stage in his life and work, notably in relation to his career as a journalist. He had made such important contacts within the contemporary press that, the very day after leaving the publishing house on 31 January 1866, he began working for *L'Événement*, the daily newspaper founded by Hippolyte de Villemessant (1812–1879) only a few months earlier. Zola's correspondence confirms that this was not a spur-of-the-moment move. In return for a monthly salary of 500 francs, he was charged in the first instance with a column which was the natural extension of his activities at Hachette: 'Livres d'aujourd'hui et de demain'

(Books of Today and Tomorrow). This was not the only dimension of the opportunity he had been given by Villemessant: in the pages of *L'Événement* that September, Zola serialized *Le Vœu d'une morte*, and, more controversially, it also published his first Salon review articles which championed Manet at the expense of established painters. This caused such an outcry that the paper's regular readers threatened to terminate their subscriptions, with the result that Zola's intended sequence of articles on the exhibition was brought to a premature close. The paper itself was suppressed by the imperial censors before the end of the year, on the pretext that, in commenting on the state of French theatre, it had strayed beyond the terms of its licence. More germane was that Villemessant had put together an editorial team of brilliant young writers whose opposition to the dictatorship of the Second Empire was increasingly outspoken.

Zola never forgot what he owed Villemessant: even thirty years later, he gratefully recalled his 'open-mindedness' and 'passionate commitment to an idea or an individual' (*EsA*, 402), which had given him both his first full-time employment as a journalist and the freedom to express his views unconstrained by editorial directives. During his years at Hachette, Zola had already published numerous articles, mainly in the provincial press but very occasionally in *Le Petit Journal* or *Le Figaro*. Joining the staff of

Hippolyte Taine.

L'Événement in 1866 fulfilled a longer-held ambition, as he had told Valabrègue a year earlier: his writing for the Lyons paper *Le Salut public*, while supplementing his income and instilling the discipline of deadlines, was mainly motivated by the hope of 'gaining access to a great Parisian newspaper' (*Corr.*, I, 406). His interchanges with Villemessant, before and after leaving Hachette, are testimony to Zola's determination to do so while subtly respecting, but also fertilizing, the wishes of his patron. In *L'Événement*, he published 125 review articles, usually of more than a single work. What distinguishes them from the notices he had sketched at Hachette is a perspective boldly differentiating recommendation and dislike. Zola once invented a supplementary category headed 'Books Not to Read' (in *L'Événement* of 9 February 1866); when this was thought to be too severe, he replaced it with the hardly less negative 'Books I Have Found It Impossible to Read'! This kind of discrimination, usually implicit, gave a critical edge to his writing which Villemessant encouraged, wholly consistent with the latter's own iconoclastic tendencies and flair for publicity.

While continuing to publish in *Le Salut public*, Zola's now professional status at long last assured him of a substantial income and opened the doors to many other Parisian newspapers. Previously paid at the rate of 10 centimes per line, he could now command 100 francs per article. Even if such commissions were intermittent, compared to his monthly salary of 60 francs as an employee of the Paris Docks, this was a veritable fortune. His notoriety, on account of his uncompromising critical stance, made him an attractive prospect for editors seeking to increase the circulation of their publications. Between 1866 and 1870, Zola published nearly five hundred articles, inclusive of those (in the case of book reviews) he recycled in somewhat amended form in the different papers and journals for which he was simultaneously writing. Towards the end of his life, Zola looked back at his time as a full-time journalist as a period when he was worn down by the daily grind, glad that his commercial success as a novelist had liberated him from it. But he had earlier acknowledged that such an apprenticeship had been instrumental in shaping his literary career. Its 'vital and energizing' importance, he insisted in 1879, was not in doubt:

> No author of distinction has wasted their time, at the difficult start of a career, in earning their crust by writing for the newspapers. On the contrary, I am convinced that such an

experience is fundamental . . . to a deeper understanding, however painful, of the modern world. (*OC*, X, 1272)

Reviewing books, for example, was an education in itself. It is doubtful, to say the least, that he read from cover to cover the hundreds of volumes to which he refers in *L'Événement* and, after its demise in November 1866, in *Le Gaulois* and elsewhere. But this activity required a less superficial gloss than the few lines needed by Hachette. The books on which he reported, sometimes at length, covered a heterogeneous range of subjects and genres: the natural sciences, medicine, fashion and cosmetics, biography and memoirs, military campaigns, Egyptian mythology, religion, marriage, celibacy, homeopathy, geography, earthquakes and maritime adventures, the supernatural, art history. At best, and well beyond what he had learnt at school, they offered Zola a passing familiarity with both mainstream and eccentric areas of topical enquiry.

Literary works, past and present, were treated with closer scrutiny if not always in great depth: a recent translation of Shakespeare was judged to be, in spite of Zola not knowing a word of English, very good; new editions of Corneille, La Bruyère, Voltaire and Hugo were accorded their due reverence, as were studies devoted to Dante, Cervantes and Goethe. But in his appraisal of contemporary fiction can be discerned the shaping of Zola's own aesthetic.[6] Popular authors, now long forgotten, were for the most part brutally devalued for their sentimentality and lack of realism. Occasionally he came across, as he termed it, 'a pearl in the nauseating stream' of novels flooding the market. The opening volume of *Les Victimes d'amour* (The Victims of Love, 1866), a trilogy by Hector Malot (1830–1907), struck him as a superb psychological and physiological analysis of sexual desire, dramatizing modern scientific principles. On reconfiguring in *Le Figaro* of 18 December 1866 the review of the novel which had appeared in *Le Salut public* the day before, he entitled his text 'Un roman d'analyse' (An Analytical Novel), ending it with the resonant endorsement of Malot, with his 'moral scalpel', as 'an anatomist inspecting the living body of the beast in man' (*OC*, X, 704).

That concluding formulation had already been used by Zola in *Le Vœu d'une morte* earlier that same year. His associated metaphors of dissection also bring into the critical frame other discursive points of reference plotted through this stage of his literary apprenticeship. Indirectly, they invoke Sainte-Beuve, ranked by him below Taine but acknowledged as 'one of the princes of contemporary criticism': his approach to biography, as Zola put it in *L'Événement* of 23 September 1866, was that of 'the morally dispassionate anatomist' (*OC*, X, 632). And Zola's review of Malot's trilogy a couple of months later echoes the prestigious critic's oft-cited response, originally in *Le Moniteur universel* of 4 May 1857, to the clinical texture of *Madame Bovary* (published in book form that same year): 'M. Flaubert wields his pen like a scalpel. Anatomists and physiologists, I find you everywhere.' It is indeed Flaubert's writing which exemplifies for Zola the criteria against which to measure the value of literary texts. Time and again, the mediocrity of much of the fiction he reviews is compared unfavourably to *Madame Bovary*. Only in the 1870s, and especially after his death in 1880, would Zola elaborate the reasons why Flaubert should be considered the quintessentially modern novelist of the period. But his extended praise of *L'Éducation sentimentale*, in *La Tribune* of 28 November 1869, already signals the uniquely distinguished place Flaubert holds in Zola's purview of the literature of his time.

Another model was *Germinie Lacerteux* (1864), jointly authored by Edmond de Goncourt and his brother Jules (1830–1870). This novel uncovers the hidden life of a domestic servant and tracks her progressive psychological and physical disintegration. Zola's review of it, in *Le Salut public* of 24 February 1865, has recourse to a lexicon privileged across his literary criticism as well as the declared theoretical tenets of the *Rougon-Macquart*. The notion of a 'medical novel', pejoratively used by its detractors objecting to its graphic details of disease and degradation, is one from which the Goncourt brothers, so Zola argues, would not demur. He assimilates their analysis of the biological fatalities of the female body and his own 'analytical' predisposition as an 'anatomist' wielding a 'scalpel' to conduct the 'autopsy' (*OC*, X, 62) of a work in order to reveal its 'organic' secrets. In his 1868 response to attacks on his own *Thérèse Raquin*, Zola specifically aligns it with *Germinie Lacerteux*'s pioneering status.

It remains true that Zola's characterization of Flaubert as another 'analytical' novelist and as Balzac's successor, in a text of 25 August 1866 (*OC*, X, 207), and of even Hector Malot as a 'son of Balzac' (*OC*, X, 700) points to the single most important influence on his literary ambitions. Zola's allusion, in his review of Malot's trilogy, to Taine's description of Balzac's *La Comédie humaine* (1829–47) as 'a huge repository of documents on human nature' is not mere indirect flattery. He cited it again in 1868, more correctly reinserting Stendhal alongside Balzac, as in Taine's

Edmond (left) and Jules de Goncourt (before 1870). Photograph by Félix Nadar.

original remark. It was only in Zola's essays of 1880–81 that the author of *Le Rouge et le noir* (1830) too would be aligned within what he considered the far-sighted predecessors of Naturalism. A brief mention of Stendhal in 1864 refers to him having 'the cold-blooded curiosity of an anatomist' (*OC*, X, 315). But in referring to both Stendhal and Balzac as 'the only two novelists of the century . . . for whom the mechanics of human existence are explored with the penetration of merciless surgeons' (*OC*, X, 735), the associative twinning is no more than strategic. In practice, it is only Balzac who secures his perennial attention.

André Gill, *Les Hommes d'aujourd'hui*, no. 4, 1878.

Having read Balzac for the first time in about 1864, Zola formalized his enthusiasm in the paper, entitled 'Deux définitions du roman' (Two Definitions of the Novel), read on his behalf at a scientific conference in Aix in December 1866: here the author of *La Comédie humaine* is acclaimed as the creator of the modern novel. And during the rest of his life Zola would remain faithful to the critical position on Balzac adopted in his letter of 29 May 1867 to Valabrègue: 'What a man! I am currently rereading him ... For me, no writer this century ... not Victor Hugo nor any of the others . . . comes close to being his equal' (*Corr.*, I, 501). In 1869–70 Zola was again rereading Balzac, reviewing the volumes of the magnificent new edition of the latter's works as they were brought out by the publishing house of Michel Lévy. The timing, coinciding with Zola's preliminary thinking about his *Rougon-Macquart* project, simply confirms the long-recognized influence of Balzac on the novel cycle. The self-conscious title of Zola's 'Differences between Balzac and Myself' (*RM*, V, 1736–7), written solely for his own benefit on the eve of embarking on the series, is an inadvertent revelation of his debt to *La Comédie humaine* as well as of his awareness of the challenges involved in working in Balzac's imposing shadow, as Zola's contemporaries knew. This is exemplified by André Gill's 1878 caricature of him saluting his great predecessor, prompted by Zola's three articles in *Le Bien public* of July 1877 that had included his calling for the erection of a statue commemorating the author of *La Comédie humaine*.

Early Works

It is instructive to correlate Zola's literary criticism during this formative period with his own early work. It is also to be reminded of the prodigious energy he displayed in his twenties – which would be sustained in the productivity of his entire career. After working hours at Hachette or while employed as a full-time journalist, he simultaneously produced a substantial body of creative work. The habit of working late was so ingrained that for many years, when working on a Sunday afternoon, he would recreate evening conditions by drawing the curtains and writing by candlelight. Zola's relativization of the inherent value of his early work is par for the course. As far as the literary merit of his verse is concerned, for example, his general comments, in 1866, on that of other would-be novelists certainly apply to himself: 'each of us has undergone that harsh apprenticeship and wisely consigned to the wastepaper basket our youthful efforts' (*OC*, X, 595). Rubbishing such efforts was extended to his second novel, *Le Vœu d'une morte*: in 1889, a new edition of it was intended to prove how far his writing had progressed since its original publication in 1866, though the demonstration was vitiated by a suppression of many of the stylistic infelicities he now disowned. On the other hand, even texts he would later dismiss as juvenilia throw light on his development as a writer.

Before 1870, Zola published four other novels besides *Le Vœu d'une morte*. Shortly after the appearance of one of them, *Les Mystères de Marseille* (1867), he collaborated during the late summer of 1867 with his friend Marius Roux (1838–1905) on its theatrical adaptation. He attended its first performance, staged in Marseilles itself on 5 October, though judging by his reports on its mixed reception (perhaps because it was four and a half hours in length!) and its truncated run, it was not a success. During these years, Zola also wrote some forty so-called *contes et nouvelles*, a hybrid French category of texts, most of them more abbreviated than what we think of as a 'novella' or 'short story'; although first published in the press, what distinguishes them from journalistic pieces is that they are patently imaginative inventions. Eight of these, the earliest dating from 1859, were collected in Zola's first published volume, *Contes à Ninon*. Four others, under the title *Esquisses parisiennes* (Parisian Sketches), were appended to *Le Voeu d'une morte* in order to fill out a book with an insufficient number of pages. Apart from further enhancing his income, Zola often used these short texts as writing exercises. Some of them anticipate the characteristics of his later work, not least in their thematic continuities.

Attempts to generate renewed interest in Zola's earliest novels have fallen back on the potentially autobiographical dimension of stereotyped plots and scenarios. That does not preclude identifying in these texts, and beyond their very personal origin, major themes of the *Rougon-Macquart*. *La Confession de Claude*, for example, is structured by an opposition between purity and corruption which recurs in many of Zola's mature novels. But to approach *La Confession de Claude* as fiction in its own right is to struggle through a mawkish effervescence too visibly related to Zola's adolescent reading of Alfred de Musset (1810–1857), the author of *La Confession d'un enfant du siècle* (1836). Zola had started working on his own confessional novel in 1862–3, when he and Cézanne were still in thrall to Musset's 'genius'. Nothing is more symptomatic of Zola's progressive liquidation of such enthusiasm for a cloying Romanticism than the scene in *Pot-Bouille* in which a volume of Musset's emotionally incontinent work is the cynical instrument of seduction of a woman overcome by its passionate intensity.

The critical reception of *La Confession de Claude* in 1865, however, does tell us something about its perceived originality at the time. It was referred to the legal authorities, who ultimately decided that it did not so 'offend public morals' that it should be censored or banned. But reviewers professed to be shocked by many aspects of it: its eschewing the comforting redemption of a 'fallen' woman, the novel's equally demystified picture of bohemian poverty, its intimate portrayals of boudoirs and bedrooms and its erotic suggestiveness. By comparison with the *Rougon-Macquart*, such realities are occluded by circumlocution. In expressing reservations about his treatment of them in *La Confession de Claude*, Zola may have had in mind the standard recently set by, and ascribed by him to, *Germinie Lacerteux*. He was nevertheless hugely pleased by the mark he had made. As he wrote to Valabrègue on 8 January 1866, while admitting that his novel had too many 'juvenile' faults:

> I have been attacked from every side . . . But I am now known, I am feared and insulted; what I have skilfully achieved is that from now on I am classed as one of those writers whose work is read with dread. (*Corr.*, I, 434)

Le Vœu d'une morte, written that summer, did not meet such publicity-seeking criteria of success. Villemessant, who had agreed to serialize it in *L'Événement* in the hope of cashing in on the noisy reception of *La Confession de Claude*, was neither the first nor the last to find this novel 'insipid'. Its conventional plot has the dying Blanche de Rionne of Zola's title delegating to Daniel the care of her daughter Jeanne. In an ensuing triangular drama, he sacrifices himself to allow his friend Georges to carry her off. Some of the secondary characters would be fleshed out in Zola's later work: Tellier, the devious politician; his empty-headed wife holding court in a fashionable salon; the wealthy and duplicitous Lorin, married to Jeanne, who is then widowed herself before falling in love with Georges. The reason why the first edition of the novel was deemed to be too short is that Zola abandoned his plan to compose further chapters of this edifying tale, designed for a serialization which, in the event, was sustained for barely a week (11–16 September 1866). He cannot but have been aware that *Le Vœu d'une morte* was a backward step.

Les Mystères de Marseille was primarily conceived with serialization in mind. Zola also hoped that, apart from adding to his income, it might light up his family name. By the time the third and final volume of this intolerably 'loose baggy monster' (to cite Henry James's legendary quip about the nineteenth-century novel in general) was published in Marseilles in July 1868, Zola had set in motion his polemical campaign in *Le Mémorial d'Aix* to rehabilitate his father's reputation. *Les Mystères de*

Marseille has so many examples of financial shenanigans that it reads like a coded indictment of those to which François Zola had fallen victim. Given his father's frustrated attempts to modernize the maritime infrastructure of Marseilles, unbearably poignant for his son, it is perhaps less surprising than it might seem that, as Nicholas Hewitt has remarked, not only is the novel's focus displaced to the city's centre and hinterland, but the Vieux-Port is 'strangely absent'.[7]

It was in the more recently founded regional paper, *Le Messager de Provence*, and at the behest of its owner, convinced that Zola's profile would help it get off the ground, that instalments of the novel appeared between 2 March 1867 and 3 February 1868, with successive breaks separating its three parts. It was consciously modelled on Eugène Sue's (1804–1857) immensely successful *Les Mystères de Paris* (1842–3). Progress on Zola's own potboiler was not slowed by artistic scruples. In a single hour, he admitted, he could polish off seven or eight pages. Which he needed to, since it ended up being 728 of them in length! *Les Mystères de Marseille* has a convoluted plot: its twists and turns (elopements, duels, escapes from prison, miraculous rescue missions and other equally implausible episodes) were designed to sustain subscriptions to *Le Messager de Provence* by prolonging the excitement of prospective readers until reaching a denouement fulfilling the imperatives of melodrama, with villains getting their just deserts.

The interest of *Les Mystères de Marseille*, in tracking Zola's development as a writer, lies elsewhere. Advertised as a 'contemporary historical novel', this is the first of his works to be given a precise context, in this case the Revolution of 1848: its insurgent crowds anticipate those of *La Fortune des Rougon* and *Germinal*. And never before had he engaged in the kind of research which the *Rougon-Macquart* would require of him: writing to Valabrègue in February 1867, he moaned that he was surrounded by a 'chaotic' pile of archival documents from the period in which the novel is set (*Corr.*, I, 473). None of his fiction before *Les Mystères de Marseille* describes so accurately an urban environment. Its hero and heroine, naive and sentimental lovers both, have to negotiate a world peopled by a cast of characters central to the *Rougon-Macquart*: criminal bankers, profiteering moneylenders, self-serving politicians, crooked businessmen and a prostitute in whose silhouette the future courtesan of *Nana* makes a preliminary appearance.

Posterity's judgement of the novel as having, as Hemmings puts it, 'no pretension to literary merit', is one with which Zola himself concurred.[8] It is, of course, too often the habit of writers to exploit their established reputation by making available their earlier work, whatever its quality. Zola, as he had done in the case of *Le Vœu d'une morte* and (in 1880) *La Confession de Claude*, thus 'allowed' *Les Mystères de Marseille* to be republished in 1884. In the preface to this new edition, he virtually apologized for what he calls the novel's 'mediocrity' by explaining that he accepted the *Messager de Provence*'s commission only because back in 1867 he was so hard up in those 'difficult days' (*OC*, I, 225) that there were some in which he had nothing to eat and had to endure the soul-destroying burdens of a journalist in order to make ends meet. It is not easy to reconcile these 'sacrifices', as Zola termed them, with what we now know about his not inconsiderable income at this juncture, let alone its further enhancement, as he confided to Valabrègue, by *Les Mystères de Marseille* earning him an extra 200 francs for each of the nine months he envisaged working on it.

Zola disingenuously justified its republication in 1884 on the grounds that the original volume was so long out of print that it had become a collector's item. His stress on the novel being based on authentic documents was designed, however, to reinforce an understanding of the integral part they played in the methods of composition adopted for the *Rougon-Macquart*. He also reminded his readers that in 1867 he had been simultaneously writing *Thérèse Raquin*, contrasting the four hours of artistic integrity devoted to a couple of its pages with the minimal effort of dashing off the next instalment of *Les Mystères de Marseille*. The coincidence of the two projects is important. *Les Mystères de Marseille* can be viewed as a first if somewhat sketchy attempt to construct a 'social history'; *Thérèse Raquin*, in its investigation of the dark recesses of human nature, is a 'natural history'. In designating the *Rougon-Macquart* as a 'social *and* natural history' of a family, Zola would ultimately bring together these two strands of his early work.

Thérèse Raquin remains the early Zola novel most often read. Its contemporary success was sustained by its theatrical adaptation in 1873 and successive reprintings, in 1877 and 1880, as well as by illustrated editions in 1882 and 1884. Marcel Carné's unforgettable 1953 film is only one of the versions of a novel whose popularity is sustained by innumerable modern editions and translations of it. Unlike *Les Mystères de Marseille*, its plot is deceptively simple. It elaborates the ironies of 'Un marriage d'amour' (A Marriage of Love), the title which the novel originally bore when it appeared in *L'Artiste* in the autumn of 1867 (and which had previously been used for a short piece in *Le Figaro* of 24 December 1866, in keeping with the preparatory function of such texts): in the throes of adultery, Thérèse and her lover murder her husband by drowning him during an outing by the Seine, but after the couple get married, guilt so corrodes their relationship that they end up committing suicide. Such a synopsis does not do justice to the significant advance in Zola's writing represented by this novel. Its descriptive texture is both atmospheric and symbolic; the structuring of its 32 chapters, built around the crime and the marriage, is handled with skill; its minor characters are grotesquely comic; the tracking of disintegration is gripping, giving to the narrative the remorseless logic characteristic of the *Rougon-Macquart*, and that logic applied here to sexual passion, from irresistible desire to impotence, is boldly explicit.

In his 1868 preface to the second edition of *Thérèse Raquin*, Zola spells out his intentions: to produce a work so focused on physiological determinants as to make it a novel of, and for, its time. In practice, it is not constrained by this barely concealed acknowledgement of what it owes to Taine, whose letter to Zola on receipt of *Thérèse Raquin* amounts to a self-congratulatory endorsement of its scientific principles and analysis. Sainte-Beuve also privately wrote to Zola, but interspersing praise with objections to the novel's excesses: the Rembrandt-like gloom of its setting, not at all the street with which he was personally familiar; the ubiquitous vulgarity of its characters; and the overuse of the word 'brutal'. A more telling contradiction of Zola's prefatory stance lies beyond such authorial epithets at odds with a declared neutrality: in the organization of the novel with more concern for suspense than science, and in its recourse to the template of a gothic horror story, complete with ghosts and hallucinatory visions.

The impact of the novel, provoking a ferocious critical debate to which its preface contributed, may have persuaded Zola to continue in a similar vein, in the shape of the last of his early novels: *Madeleine Férat*, written in the summer of 1868. As mentioned in the Introduction above, its autobiographical dimension also bears the imprint of Zola's reading of Michelet and, more recently, of Lucas' treatise on heredity. He clearly tries to give the novel's amorous triangle the same kind of scientific rigour he claimed for *Thérèse Raquin*. And the scenes in *Madeleine Férat* in which spectres of the past haunt the protagonists are as dramatically positioned. But the novel's weaknesses are those of *La Confession de Claude*, and also explained by the fact that *Madeleine Férat* is based on the three-act play, with the same title, that he had unsuccessfully tried to have staged in 1865. That the novel marked a regressive phase in Zola's literary apprenticeship was clear to Taine. He had underlined to Zola, in his response to *Thérèse Raquin*, that 'a novel should always portray the whole of society'; in his letter of early 1869, about *Madeleine Férat*, he doubled down on this advice in a reminder that 'the future of the novel' lay in Balzac's exploration of the society which had emerged since 1789, and that Zola, with his concern for the truth, need only look around him to recognize it.[9] *Les Mystères de Marseille*, while framed by a historical context, has characters largely drawn only from the upper echelons of society. *Thérèse Raquin* and *Madeleine Férat* are exclusively private dramas, devoid of verifiable references to time and place.

Political Journalism

That Zola had failed to take on board the kind of advice proffered by Taine in 1867–8 is all the more unexpected given that it was precisely at this moment that, together with his reading of Balzac and his own Parisian experience, his proximity to the political turmoil of the final years of the Second Empire was registered in his polemical journalism. From 1867 onwards, Napoleon III's power was unravelling. Increasingly violent protests against his dictatorship were met with force. But, in the classic move of authoritarian regimes seeking to assuage dissent, some freedoms were partially restored. That of the press, in May 1868, which saw the founding of 140 newspapers, offered Zola the opportunity to engage directly with the issues of the day. Between that May and the Second Empire's collapse in 1870, Zola wrote for a number of opposition papers, notably *La Tribune* and *La Cloche*, publishing in total 84 articles denouncing a slew of imperial policies.

Zola did not need to tailor his convictions to the needs of militant editors-in-chief. While investigating possible charges of indecency against *La Confession de Claude*, the public prosecutor had looked into its author's background and reassuringly concluded in his report of 8 December 1865 that Zola 'had no clear-cut political opinions'. He seems to have been unaware of his left-wing contacts at Hachette or the satirical thrust of some of his first *contes*. One of the latter, 'Les Aventures du grand Sidoine et du petit Médéric', the last and longest of the *Contes à Ninon*, was written in 1863–4, long before Zola's contribution to republican discourse, and was couched as an allegory; but Sidoine's speech from an Egyptian throne is transparent in its denunciation of many aspects of imperial policy. Less disguised was the mocking tone of Zola's 1865 review article (which no newspaper editor dared to print but which Zola included in *Mes haines* the following year) devoted to Napoleon III's self-regarding if anonymously published *Histoire de Jules César* (OC, X, 157–67). More generally, his literary criticism is increasingly angled to counter the arbiters of public taste. A review in *La Tribune* of the contemporary literary scene was the pretext for an attack on the philistinism of Napoleon III and his ministers, and on the censorship laws responsible for the artistic conformity of the age. Whether or not it is fair to write of Zola's 'tepid republicanism prior to 1868',[10] there is no doubt that his sympathies were radicalized by his involvement in the opposition press during the closing years of the Second Empire. Zola's photograph was in police files in 1869, and in August 1870 he received a summons to appear before the courts on account of his savage denunciation of imperial foreign policy. Only the outbreak of the Franco-Prussian War saved him from certain prosecution.

Zola learnt much from working for the opposition press. His contributions to it also honed his linguistic skills. It was there, too, that he came across general preoccupations which he would make his own. Between his polemical articles of 1868–70 and the early *Rougon-Macquart* the thematic continuities are striking, both in substance and in tone. But his journalism was also formative in another sense: Zola's reinforced awareness of the political leverage of the press would be a lesson never forgotten, for there is a continuity of style between that of the combative columnist of this period and Zola's intervention in the Dreyfus Affair a quarter of a century later: in an eviscerating prose, withering irony assailing official discourse, antagonistic rhetorical devices in the service of an oppositional stance, and arguments deploying the imaginative turns of phrase characteristic of Zola as both novelist and journalist.

Widening Social and Artistic Circles

After his initial isolation on settling in Paris, one of the most formative dimension of Zola's years in the city before 1870 was that of his ever-widening circle of social and professional contacts. This is attested to by the enlargement of his correspondence. By 1868 the number of different recipients of his letters was twenty times as many as when he first arrived in the capital. Beyond what was a small group of faithful friends, they are testimony to a network vastly expanded: of fellow journalists, newspaper barons, publishers, literary critics and intellectual mentors. In addition, Zola got to know a variety of significant writers: Daudet at Hachette in 1863; the Goncourt brothers, so gratified by his review of *Germinie Lacerteux* that they promptly asked him to call on them; Flaubert, whom he first met in 1869.

Far from the hovels in the Latin Quarter he had known, Zola also had occasion to make an entry into high society: *Thérèse Raquin*'s serialization in *L'Artiste* had earnt him another 500 francs; it also deepened his amicable relations with the journal's owner, Arsène Houssaye (1815–1896), who had earlier agreed to publish Zola's study of Manet in the 1 January 1867 issue of *La Revue du XIXe siècle*. Zola was thereafter regularly invited to the legendary Tuesday soirées hosted by Houssaye at his mock Renaissance-Venetian mansion, with its sumptuous decor, on the avenue de Friedland. Guests at these included not only stars of the Parisian stage and *demi-mondaines* (half-respectable courtesans), but the great financiers of the epoch and some of the major political figures of the regime. It is not by chance that in Zola's work-notes for *La Curée* we find the name 'Houssayes' (both father and son) as a shorthand reference to the glittering but corrupt social world that novel depicts.

His feelings about entering this world are difficult to gauge. We can picture a younger and less confident Zola at such gatherings in the last years of the Second Empire from a passing comment Alexis made in 1882:

> his innate shyness prevents him from shining in a social setting. Not that he has greater difficulty than anyone else in making conversation; but faced with people he doesn't know or who are not interested in him, he remains closed up.[11]

Alexis was attempting to answer critics who accused Zola of being unsociable. An article Zola wrote in 1868 is, however, equally illuminating: in *L'Événement illustré* of 13 May he recounted an evening spent 'in a salon where most of the guests were from the world of high finance' (*OC*, XIII, 82–3). Although the scene may be totally fictitious, it nevertheless offers a true reflection of his anxieties in such a situation. Satirical intentions are no doubt responsible for the stress Zola lays on the boredom and weariness inspired in him by the occasion. But he also speaks of his gaucheness in the eyes of the assembled company, who greet his ill-chosen remarks with 'a little contemptuous smile', and from which, in the article's account, he finally makes an undignified and embarrassed exit.

Evidence of Zola's personal awkwardness is also to be found in a passage from *Madeleine Férat* the same year, the context of which describes the protagonists' experience of Parisian high society after their return from the country. A portrait of Zola himself is revealed in Guillaume's censorious attitude towards female glamour: 'invisible among the black frock coats, he spent entire evenings in the bay of a window, watching with inflexible seriousness the shimmering naked shoulders paraded in the candlelight' (OC, I, 873). In *Le Vœu d'une morte*, Daniel overhears the dignitaries at the soirée given by M Tellier 'talking about women and horses, without being able to tell which of their tender and gross remarks applied to which' (OC, I, 174–7). A semblance of indirect speech soon gives way to Zola's unequivocal voice: having been at first dazzled by the spectacle, Daniel understands that he has been duped by outward appearances, realizing that its habitués are as superficially decorative as porcelain figurines. And in the light of Zola's obsessive fear of being buried alive, it is worth underlining Daniel's reaction on first entering the salon:

> he felt the same sense of being suffocated and blinded as a swimmer diving into the water: . . . he couldn't breathe. He remained motionless for a moment . . . struggling against the malaise taking over his whole body. (OC, I, 172)

In *Madeleine Férat*, the lovers throw themselves into the social whirl in order to find relief from their inner torment. But as the effect wears off, we have the same movement as in the earlier novel, from initial fascination to moral disgust. There is in Zola's work, it can be argued, a conception of high society which can be considered in isolation from his direct, if limited, personal experience of it. At its core is its artifice, underlined by Zola's use of theatrical metaphors, his insistence on masks and marionettes, beneath which lie the twin evils of greed and sexual depravity. Angus Wilson, among others, has noted in Zola 'a harsh moral sense at work'.[12] If the texts cited above are coloured by moral revulsion, there is also a certain 'moralizing' dimension overlaid on the world of high society depicted in the *Rougon-Macquart*.

The Art Critic

Another world with which Zola became more familiar, and more comfortable, during this period was that of the painters of his time. If he continues to enjoy a reputation as one of the most important art critics of the nineteenth century, it is inseparable from his personal relationship with Manet and the early Impressionists.[13] Emblematic in that respect is Henri Fantin-Latour's collective portrait, *Un atelier aux Batignolles* (A Studio in the Batignolles District) (1870, Musée d'Orsay, Paris), exhibited at the Salon of 1870. It shows Manet at his easel, the de facto leader of the pictorial avant-garde, around whom in solidarity are ranged artists including Monet, Renoir and Frédéric Bazille, the promising young painter who died, aged only 28, in the Franco-Prussian War. In his review of the 1868 Salon exhibition, Zola had juxtaposed his and Monet's fine landscapes. Among the group represented in the painting, Zola is the *only* writer. It is testimony to the status he had achieved in vigorously defending the work of such painters over the previous five years. He would continue to do so in the future. But Fantin-Latour's picture marks the culmination of another formative experience stretching back to the early 1860s.

Zola had long had an interest in the visual arts. During his early years in Paris, his social life initially revolved around the 'Aix School' of painters he had known in Provence; those who, like himself, had gravitated to the capital and most of whom are now forgotten. He was not overly impressed by their work, even though they occasionally had paintings accepted at the annual Salon. The exception was Paul Guigou (1834–1871), whose premature death Zola lamented in a text dating from 1872 (*EsA*, 220), paradoxically recognized for his talents by having been banished to the Salon des Refusés in 1863. That turning point in the history of French painting figures largely in Zola's thinking about the evolution of modern art. Napoleon III's apparently liberalizing decision to mount such an exhibition, allowing the general public to judge for themselves the works rejected by the admissions jury (in the hope, of course, that they would concur with its decisions), had the unintended consequence of creating a community of artists newly energized in their determination to dismantle the institutional structures constraining their originality. As in Zola's literary criticism, it is this conjunction of culture and politics which is the subtext of his extended commentary on the painters of his time over three decades. It is first visible in art criticism inflected by what he saw and who he knew before 1870.

Henri Fantin-Latour, *Un atelier aux Batignolles*, 1870, oil on canvas.

The painter Zola saw most of, to start with, was Jean-Baptiste Chaillan (1831–?), a fellow student of Cézanne's in Aix, with whom he often went to the Louvre to watch him copy the Old Masters and who would be the model for the near-homonym Chaîne in *L'Œuvre*. 'He really is a mediocre copyist,' Zola wrote to Cézanne in April 1860, 'but when it comes to having to create anything of his own, he is absolutely hopeless' (*Corr.*, I, 151). What lies behind this same letter is Zola's urging Cézanne himself to come up to Paris. This was a challenge: his letters to other friends rush from the excitement of Cézanne's imminent arrival to the despairing and soon-to-be confirmed expectation that the painter would shortly be packing his bags and returning to Provence. But arrive he finally did: a short-lived experiment in 1861, but itself responsible for putting Zola in renewed contact with members of the 'Aix School', and a much longer stay, between November 1862 and the summer of 1864. This was when Cézanne completed his seminal role in Zola's artistic education.

Its elementary lessons are recorded in the prolix interchanges of their earlier correspondence. Their letters of 1858–60 are much concerned with pictorial and aesthetic preferences. During his first visit to Paris, Cézanne took one stage further Zola's growing familiarity with the art of his times. Only a year before, Zola was still countering realist practice by naively affirming that Jean-Baptiste Greuze (1725–1805) had always been his favourite painter and that Ary Scheffer (1795–1858) was a genius. He rapidly tired of the idealist sentimentality of these two painters, perfectly attuned to that of his adolescent poetry and its residue in *La Confession de Claude*. Whether or not he was as dazzled as Cézanne claimed to be by *everything* they had seen together at the Salon of 1861, the painter's euphoric reaction to work shown there by Gustave Doré (1832–1883), together with his sustained admiration for Gustave Courbet (1819–1877), may be indirectly linked to Zola's first-ever critical pieces on the visual arts: on Doré two years later and his long essay on Courbet in 1865 (*EsA*, 435–7, 416–29).

During Cézanne's more extended stay in the capital, their joint exploration of the city left a more permanent mark. Together with Cézanne, Zola visited the Salon des Refusés in 1863. The painter also took him on a round of studios, thereby complementing Zola's privilege of seeing up close Cézanne himself painting in both Paris and Provence. Evidence of Zola's increased understanding of pictorial craft can be found in *Thérèse Raquin*: Laurent, Thérèse's lover, is a painter who, before taking up his palette and brushes, prepares his canvases, as Zola describes it, with meticulous care. It was at the Académie suisse, where Cézanne worked in the mornings, that Zola came into contact with a number of artists at their easels: Pissarro, Armand Guillaumin (1841–1927) and Cézanne's friend, the Puerto Rican painter Francisco Oller (1833–1917). Cézanne's own new acquaintances included Guillemet – through whom Zola met Bazille, who then extended this network by introducing him to Renoir. We do not know whether such introductions consisted of anything more than a handshake. But he spent time with them, notably Monet, at the riverside hamlet of Bennecourt, watching them painting *en plein air*. He also joined these young painters at Pontoise, where Pissarro lived and worked between 1866 and 1869. And it was during this same period that Zola started to organize Sunday evening gatherings of writers and painters. It was only half-jokingly that he would tell Valabrègue in 1867 that he was so exclusively 'surrounded by painters' (*Corr.*, I, 473) that he had nobody with whom to converse about literature. What is not in doubt is that this expanded circle, for which Cézanne was primarily responsible, is unambiguously, and even at twenty years' distance, celebrated in *L'Œuvre*: in its initially happy social occasions; in its fictional characters' debates; and in the chapter recalling Zola, Cézanne and their friends as an army on the march, united in their renegade 'passionate love of art' (*RM*, IV, 124), culminating in the critical battle sparked by the Salon des Refusés.

This apprenticeship is one he served not only in the company of the painters of his circle at the beginning of his career as a writer, but through a growing familiarity with the visual arts, prolonged and enriched over the following decades. His was not a bookish education. From his correspondence, one can track Zola's presence at the annual Salon, even in the years when he was not reviewing the exhibition. His visits to the Louvre and the Musée du Luxembourg were an equally unbroken habit. In 1859, shortly after moving to Paris, he was already distinguishing himself from those who 'flatter themselves that they know about painting and yet who I see at the Salon unable to see the difference between a horse and a donkey' (*Corr.*, I, 112). He immodestly alerted friends stuck in Aix to his newfound cultural expertise: in a letter written immediately after visiting the Salon of 1861 in the company of Cézanne, Zola refrained from conveying his impressions of the exhibition on the grounds that they would be meaningless to the uninformed: 'Although I love the arts,' he wrote to Baille, 'I can hardly talk to you about the latest trends displayed by our artists. You don't know their names and know nothing about their separate schools, and so even the briefest report would be of no interest to you' (*Corr.*, I, 288).

The unique position which Zola occupies in Fantin-Latour's collective portrait, as much a manifesto as an anecdotal record of artistic friendships, is testimony to his role in mediating the originality of the painters he met in the 1860s. Zola's book reviews already implicitly underline his sympathetic critical perspective. Almost four dozen of them were devoted to treatises on aesthetics, scholarly studies by art historians, and illustrated editions. In 1866, coinciding with the Salon articles marking him out as a radically new critical voice, Zola reviewed an art-history manual by Louis and René Ménard. Here he damns without faint praise a book 'representing the very worst' of the rules of painting 'sanctified' by the École des beaux-arts as the pedagogic and administrative arm of the Ministry of Fine Arts. As he wrote in another review of the same publication three days later, 'in artistic matters, my personal opinions are diametrically opposed to those of its authors' (*OC*, X, 666).

In Zola's giving expression to those opinions, it was precisely their exclusively personal legitimacy to which traditional art critics objected.

He did not conform to the professed neutrality of commentary on the annual Paris art exhibition. The personal pronoun heading his own review of that of 1866 (*Mon* Salon), as it did in the case of *Mes haines* (also 1866), in which Zola reprinted his essays on Doré and Courbet, was deliberate: it was intended to stake out his own originality, at odds with both critical and pictorial orthodoxy. Much later, in 1896, Zola admitted that only his youthful bravado justified such excessively provocative headings (*EsA*, 402). The immediate consequence of the outrage greeting his first series of Salon articles in *L'Événement* was to make it difficult for him to persuade any other paper to commission such a review thereafter. Only in 1868 did his badgering of newspaper editors pay off.

What his 1866 articles did do was establish his radical credentials in the eyes of the painters of his social circle. They served to strengthen his links with its members, as is evident from two paintings of that year. First, the witty expression of solidarity in Cézanne's portrait of his father reading *L'Événement* (National Gallery of Art, Washington, DC), the title itself making of his friend's articles an 'event', with Zola's contrary perspective, upending conventional criteria, reflected in that title appearing upside down. Second, Renoir's *Cabaret de la mère Antony* (Nationalmuseum, Stockholm), in which the newspaper is spread by Sisley across a table. The thirteen Cézannes owned by Zola were tokens of friendship. Those in his private collection given to him by the likes of Guillemet, Pissarro and Monet were tokens of gratitude, which can be related to specific instances of Zola's championing their work.

It was Zola's relationship with Manet, however, which was even more decisive in shaping this phase of his career as well as his aesthetic. He had seen the painter's *Déjeuner sur l'herbe* at the Salon des Refusés and his *Olympia* (both 1863 and Musée d'Orsay, Paris), the latter accepted for the Salon of 1865. But in the wake of both of Manet's submissions being rejected the following year, Zola devoted an entire article to him in *L'Événement* of 7 May 1866. Part of its impact lay in Zola's chutzpah in inserting in a review of the works exhibited at the Salon of 1866 a text about an artist excluded from it. Compared to those on show there, his detailing of Manet's originality served as a further illustration of the narrow-mindedness of the members of the admissions jury, whose members were subject to an ad hominem introductory diatribe. This text, shorn of its attack on the jury, formed the basis of the first-ever comprehensive study of Manet which Houssaye published in the 1 January 1867 issue of *La Revue du XIXe siècle* before it appeared, in slightly revised

Paul Cézanne, *Le père de l'artiste lisant 'L'Événement'*, 1866, oil on canvas.

form, as a pamphlet (*EsA*, 466–97). Zola's positioning of Manet within the modernist advance, whether or not his analyses of individual paintings receive complete assent, remains a celebrated chapter in our histories of nineteenth-century French art.

That, at this stage in Zola's thinking about its evolution, Manet was for him the pre-eminent painter of his generation can be approached in a number of ways. His perspective on Manet is a mirroring one, not least because he was *not* Cézanne. In that sense, Zola's engagement with Manet is a process of negative self-definition. However long, deep and troubled, Zola's friendship with Cézanne is coloured by a frustration aimed at his pictorial inconsistencies as well as his personality. By contrast, as projected in Fantin-Latour's 1867 portrait of Manet (Art Institute of Chicago), this worldly, well-dressed and sophisticated gentleman was not at all, as Zola stressed, the 'mocking dauber' (*EsA*, 152) of sneering caricature and popular mythology. The identification of Manet's art with his own extends to a desired social and sartorial persona, in absolute contradistinction to that of Cézanne, with his dishevelled attire and calculated bad manners. His many self-portraits make no attempt to disguise his ill-fitting personality. All Zola's advice to Cézanne, from budgets to self-discipline, adds up to 'Be more like me.' At the very moment he is once again entreating Cézanne to get back to his easel, Zola writes of Manet's rigorous work habits. And he implicitly reproaches Cézanne's procrastination in his view of Manet's contrasting productivity and refusal to be discouraged.

One of the reasons for the critical privileging of Manet is the extent to which his development structurally conforms to Zola's, having (in the latter's view) left behind wayward beginnings, anxieties of influence and theoretical indirections. Zola's pioneering January 1867 study of the painter, mentioned above, is overtly generated by a visit to Manet's studio during which he saw between thirty and forty canvases being prepared for the 1867 Paris Universal Exposition. In fact, Zola only focuses on 15 of the 56 works ultimately shown instead at the painter's private exhibition at the place de l'Alma. What is revealing is that the vast majority of Manets chosen for detailed commentary can be correlated, and even in the space allocated to each of them, to the hostility of their reception. This is also to be reminded of Zola's valorization of negative publicity in the case of his own work, further substantiating his rule of thumb, formulated in his *L'Événement* Salon review of 15 May 1866 that posits an inverse relationship between creative originality and artists catering for the expectations of a philistine public (*EsA*, 162).

Henri Fantin-Latour, *Édouard Manet*, 1867, oil on canvas.

There is no reason to doubt the sincerity of his appreciation of Manet. It is clear, however, that Zola's championing of the painter was also an opportunity to write about himself, both directly and by implication. He underlined his own audacity and courage as a critic; he referred to the hostility he would incur as a result of his admiration for the painter's work; and while both of them were subject to mockery, he was certain that 'one day, we will be avenged' (*EsA*, 155), predicting that Manet's masterpieces, *Le Déjeuner sur l'herbe* and *Olympia*, would in due course find their deserved place in the Louvre. Much more specifically than Cézanne might have imagined on the basis of *La Confession de Claude* being dedicated to him and Baille, it was in response to *Manet*'s critics, who had attacked him for his 'deliberate brutalities' and 'systematic violation' of good taste, that Zola was in effect answering those who had criticized his first novel for its 'crudity of tone' and 'hideous realism'.

The central principle underlying Zola's art criticism, first enunciated in his 1865 essay on Courbet but most fully elaborated in his writing on Manet, is his oft-cited definition of a work of art as 'a corner of creation viewed through a temperament' (*EsA*, 419). In the paintings of Laurent in *Thérèse Raquin* there is dramatization, or demonstration, of individuated artistic representation of the kind he insisted was responsible for

Paul Cézanne, *Self-Portrait*, *c.* 1877, oil on canvas.

Manet's originality. The homicidal character of the novel obviously bears no resemblance to any real-life painter. But stripped of fictional context, the reference to Laurent's 'organism' and the remark that 'it is difficult to penetrate its depths' echo Zola's self-appointed task to dissect 'the anatomy of an organism' in his study of Manet. In the novel's explanation of 'the birth of an artist' it is Laurent's particular temperament, with its singular neuroses, which produces 'beautiful works, suddenly made personal and alive' (*OC*, I, 629). It is also the virtually simultaneous writing of the novel and Zola's texts devoted to Manet which explains *Thérèse Raquin*'s thematic reconfiguration of motifs in *Olympia*. Reviewers of the novel, quite possibly prompted by Zola, leapt on some of the parallels: 'The bedroom contains every horror, even including Manet's cat which has hitherto only appeared in a painting.'[14] Such analogies reinforced a superimposition of critical frames more explicit than in the case of the reception of *La Confession de Claude*. As Zola writes in his preface for *Thérèse Raquin*, rejecting charges of prurience directed to what he calls his own 'canvas': 'I have found myself in the situation of those painters depicting nudes, not for a moment subject to desire, who are profoundly surprised when a critic declares himself shocked by their portrayal of living flesh' (*OC*, I, 520).

To trace Manet's development from his reliance on tradition to the free expression of an original pictorial 'language' was to outline Zola's own career as a writer. What is more, he offered his 1867 study of the painter as an example of his own critical method: 'My study of Manet is a simple application of my way of approaching all artistic matters, and . . . I leave it to others to judge in this essay the merits and defects of my method' (*EsA*, 468). This study is inevitably marked by the pseudo-medical jargon of other texts contemporary to it. Zola's labelling of Manet as 'an analytical painter' in January 1867, akin to writers he places in an analogous category, prefigures his notion of 'naturalist painting' in his Salon articles of 1868. His own role as novelist and critic, and Manet's talents as an artist, would all be increasingly defined by Zola according to the criteria of a developing, if still inconsistent, Naturalist aesthetic.

Zola's efforts to link his name with Manet in the public mind had continued throughout 1867. A projected illustrated edition of his *Contes à Ninon*, mentioned earlier, is a case in point. Manet, more uneasy about such blatant exercises in publicity, hesitated before approving Zola's suggestion to republish his January study in brochure form to coincide with the opening on 24 May of Manet's private exhibition. Zola reported to Valabrègue on the 29th that although this had been financially disappointing so far, he hoped that his pamphlet would 'light the gunpowder' (*Corr.*, I, 500). Manet ended up by thanking him for his valuable help. It may have been in recognition of this, together with the fact that the *Contes à Ninon* project came to nothing, that Manet proceeded to paint Zola's portrait (1868, Musée d'Orsay, Paris). He sat for this between November 1867 and February 1868. In evoking his sittings, the remark that Manet 'copied me as he would have copied some human beast' (*EsA*, 180) is a further rehearsal of the formula he had invoked in his review of Hector Malot's trilogy two years earlier, as well as exemplifying the cross-fertilization of his writing as a novelist and critic.

The portrait was shown at the Salon of 1868 and given to Zola himself, who would later give it pride of place in his Paris apartment. At one level, it had the same tactical function as Zola's earlier pen portrait of the painter's appearance. It was now Manet's turn, in other words, to reciprocate by presenting Zola to the public, equally concerned to substitute for common misperceptions an image of cultural and sartorial sophistication. The uncomplicated view of the painting is that in its general conception and iconographic reference to Zola's writing on Manet, the portrait testifies not only to their friendship but to a common aesthetic programme. On the other hand, Manet's visual wit may also make of it a commentary on the limitations of Zola's writing in support of his paintings. Less subject to equivocation is Zola's fulsome dedication of *Madeleine Férat* to Manet, dated 1 September 1868. It is by no means the last of their interchanges and mutually informing influences on each other's work, but his publicly linking his name to the painter's confirms where Zola now felt he stood.

His understanding of contemporary artistic issues was undoubtedly further shaped by his presence at the meetings, from January 1866 onwards, of Manet and his friends at the Café Guerbois, at no. 11, grande rue des Batignolles, in the very heart of the quarter where the majority of them lived and worked. In *L'Œuvre*, it is renamed the Café Baudequin and transparently identified as 'the cradle of a revolution' (*RM*, IV, 79). Initially informal and intermittent, the meetings there rapidly became a ritualized Friday evening occasion. In a side room, where noisy companionship did not preclude serious aesthetic debates, there would assemble an astonishing range of artists and critics, ever-expanding over time. These included Bazille, Fantin-Latour, Guillemet, Jean Béraud (1849–1935), Marcellin Desboutin (1823–1902) and Alphonse Legros (1837–1911), as

Édouard Manet, *Émile Zola*, 1868, oil on canvas.

well as those who would figure at the inaugural Impressionism exhibition in 1874: Zacharie Astruc (1835–1907), Édouard Béliard (1832–1912), Monet, Edgar Degas (1834–1917), Auguste Renoir (1841–1919), Guillaumin and Félix Bracquemond (1833–1914). James McNeill Whistler (1834–1903) and the Belgian painter Alfred Stevens (1823–1906) sometimes joined this brilliant gathering of artists, as did Antonin Proust (1832–1905), in due course one of Manet's most influential commentators as well as a future Minister of Fine Arts. Manet himself, with his discursive vigour, invariably dominated proceedings, as Zola remembered in preparing *L'Œuvre* in the notes for which his fictional painter assumes a similar role.

It was at this same moment that Zola put his own soirées on a more systematic footing, now on a Thursday. To these were invited Cézanne and other Aixois friends as in earlier years, but also habitués of the Café Guerbois, Zola thereby becoming one of the key players bringing together the 'École des Batignolles' celebrated by Fantin-Latour's collective portrait. Slightly at odds with the painting's compositional planes, the Zola who appears in that painting suggests he had an agenda of his own. He also displays a self-confidence not wholly consistent with the image of him in Manet's iconic 1868 portrait. And contemporary perception of his appearance and personality is even less suggestive of confidence. On meeting him for the very first time, also in 1868, the Goncourt brothers found him impenetrably enigmatic: 'a well-built young man . . . with delicate porcelain-like features . . . a mixture of male and female like those of his characters . . . but sickly, living on his nerves . . . racked by anxiety, troubled and suffering'.[15]

On the other hand, the art critic Armand Silvestre (1837–1901), recalling the special place occupied by the novelist in the midst of heated discussions at the Café Guerbois at roughly the same date, offered a portrait of the newly acquired persona subsequently projected in Zola's studio photographs of the 1870s:

> he was then still battling . . . but his certainty of future triumphs was visible in the serenity of his remarks . . . formulating them with clarity and without raising his voice . . . speaking with the calmness of those sure of themselves.[16]

The contradictions are doubtless explained by the Goncourts' awareness of a writer whose literary ambitions, as their 'admirer and pupil' (as they reassured themselves in prefacing the record of their first impressions of Zola cited above) outlined a putative novel cycle to them, might put their own achievements in the shade, and Silvestre's retrospective 'insights' once these ambitions had been realized. But both assessments, however distorted by time or prejudice, speak of a tension between Zola's private and public selves never fully resolved.

ZOLA'S RECOLLECTIONS of his 'disappointment' on first arriving back in Paris in 1858 fitted in perfectly with the nineteenth-century literary stereotype of the young hopeful making his way to the French capital from provincial obscurity. This is most famously tracked in Balzac's *Illusions perdues* (1843), the second part of which is ironically headed 'Un grand homme de province à Paris' (A Provincial Grandee Goes to Paris). Its connotations are of a 'somebody' brought down to the size of a 'nobody' by an urban experience far beyond an outsider's understanding of how to master it. Zola's admirers have been unable to resist the appeal of such a literal and metaphorical itinerary.[17] To stitch together the multiple dimensions of his formative years between 1858 and 1870 is to arrive at an inversion of the above Balzacian destiny. In Zola's case, as a result of his apprenticeships, a 'nobody' had indeed become a 'somebody'.

3
Writing the *Rougon-Macquart* I: From Planning to Realization

The following two chapters cover more than half of Zola's adult life: the 25 years between starting to plan the *Rougon-Macquart* in 1868 and completing the novel cycle in 1893. Their scope, however, is not restricted to that monumental project by virtue of the fact that, at the same time, he was writing much else: hundreds of letters each year, newspaper articles (for the provincial as well as Parisian press), short stories, art criticism, plays (both free-standing and theatrical adaptations of his own novels), prefaces to the work of others and critical essays aimed at a reading public in France and abroad. To filter out, in the interests of clarity, these diverse activities is at one level to blur their interconnectedness: they are literally simultaneous in the sense that, on most days, Zola would work on his novels in the morning and devote the afternoon to his journalism and other texts. Evenings were spent correcting proofs, those for the serial publication of his novels being the stage in the creative process where he inserted the most extensive revisions. On most Sundays, he caught up on his correspondence, much of it professional rather than private. Where these activities intersect is in the cross-fertilization of ideas and the explicatory light which his non-fictional writing deliberately shines on the aesthetic principles informing the *Rougon-Macquart*. Nor can the series itself be considered in isolation, for it draws on, and develops, themes already visible in Zola's earlier work, some of which have their origin in his private life; it also anticipates those to which he would return in novels written after it.

PAUL ALEXIS' 1882 BIOGRAPHY retails a narrative of Zola's construction of his *Rougon-Macquart* designed to reinforce a certain image of the novelist at work. In this telling, his literary achievement is the result of a single-minded focus on a grand design, with its constituent parts unproblematically produced one after another, year after year. In Alexis' interim summary, there is little sense of changes of plan or interruptions. There is none in respect of periods of intense self-doubt or the ways in which Zola's novels themselves put question marks over his whole project. Dealing only with the first nine of the *Rougon-Macquart*, Alexis could not foresee, of course, either how long it would take Zola to bring the series to its conclusion or, more significantly, how it progressively amplifies the writer's ambitions.

In one important respect, however, Alexis' account, aided and abetted by Zola himself, has had a lasting impact: by their joint emphasis on the role of research within the writer's methods of composition, there has survived a perception (even after modern scholars have tried to correct it) that Zola's novels simply rework, however creatively, his documentary sources. In response to the hostile critical reception of many of the *Rougon-Macquart*, Zola himself had default recourse to such a misleading account. Indeed, the timing of Alexis' version, in 1881–2, is not arbitrary: it appeared at the same moment as Zola's major theoretical works. In 1880 the publication of *Les Soirées de Médan*, a collection of texts put together by Zola and members of his literary circle, was equally militant in intent: in referencing his country home, its very title underlined his leadership of an apparently homogeneous group of like-minded writers. But, beyond a polemical context at this moment at its most acute, all such declarations have been responsible for a distorted view of Naturalism, the aesthetic commonly associated with Zola himself.

To explore the writing of the *Rougon-Macquart* is to gain insight into the complexities and contradictions of that aesthetic. Moreover, the development of Zola's series bears the imprint of the two decades of French history during which he was at work on it. Specific historical events modified original intentions, none more so than those of 1870–71. Of greater importance is the fact that, precisely because the process of writing the novels was extended into the *fin de siècle*, they opened up perspectives increasingly wider than the historical subtitle of Zola's series ('the natural and social history of a family under the Second Empire'). His experience of the reign of Napoleon III determines his representation of it through the prism of his polemical journalism in the late 1860s. Over the course of the more than twenty years during which he was writing the *Rougon-Macquart*, however, the Second Empire is left behind, both literally and as the singular context for his family saga. Its defined temporal span is subsumed in a properly historical *vision*: one that is both contemporary and timeless.

Planning the Series

Zola's initial idea was that the *Rougon-Macquart* should consist of ten novels. This is what he told the Goncourt brothers during his meeting with them, evoked at the end of the previous chapter, in December 1868. This coincides with his reading of Lucas' treatise on heredity, immediately after which a related set of notes includes a 'memo to self': 'Find the novels' (*RM*, V, 1731). It is here that he compiled a list of ten subjects to be treated, in what is a tentative outline of his novel series. Zola distributed these into a preliminary division of society into four 'worlds': the proletariat; commerce; the bourgeoisie; and what he calls *le grand monde*, conceived as that of a political as much as a social elite. Aware that this division did not adequately accommodate all the possible characters his annotation of Lucas had led him to imagine, Zola also appended 'a world apart', into which he could slot a prostitute, a murderer, a priest and an artist.

This supplementary frame is consistent with a historically acute understanding of the erosion of neatly divided social structures by marginalized protagonists moving within and across them: in *La Conquête de Plassans*, the priest's pernicious influence dissolves boundaries between classes; in *La Bête humaine*, the murderer brings to light political scandal as well as disturbing the regulated cogs of a modernity represented by the railway system itself; in *L'Œuvre*, the radical painter challenges bourgeois expectations and cultural traditions; but nowhere in the series would this erosion be more powerfully depicted than in *Nana*, in which the pervasive symbol of the courtesan's infiltration of all reaches of the social hierarchy is that of a contaminating fly. Only during the writing of the *Rougon-Macquart* would the delineations of Zola's self-contained, if vague, 'four worlds' also dissolve, equally subject as they are to the corrosive forces of rapacity, political self-interest and sexual promiscuity.

Early in 1869 Zola set about securing a contract for his series by approaching Albert Lacroix (1834–1903), who had published four of his early works: *Contes à Ninon*, *La Confession de Claude*, *Thérèse Raquin* and *Madeleine Férat*. This was not straightforward: the subclauses of Lacroix's contracts were cannily drafted, resulting in Zola's earnings for the 1,500 copies of *Thérèse Raquin*, for example, amounting to no more than 450 francs. This was better than in the case of the *Contes à Ninon* in 1864: Lacroix had only committed to paying any royalties at all if sales of this collection of short stories warranted a second edition. Which they did not. For the *Rougon-Macquart*, royalties were agreed at 40 centimes per volume sold. There is something characteristically malicious in the Goncourts noting, in the record of their meeting with Zola, that their upstart rival was looking for 6,000 francs for his series. He did in fact negotiate a monthly contract of 500 francs in return for two novels per year, optimistic by any standards. But he also had to sign, in advance, repayments to the publisher in the event of sales or his assumed productivity failing to cover that income. He later told a journalist that, after Lacroix went bust in 1872, he himself was, as a result of these forced guarantees stretching for years ahead, left with 20,000 francs of debts to his publisher's creditors. There is no evidence that Zola felt bound to honour the punitive consequences of contractual arrangements, in any case of dubious legality, which the artful Lacroix had put in place, sure in the knowledge that, in negotiating these with a very ambitious young writer, he held all the cards.

The financial viability of the series, and ultimately Zola's own wealth, would in the future be underpinned by Georges Charpentier (1846–1905). In July 1872 he not only bought out for 800 francs the rights to the two novels of the *Rougon-Macquart* which Lacroix's bankrupt firm had already published, he also put Zola's contract on a new footing, again on the unrealistic assumption of two novels per year but now based on 3,000 francs for each one. In acknowledgement of the economic return on his investment in Zola's writing, Charpentier then incrementally revised upwards his royalties from Lacroix's original percentage to 75 centimes per volume by 1892, as well as ceding to Zola from 1875 onwards all serialization and translation rights. By then, because Charpentier applied these new rates retrospectively, he owed Zola 10,000 francs in back payments. His generosity, or just plain decency, was based on both principle and a commitment to artistic values exemplified by novelists whose work he also published, including Flaubert, Daudet, Edmond de Goncourt, Guy de Maupassant (1850–1893) and Joris-Karl Huysmans (1848–1907).

These and other prominent cultural figures formed the kernel of Marguerite Charpentier's weekly gatherings at which writers mixed with composers, actresses as famous as Sarah Bernhardt (1844–1923) and some of the Impressionist painters Charpentier's wife supported. Zola was a member of this social circle, in which he felt more comfortable than at Houssaye's pretentious residence in the late 1860s. The relationship with Charpentier himself rapidly evolved from its commercial beginnings. In *Le Figaro* of 13 June 1896, on the occasion of Charpentier's retirement and comparing him favourably with other publishers of his acquaintance, Zola recalled that 'over the last quarter of a century . . . the friendship with my own publisher has been so affectionate and unshakeable that I've never had to ask him for a statement of account' (*OC*, XIV, 804).

Zola and his wife were almost part of the family immortalized in Renoir's *Portraits de Madame Charpentier et ses enfants* (1878, Metropolitan Museum of Art, New York). In that painting, the small boy to his mother's immediate right, Paul (often mistaken for a girl because of his blond ringlets and the dress he is wearing), was Zola's godson; the letters exchanged with his parents in the spring of 1895 when Paul, aged only twenty, became the second of their two sons to die prematurely speak of a grief profoundly shared (*Corr.*, VIII, 220–21). Left without an heir, Charpentier gave up his business, selling it to Eugène Fasquelle (1863–1952), who sustained with Zola a trust so exceptional that both the publishers of the *Rougon-Macquart* – after, of course, Lacroix – virtually acted as his private bankers: handling all financial matters linked to his professional activities, but also offsetting his income by dealing with many of his personal bills. In a November 1901 letter to Alexandrine, he reported that he had withdrawn from the publishing house 5,000 francs in cash for 'your return' (knowing all too well that she would be resuming her Parisian shopping habits after her two-month stay in Italy) (*LA*, 777). The Zola and Charpentier couples spent holidays together in the late 1880s, starting at the Charpentiers' villa near Royan named 'Le Paradou', in homage to the garden setting of the same name in *La Faute de l'Abbé Mouret*, published in the year it was built. Thereafter the Zolas sometimes took holiday rentals within reach of it. On his retirement, Charpentier had responded privately to Zola's tribute by assuring him that their uncommon friendship would survive into the future. It manifestly did: in his courageous support for Zola during the Dreyfus Affair, including visiting the writer in his London exile, and not least in his physical presence next to Zola at some of its most publicly threatening moments.

To engage Lacroix's interest in his proposal in 1868–9, Zola had provided him with synopses of envisaged novels as well as a detailed elaboration of his series' introductory frame, *La Fortune des Rougon*. These do not exactly correspond to the first ten novels as we have them today: two of the synopses are amalgamated in a single novel; another is redefined by the fall of the Second Empire the year after submitting his prospectus to Lacroix. Overlaid on an earlier preliminary list of the subjects he wanted to treat, those that survive suggest that his priorities were, after *La Fortune des Rougon*, novels devoted to the speculative frenzy associated with the rebuilding of Paris, the role of priests in society, politics, the working class, art and the judiciary: respectively, if reshaped, the future *La Curée*, *La Conquête de Plassans*, *Son Excellence Eugène Rougon*, *L'Assommoir*, *L'Œuvre* and *La Bête humaine*. On the other hand, the idea of writing a whole novel about a procuress evaporates, with the figure relegated to that of a secondary character making intermittent appearances elsewhere. One of these, however, is so integral to his plotting as to suggest that Zola did not want to dispense entirely with the role in a corrupt society played by a woman arranging marriages and sexual liaisons behind the scenes: in the second chapter of *La Curée*, the shadowy activities of Sidonie Rougon are described at length, and she is conceived as representative of the 'classical school' (*RM*, I, 424) of the stereotype, ultimately defeated by a more modern rival in Mme Lauwerens.

But Zola's preliminary thinking about his novel cycle, both in his private notes and in his outline of it for Lacroix, remains instructive. In comparing his project with Balzac's *La Comédie humaine*, Zola's declared ambitions included the multiple ways in which his own work would be 'utterly different': in its restricted focus on a single family rather than spread across 3,000 characters; in its neutral rather than judgemental perspectives, restricting his own to that of a scientist rather than adopting Balzac's moral and philosophical standpoints; and, in contrast to what he considered the latter's exclusive interest in Catholicism and the monarchy, 'mine will be a mirror of the whole of contemporary society' (*RM*, V, 1737), underlining (with his pen) that the only function of historical context would be to complement other determinants of human behaviour. The thrust of these notes is rehearsed for the benefit of Lacroix, in the stress that his series would span the Second Empire 'from the *coup d'état* of 1851 to the present day', simply recording the era rather than inserting his own point of view. He would do for the Second Empire, he claimed, what Balzac had done for the July Monarchy, but 'more systematically' in the application of underlying 'scientific' principles (*RM*, V, 1755–8).

Zola had promised to himself 'to leave politics aside', and he assured Lacroix that he would proceed 'without any democratic prejudices . . . not as a socialist, but simply as an artist'. This claim to write with the objectivity of the dispassionate observer, doubtless to assuage possible anxiety about falling foul of imperial censorship, is yet another intention contradicted by the novels of the series. To further reassure his publisher, he indicated that there would be 'heroes' as well as 'villains', and, with an eye to commercial considerations, Zola stressed that each episode could stand alone. This remains as true for readers today as it did for contemporary ones, although many of the novels include passing reference to the family origins and previous life of their protagonists. He had noted that he would abjure the Balzacian technique of reappearing characters. In practice, even in the margins of each episode, it is possible to trace fictional destinies threaded through the *Rougon-Macquart*. In some cases, Zola felt obliged to reread an earlier novel to ensure consistency: for *Nana*, he rehearsed the courtesan's sexually wayward beginnings as they are signalled at the end of *L'Assommoir*; in detailing the figure of Claude Lantier in *L'Œuvre* he copied out verbatim his pen portrait in *Le Ventre de Paris*; for the concluding novel of the series, *Le Docteur Pascal*, Zola revisited all the *Rougon-Macquart* in order to provide an epilogue to each of them.

The interior monologue of Zola's preliminary thoughts on his series resembles that of the preparatory notes for each of its novels. All such musings are punctuated by the imperative ('Il faut') of what 'I must' do. This applies to his invocation of other writers. As in the case of Balzac, the Goncourts were also contrasted with what he felt was necessary in order to more precisely define his own originality. At the end of their 1868 meeting with their 'admirer', so their diary entry records, Zola had reiterated his conviction that the brothers' novels provided the template for every writer following in their footsteps. Unknown to them, though they may have suspected it, Zola was at that very moment thinking otherwise: 'the Goncourts will be so crushed by . . . the length of my chapters . . . that no one will accuse me of imitating them' (*RM*, V, 1745). Their novels are so fractured by chapter divisions (70 in *Germinie Lacerteux*, 154 in *Manette Salomon* (1867)) that they string together a sequence of scenes without the internal 'logic' of, and 'breathless' immersion in, his own novels.

This compelling quality could be achieved, Zola thought, by limiting each of the novels to twelve or thirteen chapters. The structuring of

L'Assommoir would in due course illustrate this tightening to brilliant effect: as the first six of its chapters track Gervaise's ascent to the peak of her hopes and happiness, so the last six of the thirteen incrementally register her decline. The intensification of such tragic irony, already signalled by the connotations of bludgeoning forces in that novel's title (the 'Assommoir' is the name of the drinking den frequented by the characters while *assommer*, in French, is 'to smash' or 'deal a heavy blow'), involves the reader emotionally in what was originally conceived as 'La Simple Vie de Gervaise Macquart' (The Simple Life of Gervaise Macquart), simple only in the rising and falling curves of a fictional destiny. Barely half of the *Rougon-Macquart*, it has to be said, respects Zola's self-imposed limits; his alternative solution was to break up a greater overall number of chapters by placing them in separate parts. This almost certainly reflects his increasing involvement in the theatre: the five parts of *Une page d'amour* are only one example of such segmentation.

In thinking about characterization, Zola turns more positively to the Goncourts: he contrasts the eponymous heroine of *Germinie Lacerteux* with Flaubert's typecasting of a 'realistically observed' Emma Bovary. And he engages in a silent argument with Taine. The latter's advice, he noted, was to generalize. But this advocacy of typology seemed incompatible with Taine's praise for Julien Sorel, the hero of Stendhal's 1830 *Le Rouge et le noir*. This character, Zola felt, was as atypical as the Goncourts', and more 'humanly interesting' by virtue of their 'torturing of the truth' at the expense of the humdrum, thereby testifying to artistic creativity (*RM*, v, 1743). Zola's compromise was to try to sustain the singularity of 'my *Thérèse* and my *Madeleine*', while not inventing characters so out of the ordinary as to make them 'monstrous'. In remembering that apprenticeship, he also cautioned himself against using too many adjectives or indulging in descriptive passages so long, as in *Madeleine Férat*, that they disrupted the 'majestic torrent' of his future narratives. That he was still intent at this stage on exploiting another lesson of his early novels is equally clear from his determination to restrict the size of his cast: 'two or three central characters, analysed in depth, and two or three secondary ones . . . either as a complement or contrast to them'. This was again to differentiate himself from Balzac's activation of 'an entire world'. In practice, that of the *Rougon-Macquart*, teeming with hundreds of both fictional characters and historical figures, does bear comparison with *La Comédie humaine*.

What also dominates Zola's preliminary thinking about the *Rougon-Macquart* is a concern for cohesion, balance and the internal rhythms of his series. He expressed the need to give it a unifying 'philosophical' thread, neither 'absurd' (as he termed Balzac's) nor so foregrounded as to impinge on his fiction. Balzac's interpolated passages of reflection must be avoided: 'I prefer to simply write as a novelist,' rather than engage in a demonstration of ideas. The underlying thread would be, he thought, materialism. This is synonymous with a vision elaborated in his series: that of a society and an era shaped by 'forces' he felt he had no need to further explain. The injunction to 'avoid using the word Fate . . . which would be ridiculous across ten volumes' had been inserted during his reading of Lucas. But the reminder here relegates the influence of heredity to the margin. Those forces that do provide the impetus of his series are those driving the members of his fictional family: material ambitions and carnal appetites.

As for balance, while ensuring that readers would be 'gripped by the throat' by his 'excessive and unforgettable . . . nightmares', as he had learnt from the reception of *Thérèse Raquin*, Zola was aware that he would have to find 'something else' so as not to overdo 'dramas of the flesh'. By organizing his series not as a linear unfolding of events (as in texts dictated by serialization) but rather as a set of overlapping perspectives, both chronological and social, he was able to implement projected symmetries and antitheses: alternating between novels set in Paris and the provinces, between those with male and female characters at the centre, between the private and public spheres, between social classes and between light and shade. *Son Excellence Eugène Rougon*, staging an official history, is followed by *L'Assommoir*'s revelation of the hidden realities of the daily grind. The year after the latter's focus on the lives of the proletariat in Parisian slums, *Une page d'amour* takes the reader to the comfortable interiors of suburban Passy. But it also exemplifies the way in which the rhythm of the series can occasionally be related to that of Zola's personal circumstances: most of that novel was composed during his five-month stay in L'Estaque in 1877 which he described as a 'retreat', relieved to have left Parisian politics and literary controversy behind, and Zola's letters from there to all his correspondents that summer speak of a marvellous interlude 'far from the madding crowd', calmly progressing *Une page d'amour* with a view of the Mediterranean from his balcony and enjoying the simple pleasures of eating shellfish and bathing in the sea. Even his wife, so he reported, was happy and much restored (*Corr.*, III, 67–142).

In planning *Au bonheur des dames*, Zola determined from the outset that, immediately after the bleakness of *Pot-Bouille*, he would write a book celebrating the energy of the times. Instead of 'giving the final word to inanity and sadness' (*Ms* 10277, fol. 1), it would represent the genesis of a dynamic period, built on hard work and collective aspiration. In depicting 'many people who are happy to be alive', enjoying their deserved success, this would be the reverse side of the preceding novel's exposé of mediocrity and failure. Even the title of *Une page d'amour* pointed to the text's parenthetical status, an isolated page in his family saga as well as in its heroine's life: as Zola later wrote, 'written between *L'Assommoir* and *Nana*, I conceived it as a contrast, an interlude of tenderness' (*Corr.*, VII, 288). Justified by wanting to include 'every kind of note' in his series and protesting at the time that, in working on a novel that would be 'totally new' whatever its limited critical or commercial success, 'he had no regrets' (*Corr.*, III, 114), Zola was impatient to move on: after the 'blandness' of *Une page d'amour*, so he confided to Edmond de Goncourt from L'Estaque in July 1877, *Nana* would be anything but ('*féroce*', or 'savage', as he termed it) (*Corr.*, III, 82). Nor was Zola averse, in the display of such alternating modes, to confounding his reading public: after the brutalities of rural life depicted in *La Terre*, the opening lines of his preparatory notes for *Le Rêve* defy critics too readily reaching for variants of 'obscenity' in denouncing his novels:

> I would like to write a book at odds with what might be expected of me. The priority must be that it should be a novel which anybody could read, even young ladies. No violent passion, therefore, nothing but an idyll. (*Ms* 10323, fol. 217)

And then *La Bête humaine*: by contrast, 'after *Le Rêve*, I want to write an entirely different kind of novel; set in the real world' (*Ms* 10274, fol. 338).

Only with the change of publisher in 1872 did Zola begin to think of expanding his series. To the original ten novels outlined to Lacroix, he added four more. At the same time, for his own and Charpentier's benefit, he inserted their protagonists in the genealogical tree he had first sketched in 1869. The four novels newly imagined comprise one which would become *Au bonheur des dames*, a second and more 'political' working-class novel (as *Germinal* would be) complementing what he already had in mind for the future *L'Assommoir*, an embryonic version of *Une page d'amour* and a 'scientific study' which looks forward to *Le Docteur Pascal*. By 1880 Zola's admission that he still had nine novels to write suggests he had arrived at the decision to give the *Rougon-Macquart* cycle its definitive and satisfyingly rounded proportions. In the same way as he had suggested a 'perfect ten' novels to Lacroix, it is inconceivable that a man so preoccupied by order and symmetry would have settled for an awkwardly incomplete figure of just more, or fewer, than twenty.

Never in doubt was the function of the introductory novel of his series, *La Fortune des Rougon*. As stressed earlier, this is where everything begins. It was sociologically necessary too that the rising fortunes of a fictional family should have their origins in a provincial backwater. But, with Eugène Rougon already there and busily preparing his ministerial future, Paris is on the horizon, as much as it had been for Zola himself in leaving Aix-en-Provence. To correlate the Rougons' material and political ambitions with the opportunities afforded by the *coup d'état* of 1851 was to fulfil his intention to portray the Second Empire's origins. This correlation was a topical theme in the opposition press at the very moment Zola was planning *La Fortune des Rougon*. In the political climate of the faltering regime, he would learn as much as he would contribute. It was while writing for *La Tribune* that he came across the historians who were to become the principal sources for the *Rougon-Macquart*, notably Taxile Delord (1815–1877) to whose work Zola freely admitted his debt: the first volume of Delord's *Histoire du Second Empire* (1868–75) was serialized in the paper in January 1869. And Delord, as an ardent republican, was hardly the model of an impartial historian. Zola would be guided by the general spirit of his work, make the same accusations as to the moral state of France, and adopt Delord's portrait of Napoleon III.

The emperor's enemies had long held ready allusion to his regime's origins as a weapon of revenge once it should appear to stumble. In *La Tribune*, on 29 August 1869, Zola contributed to such republican propaganda. The overt pretext was a review of the study of the uprising in the Var which he had already consulted to fill out some of the historical details of *La Fortune des Rougon*. It is the clearest proof of the extent to which Zola's journalistic activities at this time account for the satirical perspective of the early *Rougon-Macquart*. But his article also implicitly drew attention to the topicality of the novel on which he was then at work. This would be further enhanced by having it serialized in *Le Siècle*, a newspaper with a huge circulation as well as being politically sympathetic to *La Fortune des Rougon*'s overt denunciation of the *coup d'état*. From Zola's initial planning onwards, the novel's sweethearts assume a symbolic role: Silvère is conceived as incarnating 'the young

Paul Cézanne, *Paul Alexis lisant à Émile Zola*, *c.* 1869, oil on canvas.

Republic', and the virginal Miette as 'Liberty', referencing Delacroix's iconic painting, *La Liberté guidant le peuple* (1830, Louvre, Paris). Their courtship seals the symbiosis of these ideals. The deaths of the couple at the hands of the supporters of the future Napoleon III allegorize the criminal origins of the Second Empire.

As the date on the back of the first page of its manuscript confirms, Zola had started writing *La Fortune des Rougon* on 4 June 1869. Towards the end of September, when Alexis, newly arrived in Paris, visited him for the first time, in the company of Valabrègue, his guests were treated to a reading of its opening pages. Two of Cézanne's 1869–70 paintings record such occasions at Zola's then address in the rue la Condamine (in the 17th arrondissement) : *La Lecture de Paul Alexis chez Zola* (private collection) and *Paul Alexis lisant à Émile Zola* (Museu de Arte de São Paulo). Much of the novel was drafted during the summer of 1869. Zola told Edmond de Goncourt on 15 July 1870 (*Corr.*, II, 223) that he was still madly trying to complete it, its serialization in *Le Siècle* having already begun on 28 June. As so often during his writing career, he was having to catch up.

On 19 July, however, France declared war on Prussia and preparations were put in place should Paris be besieged. On 8 August, faced with a rapidly deteriorating political and military situation, *Le Siècle* suspended publication of Zola's novel in order to give greater coverage to the impending crisis. He would not see its publication resumed until March 1871. In a letter to Goncourt on 22 August 1870, Zola described himself as 'a miserable novelist with nothing to do'; 'this appalling war', he wrote, 'has wrenched the pen from my hand. My suffering is that of a directionless soul. I'm just wandering aimlessly through the streets' (*Corr.*, II, 223–4). Accepting Goncourt's invitation to lunch on the following Saturday, the same restless Zola expressed his eagerness to engage in 'some quiet conversation', away from everything that was getting on his nerves. By no means had he given up his literary ambitions. In his *Journal* entry for 27 August, Goncourt reported that Zola had again entertained him with details of his planned novel cycle. Frustration at not being able to get on with it was Zola's immediate reaction to the outbreak of the Franco-Prussian War. But this interruption to the writing of his series would in fact have enriching consequences for its overall design and thematic emphases.

Interlude: The Franco-Prussian War

It sometimes seems as if the Franco-Prussian War of 1870–71 has been bracketed out of the history of post-Revolutionary France. Only in 2014 was a museum commemorating it opened at Gravelotte, in Lorraine. That it has not been entirely forgotten is partly due to the great war novel that Zola wrote some twenty years after it, *La Débâcle*. Its subject is his country's humiliating defeat in this conflict. Both its fictional transposition in that novel and the shadow it casts over the *Rougon-Macquart* as a whole testify to the Franco-Prussian War's influence on Zola's life and work. As late as 1878, he was still lamenting 'the political and social catastrophes from which we have not yet recovered' (*OC*, XII, 564).

This is also to be reminded of the equally shaping influence of the Franco-Prussian War on modern France, and its geopolitical consequences for Europe.[1] Ever since, it can be argued, the country's national identity and foreign policies have been inseparable from the perception of the threat across the Rhine. For two world wars (and, as a consequence, the dynamic of Franco-German relations in the second half of the twentieth century) can be traced back through a causal pattern which originates in the Franco-Prussian War. As a direct result of it, by the Treaty of Frankfurt in May 1871, France lost its eastern provinces of Alsace and Lorraine, an amputation only avenged by the terms of the Treaty of Versailles (1919), which, in turn, provided Hitler with the opportunity to reverse them. Zola was writing the *Rougon-Macquart* during a period dominated by a revanchist political and military discourse. And only that wider context explains the significance of the Dreyfus Affair and his historic intervention in it.

La Débâcle skilfully inserts, not least for the benefit of earlier generations of readers subject to collective amnesia, allusions which outline the dramatic events of 1870–71: the novel very precisely explains, however unpalatable, the multiple reasons for France's defeat. The apparently bizarre *causa belli* of the Franco-Prussian War was a dispute over the Spanish throne, vacant since 1868. In supporting the candidature of King Wilhelm of Prussia's obscure relative, Prince Leopold of Hohenzollern, Chancellor Otto von Bismarck (1815–1898) had found the perfect pretext to draw France into a war necessary to drive the southern German states into a powerful union with Prussia. Consternation in France, at the prospect of having to guard its Iberian frontier too, escalated into an ultimatum to withdraw the Hohenzollern candidacy (referenced by Zola in *La Bête humaine* as a beacon on the road to catastrophe). In the ensuing diplomatic manoeuvring, during the first two weeks of July 1870, France played into Bismarck's hands.

Zola was not blind to this: in an October 1870 article headed 'La Tête de Bismarck' and calling for his head, he recognized that 'Bismarck, at present, is the brains of Prussia.'[2] Allusions to him across the *Rougon-Macquart*, after the Franco-Prussian War, are marked by a grim authorial irony. In *Nana*, Bismarck's personality and politics are a source of blithely unaware chattering among the most distinguished representatives of the imperial regime he would destroy: one of them discounts the importance of a man she considers a stupid boor whose prominence she cannot understand, and even the mere suggestion that he would conduct a successful war against the French is greeted with mirth. In *L'Argent*, Bismarck makes an appearance at the Paris Exposition of 1867, where the immense popular success of the Krupp guns put on display by Germany needs no authorial comment. He is seen following his monarch around Paris like a 'faithful dog', but, in Chapter Eight, at the ball held at the Ministry of Foreign Affairs, he is a sinister presence in his own right: as he watches Saccard pass with his latest female acquisition, he reflects on the degraded values of his French hosts. Zola's portrait here of Bismarck's brutal genius is more knowing than the unheeding curiosity of his characters: resplendent in his cuirassier uniform, with his colossal profile, echoing laughter and massive jaw framed by whiskers likened to those of a 'barbarian conqueror' (*RM*, v, 259), Bismarck has France in his sights. In *La Débâcle*, the French soldiers so underestimate him that they delude themselves about the vengeance they will so easily wreak on him, encouraged by baseless rumours of his personal cowardice.

Relying on its alliance with Italy and Austria, and supremely confident of crushing the pretensions of an incipient German empire, France fell into Bismarck's trap. The final pages of *Nana* are reprised in the opening ones of *La Débâcle* which evoke the chauvinistic rejoicing in Paris at the news of the declaration of war, 'when crowds swept down the boulevards, and bands of people brandished torches crying "To Berlin! To Berlin!" and singing the *Marseillaise*' (*RM*, v, 408). And, from then on, Zola does refer us in the novel (often through the conversations of his characters or the newspapers they come across by chance) both to significant moments in the war and to the salient features of the doomed French resistance to the Prussian invasion.

In the interests of economy, Zola only indirectly refers in *La Débâcle* to the succession of defeats experienced by French armies prior to the culmination of such military disasters at the Battle of Sedan on 1 September 1870. The novel's focus is on a single regiment brought up so close to that defeat that its poorly led soldiers are part of the surrender of Napoleon III's army the next day, with the emperor himself among its 104,000 prisoners. When the news reached Paris on the 4th, the end of the Second Empire was formally voted by a pressured legislature, with responsibility for the war transferred to a government of National Defence provisionally led by Léon Gambetta (1838–1882). After Sedan, the German 'avalanche' (as it was termed in the press) swept on. Paris was besieged and its population reduced to virtual starvation before its capitulation on 28 January 1871. Before that, on the 18th, coinciding with the anniversary of the coronation of the first Prussian king in 1701, and in the very same Hall of Mirrors, at Versailles, where revenge would only be exacted half a century later, France was subjected to the spectacle of Wilhelm being proclaimed as emperor of Germany, thus bringing Bismarck's grand strategy to a successful conclusion. For Zola, however, it was Sedan itself which was the key moment in the Franco-Prussian War, even if it may not have been as important as other battles. It was *the* 'débâcle' in its multiple senses: for an army, an emperor and his empire, a dictatorship, a society and an era. Sedan allowed Zola, as he put it to his first English biographer, 'to show France . . . irrevocably fated to disaster'.[3]

Sedan was indeed only the beginning of that disaster. There was worse to follow. Faith in Gambetta's ability to prosecute the war had been progressively undermined throughout the winter of 1870–71 by a virtually unbroken sequence of military reverses, most acutely felt in Paris by the abortive attempts to break through the German encirclement of the city. Having undergone the fruitless suffering of four months' siege, the disaffected population felt betrayed by the government's negotiation of an armistice, on 28 January, and the ensuing elections, which returned a conservative-leaning (and largely provincial) majority pledged to end the war at any price. On 8 February 1871, Adolphe Thiers was confirmed as president of the Third Republic, having agreed a draft treaty which included the further humiliation of the entry of German troops into the capital. All the imposed peace terms were accepted by the National Assembly, meeting in Bordeaux, on 1 March. But it was less Thiers' seminal role in this agreement than his subsequent actions in response to the Commune which most severely tested Zola's long-standing admiration for him.

When Paris's municipal council refused to accept the authority of the National Assembly, as Zola would later judge, Thiers was confronted by a political situation handled with unforgiveable brutality. The National Guard in the capital appointed a central committee and seized cannon belonging to the regular army on 18 March. The election of the Commune, both to run the city and as an alternative government, effectively marked the beginning of a civil war. This continued through the spring, with Paris besieged for a second time, now by French forces under the orders of Thiers' 'official' government, which had moved to Versailles. Only between 21 and 28 May (known as the 'Bloody Week') did these forces succeed in taking back control of the city, and then at a terrible cost. On both sides there were calculated atrocities and an almost unimaginable barbarity. The Versailles troops worked their way through the barricades in indiscriminate slaughter compounded by mass executions. Summary courts martial and deportations would continue into the months and years ahead, the last of them in 1875, with a general amnesty declared only in 1880. It is estimated that some 30,000 French died at the hands of their countrymen during that one week in May 1871, more deaths than in any single battle of the Franco-Prussian War. As the Communards retreated, they set fire to the city. Paris was in ruins. The Third Republic had been born in what Victor Hugo called *L'Année terrible*. Zola's *La Débâcle* is the story of that 'terrible year'. More generally it informs his understanding of his times, given expression in the writing of the *Rougon-Macquart*: in its novels characterized by the tensions between a residual belief in human perfectibility and a vision of the Apocalypse so fearfully prefigured in the events of 1870–71.

Zola took no part in the war that brought about the fall of the Second Empire. Critics of *La Débâcle* would later throw this fact in his face with scorn. As the only son of a widow, he was exempted from military service and, in any case, his eyesight would have excluded him from conscription: at sixteen, he had noticed that he could not read posters at a distance; by the age of twenty he was wearing pince-nez; the dangling monocle in Manet's 1868 portrait of him suggesting a perceptual blank, clinically verifiable but also perhaps hinting at the critical limitations of the novelist's pictorial insights; and, on the outbreak of hostilities in 1870, Zola's myopia prevented his being admitted to serve in the National Guard.

With his wife and mother, Zola left Paris on 7 September. Writing to Edmond de Goncourt on the day of his departure, he told him that he was heading for the Midi not only on account of the two women being in a state of terror but because doctors had recommended that Alexandrine's health would benefit from warmer climes (*Corr.*, I, 225). His hopes, as he assured Goncourt, to return to the capital as soon as possible to take part in resistance to the Prussians were rehearsed in a 1924 article by one of Zola's godsons, Émile Solari (1873–1961). This was composed with the help of Zola's wife's recollections and doubtless intended to counter residual anti-Dreyfusard aspersions about his patriotism.

After a few days in L'Estaque, where Cézanne was living, Zola and his charges set up house in the suburbs of Marseilles. As his income as both journalist and novelist had dried up altogether, he began his search for an alternative source. On 19 September he wrote to Marius Roux suggesting that, building on their previous collaboration, they might edit a newspaper together (*Corr.*, I, 225–6). The first number of their paper, the strongly republican *Marseillaise*, was announced for 27 September. But it was soon in financial difficulties. On 29 October, Roux and Zola agreed to sell out their controlling interests in the paper to *Le Peuple* in return for a guaranteed salary as editors. But this clause of the agreement, not unlike Zola's contracts with Lacroix, was conditional on the paper reaching certain sales targets (in this case, of over 6,000 daily copies). By the middle of November, with the disappearance of the revolutionary climate which had favoured its birth, it was clear that the days of the *Marseillaise* were numbered; Zola, as resourceful as ever, was already setting various wheels in motion to secure ways in which he could earn a living in order to provide for his wife and mother.

His first idea was to get himself appointed as a sub-prefect of Aix-en-Provence. That Zola's contacts there failed to produce results did nothing to mitigate his long-standing resentment of the city. Locals who might have followed the serialization of *La Fortune des Rougon* since it had started appearing the previous June would have been left in no doubt as to its author's view of their deeply conservative politics. If there was a further slight in frustrating Zola's appointment, it was repaid in *La Conquête de Plassans* three years later: the portrait of the wily Delangre, re-elected with a crushing majority over the anti-Bonapartist opposition, was based on the real mayor of Aix between 1852 and 1863, but Zola must have enjoyed adding to his fictional one the demeaning detail of his being cuckolded.

Zola then decided to press his nomination at the seat of the provisional government, which had relocated to Bordeaux in response to the Prussian advance on the capital. On 11 December, Zola set off on the arduous cross-country train journey from Marseilles to the Atlantic seabord, arriving there on the following day. In Bordeaux he spent much of his time in fruitless meetings before learning that the post in Aix was indeed out of the question. In a despairing mood, he made plans to return empty-handed to Marseilles, although the collapse there of his and Roux's newspaper on 16 December left him the option of seeking an appointment elsewhere than in the Midi. But he postponed travelling back in the hope that something would turn up. By doing so, Zola resumed contact by chance with Alexandre Glais-Bizoin (1800–1877), one of the founders of *La Tribune* whom he had got to know while on its staff before the war. Returning from a self-imposed political exile after the *coup d'état*, Glais-Bizoin had been so prominent an opposition deputy from 1863 onwards that he was offered a ministerial portfolio in Gambetta's cabinet. In that capacity, he promised to engage Zola as his private secretary, a not very demanding post he would retain until the change of government on 8 February 1871. On 21 December Zola could write with relief that the appointment had been confirmed and make plans for his wife and mother to join him in Bordeaux, which they eventually did on 26 December 1870.

Had Zola secured a post as a sub-prefect, it would have been an incongruous parenthesis both in the writing of the *Rougon-Macquart* and in his life. He was in fact offered Quimperlé, in Brittany, and Lesparre, near Bordeaux, but had turned them down as he was still unreasonably confident of obtaining Aix and felt these back-of-beyond posts were financially unacceptable. In February 1871, through the good offices of Glais-Bizoin, Zola was appointed to the *sous-préfecture* of Castelsarrasin, only for the holder of the post to appeal successfully to Gambetta to have the nomination overturned. But with the signing of the Armistice that month, Zola's political education took a different turn. He immediately arranged to resume his journalistic activities by sending a parliamentary chronicle to the *Sémaphore de Marseille* and to *La Cloche*, an arrangement that would be continued after the National Assembly moved from Bordeaux to Versailles.

This commission, like so many other facets of Zola's experience as a journalist, left its mark on his fiction. He had a ringside seat for the political stage in a literal sense, the sessions of the National Assembly being held in Bordeaux's principal theatre. The novel most obviously indebted to his being one of its spectators is *Son Excellence Eugène Rougon*, the satirical tenor of which is sustained by an emphasis on the theatricalization, precisely, of political life. As do his 22 'Letters from Bordeaux' (19 February–22 March 1871) and, also in *La Cloche*, his 228 parliamentary reports mostly headed 'Letters from Versailles' (23 March 1871–3 May 1872). The novel similarly charts the arbitrary entrances and exits of 'actors' in a pantomime, motivated by personal antipathies and unholy alliances. Rougon's powers of oratory are those of Thiers, on which Zola reported in the press with an awe not unrelated to his own lack of them, but also with cynicism as he watched the docile audience mesmerized by speeches designed to secure ratification of Thiers' controversial policies.

Publishing statistics habitually position *Son Excellence Eugène Rougon* as the least read of the *Rougon-Macquart* series. And Henry James was sadly misinformed in asserting that it had 'obtained a success not hitherto enjoyed by the productions of this remarkable young writer'.[4] But he was not wrong in stressing the 'cleverness' and 'transparent veil' through which 'actual persons' are represented. Notwithstanding Zola's own preliminary anxieties on this score, his achievement paradoxically lies in the absence of the kind of compelling plot characteristic of his more popular novels. In the serialized version in *Le Siècle* in the early months of 1876, it bore the quasi-Balzacian, if underwhelming, title of

Scènes de la vie politique sous le Second Empire, indicative of its fragmented design. As Zola had witnessed at first hand the banal machinations of parliamentary decisions and manufactured 'dramas', so the barely structuring vicissitudes of Eugène Rougon's rises and falls (in the plural) make it appropriate that the narrative ends without a conclusion other than the suggestion that his career will go on. The poet Stéphane Mallarmé (1842–1898), in his letter to Zola of 18 March 1876 (cited in *RM*, II, 1507–8), expressed his admiration for the novel's admixture of fiction and history, while retaining what he called 'the anecdotal, ephemeral and fortuitous' dimensions of the latter. There now exists a consensus that *Son Excellence Eugène Rougon* deserves to be ranked alongside Stendhal's *Lucien Leuwen* (1834–5) as one of the finest political novels of the nineteenth century. But, as a result of what he had been forced to endure as a parliamentary correspondent, it also reflects Zola's doubts about the efficacy of elected government always at risk from opponents to democratic principles.

On 14 March 1871, Zola left Bordeaux on the government train. Whereas in February he had complained that it was no time to be a creative artist, the prospective return to the capital – now that the Peace Treaty with Germany had been signed – lifted his spirits, only for these to be dashed again when the Commune broke out four days after getting back to 14 rue La Condamine, where he and Alexis had been pictured by Cézanne. Zola later told the painter that for the best part of the next two months 'I lived in a furnace, night and day and, towards the end, with shells whistling overhead and falling into my garden' (*Corr.*, II, 293). From the date of his return until 20 April, Zola continued in his role as parliamentary correspondent, making the daily train trip out to Versailles, where the National Assembly had relocated on 11 March. During this period, he was arrested briefly by both sides: by the Communards in Paris on 21 March and two days later by the authorities in Versailles. In his own account, in *La Cloche* of 23 March, he made light of these incidents, giving ironic thanks that there wasn't a third faction which might also consider him to be a 'very dangerous person' (*OC*, XIII, 431). It says something about the man that, from his Paris address on 12 June and in the midst of all these upheavals, Zola somehow found the time to write a moving letter to the recently widowed wife of one of his mother's brothers.

His first article for *La Cloche* had appeared on 19 February. Zola continued to write for it until the end of 1872, producing in total some

159 articles in 1871 alone. Circumventing postal restrictions during the Versaillais siege, Zola also managed to sustain a flow of unsigned articles to the *Sémaphore de Marseille*, keeping his provincial readers abreast of the violence in the capital. These 27 'eyewitness' reports, from 10 May to 7 June, deliberately gave the impression that he was still in central Paris, watching the construction and subsequent destruction of barricades against a backdrop of political developments. In fact, on the first of those dates, justifiably fearful of the impending entry of Thiers' troops into the city (as would happen on the 21st), Zola had successfully taken advantage of small gaps in its encirclement to make his way, via the suburbs of Saint-Denis, to the Bennecourt region west of the capital.

Having told his wife and mother to urgently pack their bags, by 14 May they had joined him in the holiday house at Gloton (some 60 kilometres (37 mi.) from Paris) that he had rented since 1869. He would only terminate its lease in August 1872. In the notes for *L'Œuvre* he refers to the property ('which we once rented', *Ms* 10316, fol. 87) in imagining his fictional painter's creatively reinvigorating retreat from Paris to the countryside. In the novel of 1886, the idyllic status of a happy interlude in a tortured artistic life is also reinforced more personally: it is here that Claude's future wife becomes pregnant. In 1871 such a fantasy was far from Zola's mind, but it was no less a nostalgic return to the secluded hamlet on the banks of the Seine where, before the war, he had watched his painter friends working *en plein air*. He remained there at least until the end of the month.

Only twenty years later, in *La Débâcle*, could Zola arrive at a considered assessment of the events of 1870–71 in which he had been indirectly caught up. Even so, a strain of hostility towards Zola's treatment of the French army in this novel would be revived in the context of Zola's public stand against the military in the Dreyfus Affair. For the most part, however, there was widespread contemporary acknowledgement that *La Débâcle* was one of his finest achievements. During Zola's lifetime, it remained the bestselling of all the *Rougon-Macquart* in providing for a whole generation a better understanding of France's national tragedy. It would have been a very different novel if it had been written in the immediate aftermath of the Franco-Prussian War. Interpretative perspective would have been subordinate to topicality and eyewitness accounts. In an 1872 review of one such collection of personal reminiscences, Zola had declared that it was still ten years too early to gain critical purchase on recent events. By the time he himself did so, the meaning and protagonists of France's defeat would be viewed from another kind of distance, both philosophical and aesthetic.

What remains invariable in Zola's writing, however, is a fundamental anti-militarism which is characteristic of his attitude at the time as well as colouring the wisdom of hindsight. It would be exacerbated by the Dreyfus Affair. Even before the formal declaration of war, Zola was one of those radical journalists exploiting the crisis as further evidence of Napoleon III's regime leading the country to disaster. In a piece in *La Cloche* of 11 July 1870, entitled simply 'La Guerre' (The War), he recalled earlier imperial campaigns abroad and aligned himself in the anti-militarist camp. On the 18th, in the same newspaper, Zola called for the voice of reason to recount 'the horror and madness of the slaughter' behind the promised glory. On 25 July, he pictured an anonymous village as 'a virgin . . . violated by war', whose shredded pastoral calm would assure its infamous future status as a 'place where two nations had massacred each other' (*OC*, XIII, 304). Two days later he continued in the same vein, including recalling how, as a boy in Aix, he had watched the smartly uniformed soldiers marching to the front, only to see them eventually return 'limping and bleeding as they dragged themselves along the road' (*OC*, IX, 442).

If such recollections, whether authentic or invented, were the common currency of that section of the press which had not succumbed to the general chauvinistic frenzy, Zola's stance was by no means opportunistic. Partially reprinting such texts in his *Nouveaux Contes à Ninon* in 1874, he expanded their personal dimension (*OC*, IX, 440–43). As a fourteen-year-old, so he recalled here, he and his schoolmates, equally enraptured by the spectacle, had followed out of the city the columns of troops heading for Crimea. In Paris, in 1859, he had seen at first hand in the place de la Sorbonne the extravagant rejoicing at the news of the French victory over the Austrians at the Battle of Magenta. Zola stripped out from the original versions in *La Cloche* the more polemical mention of the imperial soldiers' bedraggled return. But he maintained the more general thesis that war was an abomination.

As long ago as 1862 he had written an anti-militarist tale, 'Le Sang' (Blood), set in a battlefield littered with mutilated corpses, as stomach-turning as Goya's drawings in his *Disasters of War* series (1810–14). At its close, the four soldiers of the story ignore the call of duty and walk off arm in arm in search of peace, leaving behind them their nightmares and agreeing that 'our job is a filthy one' (*OC*, IX, 74). Such pacifist idealism would not prevent Zola later calling on his countrymen to fight the Prussian invader to the death. But it does reveal, in the future author of *La Débâcle*, a visceral disgust for the physical realities of war. His long-standing anti-militarism is equally evident in his own contribution (subtitled 'An Episode from the Invasion of 1870') to *Les Soirées de Médan*. The collection as a whole (including, most famously, Maupassant's *Boule-de-suif*) is aimed at demystifying military glory at a time characterized by enthusiasm for renewed conflict with Germany. Zola's text is bathed in an uncomplicated sympathy for innocent victims. But both in tone and in their limited purview, his tale and his polemical articles stand significantly apart from his picture of war in *La Débâcle*.

That novel underlines the distinction to be made between Zola's consistent rejection of militarism, on the one hand, and, on the other, a philosophical conception of war gradually accommodated within an evolutionary vision of an eternal conflict between the forces of Life and Death: 'I want to show war as it really is,' Zola wrote in its preparatory notes, 'the essential struggle for life, Darwin's grand and distressing idea, to which the individual is subordinate, crushed like an insect by the forces of... nature' (*Ms* 10286, fols 6–7). This vision receives its ultimate expression in *La Débâcle*. In an article in *Le Figaro* of 1 September 1891 (*OC*, XIV, 827–31), on the twenty-first anniversary of the Battle of Sedan, Zola insisted that the certainty of France's defeat had to be seen not just in terms of military inferiority, but also within the biological necessity of the strong and the young devouring the old and the weak. Prussia's application of modern technology to the science of war is part of this scheme, but largely incidental in providing the catalyst of France's recognition of its own fatal decline. As much as by longer-range artillery, the French are destroyed, in *La Débâcle*, by what is repeatedly described as 'an invincible and logical force' out of sight. In the same way as Tolstoy's *War and Peace* transcends the Napoleonic campaigns which are its own context, Zola's novel thereby retains its power over and beyond a particular time and place. However vouchsafed its accuracy may be, it reworks events in such a way as to continue to engage the reader at the level of the timeless conflict between historical forces and the human beings subject to such fatalities beyond their control.

Starting work on *La Débâcle* in May 1891, it was from twenty years' distance that Zola could finally bring the Commune into the same interpretative frame as the Franco-Prussian War. His attitude towards that uprising has been much criticized, often by those wedded to the tradition of the resistance, on the part of French intellectuals, to an oppressive establishment. Such is Zola's selective use of his sources in the writing of *La Débâcle* that he omits any mention of the idealism of the Commune or its well-intentioned social reforms. It has even been suggested that his treatment of it in the novel was distorted by his desire, at the time, to be elected to the Académie Française. His view of it was in fact fixed and hardening long before 1892.

In 1871 Zola had been appalled at the carnage but moved from a refusal to take sides to a position of increasing hostility. He was severely critical of the Versaillais repression, mixed with compassion for its victims. But the Commune was for Zola a demented nightmare, with its leaders characterized by their demagogic hysteria: 'they are revolutionary idealists, with their doctrinal heads in the clouds,' he wrote in *Le Sémaphore de Marseille* of 4 May 1871, 'slipping in their own blood, felled as criminals while thinking of themselves as martyrs.'[5] The swaggering Chouteau, in *La Débâcle*, is precisely the type. Viewed with similar authorial scepticism are the plotters of revolution in *Le Ventre de Paris* and *Germinal*. The latter is indelibly marked by Zola's lack of sympathy for the Commune. Even the hero of the novel, Étienne Lantier, is not invulnerable to the charges Zola had levelled against its leaders more than a decade earlier: Zola traces a self-aggrandizement in which the character sees himself as an 'apostle' of truth, ultimately despising the ignorance of those who reject his leadership. The experience of the Commune also informs Zola's nightmarish vision of the unleashed mob of striking miners breaking out of the passivity of their unrelenting suffering. He had intended that, as he put it in the work-notes for *Germinal*, 'the bourgeois reader should feel a *frisson* of terror' at the spectacle. In his evocation of collective violence, however, there is more than a hint of Zola's own disgust. Unforgettable his crowd scenes may justly be; here revolution and anarchy are perilously synonymous.

In his reports, between 1871 and 1876, on Courbet's indictment for his alleged role in the destruction of the Colonne Vendôme, there is no mistaking where Zola stands: the painter's association with the rioters directly responsible for it is conflated with the Commune itself as an essentially pathological phenomenon, a symptom of debilitated brains and frustrated patriotism erupting in contagious madness. In 'Jacques Damour', a text of 1880, he treated the topical subject of the return of a Communard from deportation; Zola's sympathy for what the character had endured in exile is dissolved by authorial irony at the expense of his renewed revolutionary fervour and his dreams 'of universal happiness achieved as a result of exterminating everybody' (*OC*, IX, 853). Zola's revulsion, qualified by pity, at the deluded excesses of the Commune is sustained across the decades. But, in a longer perspective, it is not incompatible with a regenerative vision of contemporary history with which his novel cycle begins and ends. Even immediately after its fires had been doused, he was writing of Paris that 'perhaps the horrible bloodletting it has experienced was necessary to calm certain of its feverish symptoms.'[6] The symbolic significance afforded to the Commune in *La Débâcle* is consistent with this diagnosis: it is seen as an extension to the Franco-Prussian War, conceived as the final purificatory ritual after which France could rise from the ashes of imperial corruption.

Representing the Second Empire

Returning to Paris in the spring of 1871, Zola's sense of rebirth and renewal was more personal. 'Our time has come,' he had written to Alexis from Bordeaux on 17 February, 'we are the men of the future' (*Corr.*, II, 280). His assertion that a five-month break from writing had done him a lot of good was equally upbeat. The strains and stresses of this period of 'rest' could be dismissed as a minor inconvenience, such was Zola's excitement at getting back to work. This newfound energy was directed, in the first instance, to radically cutting the last chapters of *La Fortune des Rougon* to fit the merely four instalments sanctioned by *Le Siècle* in order to resume and complete the serialization of the novel. These appeared on 18, 19, 20 and 21 March. They did not secure much attention from the paper's subscribers, given that it was on the 18th that the Commune seized power in the capital. Nor was it helpful that the instalments bore an unexciting new title: *La Famille Rougon*. Correcting the page proofs for the publication of the novel in volume form, however, sustained Zola's euphoria. Repeating to Cézanne too that 'our time has come,' Zola's letter of 4 July compares his editorial task to the pleasure he had experienced in publishing his very first book: 'After all these disruptions, I feel as young as when I was waiting impatiently for the printed sheets of my *Contes à Ninon*' (*Corr.*, II, 294).

However, for both *La Fortune des Rougon* and his series as a whole Zola now had a problem. When he had started writing the *Rougon-Macquart*, he had been keenly aware of the topicality of *La Fortune des Rougon*'s focus on the Second Empire's beginnings. Its cataclysmic demise in 1870, by comparison, threatened to relegate the *coup d'état* of 1851 to a footnote. Zola's somewhat desperate response to the associated risk to his novel was to stress its renewed interest. Through the seventeen publicity notices he prepared for the Lacroix edition published on 21 October 1871, that emphasis sought to justify the publication of *La Fortune des Rougon* on the grounds that 'in the context of the bonapartist plots so prevalent today, the novel is highly topical.'[7] On reflection, neither Zola nor his publisher thought it worthwhile to insert such unconvincing notices in the press.

The fall of the regime had been predicted with relish by its opponents well before 1870, though few of them had foreseen its imminence. In *La Fortune des Rougon*, its prospective downfall is not envisaged, save perhaps in the analogies evoked between Austerlitz and Waterloo in the moments, respectively, of Félicité Rougon's triumphs and humiliations, the two classic poles of Napoleonic fortunes exploited to fuller effect in Chapter Ten of *L'Argent*. Only in an 1872 article did Zola retrospectively put the beginning and the end of the Second Empire into the same metaphorical frame: founded in blood, the regime had perished in blood, with the *coup d'état* of 1851 viewed not merely as a crime but as 'the night when France received its first fatal wound' (*OC*, XIV, 176). More immediately it was necessary for him to revise the version of his introductory novel's preface drafted before the collapse of the Second Empire. In this, now dated 1 July 1871, Zola was able to expand the novel's intended function within his series as a whole by making the 'betrayal of Sedan' the climax of the historical drama opened up by *La Fortune des Rougon*:

> the fall of the Bonapartes . . . has given me, as an artist, the terrible and necessary denouement to my work . . . which is now a closed circle . . . making it the picture of a dead reign, a curious era of madness and shame. (*RM*, I, 4)

At this stage, Zola was still clinging to his intention to devote a novel to either the Italian campaign against Austria or the Crimean War in order, as he had told Lacroix, to reveal the realities of war, explored through the ambivalent attitude of the troops Napoleon III had sent into battle. The 'artist' in him, elaborating the notion of a 'closed circle', rapidly decided that history itself offered him a more aesthetically satisfying overall design for his *Rougon-Macquart* series. Even in his preliminary outline of it, in 1868–9, Zola had envisaged his fictional family's rise and subsequently inevitable fall, but not the symbolic value this would assume. For a writer concerned, from his earliest novels onwards, with organizing his narratives around a singularly dramatic event, the crushing finality of the Franco-Prussian War provided a fifth act with affinities to classical tragedy. Shakespeare was one model, with the five parts of *La Terre* explicitly gesturing towards the plot of *King Lear*; Racine was another, Zola's notes for *La Curée* asserting that 'what I'm really going to do is write a new *Phèdre*' (*Ms* 10282, fol. 298). While the series is too long for the reader to grasp its overarching pattern of inexorability, many of its individual novels accelerate towards catastrophe. Nowhere is this more obviously related to the Franco-Prussian War than in the final pages of *La Bête humaine*: loaded with patriotically inebriated troops in cattle trucks being transported to the Rhine after France's declaration of war, a driverless train hurtles towards its doom. Imminent catastrophe in other novels is not always as overtly that of the country's shattering defeat in 1870–71. But the latter is inseparable both from the pessimistic dimension of Zola's representation of human experience, shared for the same reason by so many of his contemporaries, and from the shaping of his plots.

It would not meet the imperatives of such a dramatic structure simply to make of the Second Empire a story of progressive decline. As Zola would do, in microcosm, in the case of *L'Assommoir*, the seeds of future disaster had to be planted within apparent triumphs. The depiction of the apogee of Napoleon III's reign is thus punctuated by the signposts of ultimate disintegration afforded by the wisdom of hindsight. In April 1879, retracing the history his generation had lived through, Zola described the causes of the regime's collapse: it was due, he wrote, to the inherent weakness of its ostentatious scaffolding, 'so riddled by corruption that the logical consequence of the war of 1870 saw it being reduced to dust, crashing to the ground at the very moment of its apogee' (*OC*, X, 1380). As he was writing *Nana* at precisely this time, it is not surprising that that novel, more than any other in his series, reflects such a statement. But the imagery of fragile pillars and of a gilded facade crumbling away is to be found again and again in the *Rougon-Macquart*'s portrayal of Second Empire society.

That imagery is first developed in *La Curée*, arguably Zola's best novel before *L'Assommoir*, distinguished by its rigorous design and skilful integration of social realities and private destinies. It was certainly the one in which his literary ambitions were most clearly invested. The idea of writing a great Parisian novel, in the footsteps of Balzac and Flaubert, had been catalysed by an article spotted in *Le Figaro* of 25 January 1869 devoted to an acrimonious parliamentary debate on the financing of the rebuilding of the capital. The subject of the article was Thiers' devastating speech two days earlier aimed at Haussmann's financing of the rebuilding of Paris, and it may have been this which attracted Zola's attention – and not just because it was Thiers, although his enduring fascination with his alter ego may have played its part. The very first notes in the preparatory dossier of *La Curée* comprise Zola's annotation of a journalistic synopsis of the speech, sympathetically embroidered by the hypothesis that Haussmann's juggling of millions of francs was the stuff of 'a novel Balzac could have written'. One has no need to guess what such a challenge would have meant to Zola, at that very moment rereading *La Comédie humaine*: here was the subject of a novel which he simply had to write.

Such was his impatience to get his introductory novel out of the way that Zola had begun planning and writing *La Curée* even before finishing off *La Fortune des Rougon*. This urgency explains why, neither for the Lacroix edition of the latter nor for the Charpentier one at the very end of 1872, did he take the opportunity to update the text in the light of the events of 1870–71.[8] Zola had taken the manuscript of *La Curée*'s first chapter with him when he left Paris in September 1870, while continuing to worry during that winter about the large file of preparatory notes for his series which he had been forced to leave behind. When he was finally able to resume work on this second episode of the *Rougon-Macquart* in the summer of 1871, Zola could hardly ignore the new historical context in which he was now writing. He was still seeking to depict the Second Empire at the apex of its political power and material prosperity. Rejecting as too didactic a denouement of bankruptcy and ruin, he noted during the preparation of *La Curée*, 'my novel will end with the triumph of the villains; only later will the Debacle take place' (*Ms* 10282, fol. 240; the capitalization is Zola's own). That remark was also dictated by a concern not to extend the novel's time frame too far into the future. It simultaneously looks forward to *L'Argent*, in which the speculator Aristide Saccard again takes centre stage only for his earlier success to be comprehensively reversed. But *La Curée* itself is only the first of the *Rougon-Macquart* novels discreetly marked by the traumatic events of the interlude since Zola had begun it.

The dates of the action of many of the *Rougon-Macquart* novels can only be adduced by calculating, as Zola himself was often forced to do, the ages of reappearing characters or inferred through interpolated historical markers. This left him open to charges of anachronism which he often struggled to deny. In an 1882 letter thanking Frantz Jourdain (1847–1935) for the information supplied for *Au bonheur des dames*, Zola regretted that his 'scruples as a historian' meant he could not use the architect's sketch of a modern department store: 'All my scenes take place before 1870, and I cannot risk incensing my critics through an anachronism' (*Corr.*, IV, 303). He more often fell back on his oft-cited caveat, in the preparatory notes for *La Fortune des Rougon*, that 'while my historical frame will be subordinate to imaginative imperatives, all the facts will be taken from history' (*RM*, V, 1759). The fall of the Second Empire, obliging him to squeeze five generations of his fictional family into eighteen years, complicated this liberation from historical integrity. He confessed to an interviewer, shortly after the appearance of *Nana*, that the timing of the regime's sudden demise had caused him considerably more difficulties than he had cared to admit in his 1871 preface to the opening novel of his series:

> I foresaw 1870, but . . . the collapse took place earlier than I had supposed it would . . . so that, in order to remain within the confines of the Second Empire . . . I've had to cheat, compressing into three or four years the decade which the depiction of Nana's life should have spanned.[9]

A preparatory note for *La Curée* reveals the liberty taken by Zola in the arrangement of its chronology to suit his purpose: 'it will be absolutely necessary to falsify the dates' (*Ms* 10282, fol. 468). One of the results of this is the anachronism of textual instances predicting, in novels supposedly taking place much earlier, the disasters of 1870–71. In *L'Assommoir*, immediately following its heroine's marriage in July 1851, the wedding party is confronted in the Louvre by Théodore Géricault's *Le radeau de la Méduse* (The Raft of the Medusa) (1818–19, Louvre, Paris): based on a shocking event (when the captain of the sinking vessel named in its title had offloaded passengers and left them to their fate), the painting was politically allegorized thereafter as representing the abandoned survivors of the 'shipwreck' of the nation. The depiction of Napoleon III is another case of anachronism: in *La Curée*, he is a shuffling caricature, hollowed out before his time, and in *L'Assommoir*, in Chapter Eleven, which starts off in about 1866, a character describes the emperor, having caught sight of him in the street, as 'an absolute wreck . . . I wouldn't give him more than six months' (*RM*, II, 734). While the date does coincide with public awareness of the bladder problems from which he would die after botched surgery only in 1873, the irony of the prediction is enhanced by the fact that opposition journalists had gleefully seized on the diagnosis to (mis) place bets on how soon it would prove terminal.

Hindsight of a less explicit kind inflects both descriptive texture and Zola's plotting. *La Curée* is one example: instead of referencing the clouds of dust experienced by Parisians during Haussmann's reconfiguration of the capital, Saccard's metaphorical demolition of the city from the heights of Montmartre (where the Commune had been sparked) is pervaded by images of fire. *La Conquête de Plassans* ends in a gigantic conflagration, consuming both Octave Mouret's house, designated as a strategic republican space, and its Bonapartist trespassers, as well as the innocent victims within it. Even the panoramas of *Une page d'amour*, as Colette Wilson has argued, are coloured by the memory of Paris set alight by the Communards.[10] She has also identified in *L'Assommoir* the legacy of the Commune: in the invasive itinerary of Gervaise's wedding party from the outlying working-class districts of the capital to its institutional heart, stampeding through its tranquil spaces in defiance of the forces of law and order represented by disapproving museum guards. Saccard had singled out the Vendôme column in imagining its surrounding streets dissolving in the heat of a chemist's still. It seems no less by chance that Gervaise and her friends move on from their raucous disruption of the Louvre to finish their excursion by clambering up, with ribald disrespect, the internal staircase of the very monument whose toppling on 16 May 1871 remained an act of wanton Communard vandalism never forgotten nor forgiven.

There is barely a novel in Zola's series *not* marked, even parenthetically, by the fall of the Second Empire. He deliberately rearranged the time span of *La Terre*, for example, to close the novel in 1870. He was faced with objections that the agricultural crisis at its centre, provoked by the influx of American wheat, did not occur until 1880. But Zola's retaining the period 1860–70 to synchronize it with the action of the novel was a reassertion of his prerogative to rearrange chronology in order to take further advantage of the aesthetically satisfying structure afforded by the catastrophe of the Franco-Prussian War. As *La Terre* draws to a close, darkening skies and Françoise's rape and murder bring pathetic fallacy and personal trauma into the same historical frame: she dies to the roll of drums assembling the recruits for war as the novel reaches its tragic climax. To their muffled but incessant beat, one character prophesies the terminal demise of the French rural economy, another is murdered, and Fouan, the King Lear figure, is buried alive by his children. Leaving to enlist in the army, Jean Macquart contemplates a burning farm and sees hanging over the landscape 'the smoke of war, with its horses, canon and the screams of a massacre' (*RM*, IV, 811).

Interpolated historical markers in the *Rougon-Macquart* also serve to chart, in retrospect, the Second Empire's decline, notably in references to Napoleon III's foreign-policy adventures: in *L'Assommoir*, we are told that Père Bru has lost three sons in the casualty-heavy Crimean War of 1854–6; the Crimean campaign had hardly been noticed, so Zola stressed in *La Curée*, by a French population preoccupied by material greed and the pleasures of the flesh; and in *L'Argent*, the fiasco of the attempt in the 1860s to establish imperial rule in Mexico through Archduke Maximilian is recalled as the first tolling of the death knell of Napoleon III's regime. Manet's *The Execution of the Emperor Maximilian* (1867, Städtische Kunsthalle, Mannheim) is an indictment made all the more devastating, as Zola himself pointed out in a *Tribune* article of 4 February 1869, by the uniforms worn by the Mexican rebels' firing squad being unmistakeably French (*OC*, XIII, 222).

The extent to which the events of 1870–71 not merely shadow but also shape Zola's writing of the *Rougon-Macquart* is highlighted by *L'Argent*, composed immediately before *La Débâcle*. Zola had intended the novel to link the worlds of politics and high finance. Its imaginative elaboration, however, takes this much further than locating in the 1867 crash of the Union générale bank (renamed in *L'Argent* as the Banque universelle) an analogue of the Second Empire's bankruptcy. In some respects, this is yet another novel in which historical allusion is predictive. The 1866 Battle of Sadowa, for example, is integrated into Zola's plotting, with the crushing defeat of France's new ally, Austria, by the Prussians resulting in a sell-off of Saccard's investments on the stock exchange; its ominous implications are voiced in the conflation of private and national fortunes:

> as everything is falling apart . . . so the prediction will come to pass . . . France will be defeated in any war against Germany! We're ready, the Prussians only have to come in and grab one of our provinces. (*RM*, V, 385)

The clear-sighted Mme Caroline considers Saccard's finances to be as certainly fated to disaster as the out-of-control train in the final pages of *La Bête humaine*: her vision of his company likens it to 'a machine powered by a surfeit of coal, hurtling along the rails to hell until that final crash when everything falls apart and explodes' (*RM*, V, 216). In a letter of July 1890, Zola made it clear that he planned to end *L'Argent* with a spectacle of disintegration 'in blood and mud' (*Corr.*, VII, 71). These are hardly images normally associated with financial disasters. Informed readers could see through them: in thanking Zola for a copy of the novel, J.-K. Huysmans was in no doubt that its denouement was that of Sedan.

More far-reaching are the ways in which *L'Argent* becomes an allegory not just of the Franco-Prussian War but also of the Bonapartist dynasty responsible, in Zola's thinking, for nineteenth-century France's convulsions and crises. In *La Débâcle*, this diagnosis is explicit. In *L'Argent*, Zola's irony suffices, substantiated by a metaphorical scheme which consistently equates the manipulation of share prices with military battles and recurrently terms losses as a 'debacle' which leave the floor of the stock exchange figuratively littered with corpses. Throughout the novel, Saccard models himself on the first Bonaparte, even planning his comeback as a return from Elba in the manner of Napoleon's escape from exile in 1815; his defeat of the rival financier, Gundermann, in their first encounter is described as his own Austerlitz; and when a co-conspirator fails, at a decisive moment, to reinforce Saccard's funds, both Zola's commentary and the fictional character's reflections inevitably evoke Waterloo. Gundermann, who finally defeats Saccard, is logically paralleled with Wellington. His name alone, however, is transparently significant. His Germanic provenance allows Zola to overlay on the events of 1870–71 the destiny of the Bonapartes, their earlier fortunes crushed in 1815 thanks to the Prussian involvement in Wellington's famous victory.

The ways in which historical perspective shapes the writing of the *Rougon-Macquart* are more complex, however, than the insertion of resonant allusions and the overlaying of allegory. Hindsight also affords a different kind of wisdom. In *La Débâcle*, Napoleon III is viewed with a sympathy anticipating Zola's 1895 statement (in the course of an interview published in *Le Gaulois* of 20 August) that he had modified his conception of him since the embittered 1860s. In this novel, the focus is once again, as in his intermittent entrances in many of the earlier *Rougon-Macquart*, on watery eyes suggesting weakness and vacillation. But, no longer caricatured by polemical excess, Napoleon III is viewed as he was, in excruciating pain from kidney stones and incapable of dominating the military situation. In sharp contrast to King Wilhem, the embodiment of Prussian confidence as he watches the encirclement of the French at Sedan, he is seen as a man both sick and vulnerable. If we are never allowed to forget that he is ultimately responsible for the chaos around him, we are left above all with the impression that he is the victim of Fate. The soldiers' diagnosis is a brutal 'Done for', more inevitable than a mere prediction, as he awaits the working out of an interlocking set of fatalities. By having one of the novel's protagonists see Napoleon III after his decision to advance to Sedan in the certain knowledge of defeat, Zola could (as he put it in his work-notes for *La Débâcle*) 'enlarge its meaning', the silhouette of the emperor against the windowpane (*RM*, V, 563) outlining the empty shadow of divested power and authority.

This is an entirely different perspective from the one found in Zola's earlier writing: in *La Cloche* of 18 February 1872, he had vigorously denounced attempts to rehabilitate the emperor's memory by giving him credit for capitulating at Sedan rather than prolong the slaughter of his men. His efforts to stop the massacre by ordering the hoisting of a white flag are seen in Zola's novel twenty years later as a restoration of his humanity. In the 1870s Napoleon III was universally found guilty, even to the point of the National Assembly declaring that he alone was responsible for all of France's misfortunes. Only in our time has his reputation been occasionally revised. But it was not merely the wisdom of hindsight which prompted Zola's own modified portrait. He subsequently explained that it was for dramatic effect that he had included the possibly apocryphal episode in which Napoleon III was jeered by his troops as they were driven into captivity. He is so helpless and bewildered among the scattered trappings of his empire that he becomes a spectacle of undeniable pathos. The forlorn figure thrown down from the pinnacle of power to be abused by the rabble allowed Zola to invoke the Shakespearean axiom: tragedy requires that even the merited fall of a tyrant should evoke our pity.

More generally, the tendency to 'enlarge its meaning' is also true of Zola's representation of the events of 1870–71 throughout the *Rougon-Macquart*. Their significance is only gradually defined, as he gets further away from the Second Empire his novel cycle purports to reconstruct. It was during the Third Republic that the majority of *La Curée* was actually written. Its serialization in *La Cloche*, begun in September 1871, was suppressed by the state censors in November. Zola's retort that the novel's satirical force was aimed only at a previous era cut no ice. As Jann Matlock has demonstrated, referencing Zola's simultaneous work as a parliamentary correspondent, *La Curée* in fact overlays on its representation of the years 1862–4 a subtle critique of the repressive policies of Thiers' government.[11] It thereby adumbrates a historical continuum between imperial dictatorship and that perpetuated under the guise of democracy. This is an increasingly important dimension of Zola's wider-angled vision of his century. And it goes some way to overcoming the objection, articulated in Taine's letter to him in 1875,[12] that the early novels of the *Rougon-Macquart* were so ferociously aimed at the Second Empire that the series risked losing sight of a more generalized analysis of the forces shaping the contemporary world.

Son Excellence Eugène Rougon, for example, extends its purview beyond a focus on the political machinations of Napoleon III's regime. This is most spectacularly staged in Chapter Four of the novel, devoted to the baptism of the emperor's son and heir on 14 June 1856. For Zola's readers in 1876, the extravagant public celebration of dynastic pretentions two decades earlier is undercut by the fall of the Second Empire; for later readers, that irony would assume a grimmer pall, the Prince Imperial (the putative Napoleon IV) having been killed in South Africa in 1879 while fighting as a volunteer with British troops.

The most significant shadow evoked by Zola in this episode is that of Napoleon Bonaparte: in the foreground of the scene are a colourful military parade and a line of carriages confidently filled by the representatives of European royalty; in the background, however, beyond the 'quai Napoléon' and adorning the entire wall of a six-storey building on the Île Saint-Louis, is an advertisement for 'a gigantic grey overcoat draped over an absent body' (*RM*, II, 97); and at the very moment the imperial parents and their infant son come into view, a spectator mockingly disturbs the collective mood by a 'look, there's the uncle', having recognized the most iconic detail of every heroic portrait of Napoleon I. This massive silhouette dwarfing a Napoleon III visibly exhausted by having to acknowledge the cheering crowds is doubly signifying: as Zola would admit in response to the critics of *La Débâcle*, in 1876 he still subscribed to Victor Hugo's belittling of the first Bonaparte's nephew as *Napoléon-le-Petit*, the title of the poet and novelist's vitriolic 1852 pamphlet, but the spectre of Napoleon III's uncle also occupies a more permanent place in Zola's political understanding of his times. At the very beginning of his novel cycle, in *La Fortune des Rougon*, his fictional family's ambitions are framed by the six engravings of Napoleonic victories decorating their domestic walls. In the preparatory notes for *La Débâcle*, bringing his series' historical panorama to a close, Zola conceives of France's defeat in 1870 as the 'punishment' for a destiny set in train by Napoleon Bonaparte. In his *The Eighteenth Brumaire of Louis Bonaparte*, written in the same year as Hugo's own denunciation of the *coup d'état*, Karl Marx (1818–1883) famously described the Second Empire as a parody of the imperial reign of the latter. Bonaparte's seizure of power as First Consul on 9 November 1799 ('18 Brumaire' in the post-1789 revolutionary calendar) also informs Zola's telescoping of two equally illegitimate Napoleonic dictatorships, more invidious than the repeated pattern of the rise and 'decline and fall' of empires which they exemplified.

Such a superimposition of time frames also serves an analysis of contemporary France grounded in a moral as much as political positioning on Zola's part. *Le Ventre de Paris* starts with the return to France in 1858, having escaped from the 'hell' of Devil's Island (in French Guyana), of a character representative of the 15,000 political prisoners deported in 1851–2 on account of their opposition to the *coup d'état*. The penal colony had been established by Napoleon III for that specific purpose and would be maintained for the next hundred years. It was where Alfred Dreyfus would be sent to serve his life sentence after his 1894 conviction. In spite of its allusions to the beginnings of the Second Empire in 1851, this novel is the episode in the *Rougon-Macquart* most topically marked by the Commune twenty years later, not least in the barely disguised homonym associating one of its prominent leaders, Gustave Flourens, with Florent, the protagonist of *Le Ventre de Paris*. In many respects, the novel prefigures 'Jacques Damour', mentioned earlier, in the context of Zola's anti-militarism. That text would be published in 1880, the year of the belated amnesty of those prosecuted for their role in the Commune. From the beginning of 1872 onwards, Zola's working on *Le Ventre de Paris* coincides with a renewed wave of deportations, transporting to brutally inhospitable overseas destinations many of the nearly 40,000 arrested in the wake of Thiers' government regaining control of Paris six months earlier. During its writing, newspapers of every shade were still transfixed by the ongoing trials, as Zola's own contributions to the press underlined. At the end of the novel, Florent's half-baked revolutionary plans lead, once again, to his arrest and deportation, ironically only a year before an earlier general amnesty: of those sentenced among the more than 125,000 arrested in Paris and the provinces between December 1851 and January 1852.

But in setting the novel in the capital's central markets, Les Halles, Zola was simultaneously able to 'enlarge the meaning' of *Le Ventre de Paris* beyond both historical singularity and recurrence. At the most prosaic level, the novel (often translated as 'The Belly of Paris') accurately details the functioning of Les Halles, largely developed after 1847 to provide the capital's inhabitants with the means to feed themselves. Zola's narrative, however, is thematically consistent with his portrayal throughout the *Rougon-Macquart* of the Second Empire as a period of sated appetites. And a rare instance of Zola's humour in this respect can be found in the retrospectively angled *Le Docteur Pascal*, the action of which takes place in 1872–4 as the only novel of the series set beyond its declared historical confines: the reader is told there that the Pierre Rougon of the opening novel of the series, on learning of the catastrophe of Sedan and on the eve of the dissolution of the regime he had prided himself as having helped found, had died in an apoplectic fit of indigestion! But food itself provides Zola with his novel's symbolic dimension, signalled as deliberately as his notes reveal he intended, in Florent being alerted to a series of prints depicting 'The Fat against the Thin', a timeless scenario with a cultural provenance going back at least as far as Bruegel's drawings in the 1560s. The characters of *Le Ventre de Paris* are accordingly divided between the corpulent and the emaciated. And the complacently well-fed's expulsion from their midst of the starving Florent is ultimately the moral of Zola's story.

Nowhere is such an overlaying of mythology on political specificity more instructive than in *Nana* – as Flaubert recognized, marvelling to Zola that its heroine 'assumes a mythical status without ceasing to be real'.[13] Here again, the events of 1870–71 are explicitly evoked: in the chapter set at the Longchamp racecourse, Nana herself becomes synonymous with France as the horse bearing her name is cheered on with nationalistic fervour, and, at the very end of the novel, her death throes are synchronized with the jingoistic cries in the streets below her room, delusionally anticipating the conquest of Berlin. In order not to limit its political symbolism, Zola leaves unsaid that her physical decomposition is probably, or plausibly, venereal in origin. The central theme of *Nana*, however, is not the fall of the Second Empire: it is the moral putrefaction of the era.

The novel's more generalizing discourse is inseparable from contemporary anxiety about the terminal decadence of the nation which the Franco-Prussian War had merely accelerated. This perception had already been current in the 1860s, exemplified by Henri Rochefort's series of articles entitled 'Les Français de la décadence' (1866). After 1870, both military defeat and the burning of Paris by the Communards generated an inexhaustible set of analogies: the parallel between the fate of France and that of imperial Rome was so apposite that the fact that three and a half centuries had separated Nero's legendary orgies from the invasion of the Goths could be ignored. Now, once again, a corrupt civilization had been destroyed by barbarians from the North.

This idea was not propagated exclusively by those hostile to the Second Empire. Flaubert, for example, had enjoyed the glittering occasions hosted by Napoleon III at Compiègne. But in his despair in the autumn of 1870, he too was haunted by the idea that the Prussian victory meant that 'we are entering a world from which the Latin race will be excluded.'[14] Nor was this a passing or individual obsession. In 1884 the first volume of Jules Barbey d'Aurevilly's *La Décadence latine* brought to the surface the fears of the men of Flaubert's generation who had lived through the trauma of 1870–71. The collective mood had many symptoms, including widespread subscription to the pessimism of the philosopher Schopenhauer and the founding of the *Revue wagnérienne* (1885), canonizing a new musical vogue embraced by Zola (as *L'Œuvre* proves) as it was by other prominent writers equally ranged against stultifying traditionalism. Zola's later novels are inseparable from this mood: it finds its fullest expression in his *La Joie de vivre*, where the character of Lazare reads Schopenhauer and plays Wagner as he composes his own 'Symphony of Suffering'. But that this was a sign of the times rather than a literary conceit is underlined by Elémir Bourges' novel *La Crépuscule des dieux* (1884), which takes its title, of course, from Wagner's *Götterdämmerung*. The scenes which close this melodramatic novel take place while French troops, mobilizing against Prussia in the summer of 1870, are passing through the streets, precisely the backdrop to the end of Zola's *Nana*.

In *Nana* itself, sexual incontinence characterizes the whole of society. Its microcosm is the novel's theatre, its equation with a brothel cheerfully voiced in conversation by its manager and patrons alike; it has little to do with the verifiable fact that, for much of the nineteenth century, Parisian theatres were a favourite site for prostitutes in search of clients. As the Second Empire recedes into the rear-view historical mirror, the generalizing reach of the *Rougon-Macquart* ensures that the metaphor applies to Zola's depiction of an entire age of moral corruption, viewed by him with a mixture of fascination and puritanical disgust. In the significantly entitled 'La Fin de l'orgie', in *La Cloche* of 13 February 1870, and in other articles in the opposition press at the time, he had been as provocative as other journalists in referencing Sodom and Gomorrah (*OC*, XIII, 259–62). But as was already evident in his early novels and his annotation of Prosper Lucas' reproductive permutations, the *Rougon-Macquart* series confirms Zola's abiding interest in the destructive power of transgressive eroticism.

In the writing of *Une page d'amour*, Zola consciously set out to differentiate it from such negativity: it was to be a universally applicable analysis of female desire constrained only by convention and guilt, 'in which', as he stressed in its preparatory notes, 'everybody should be able to identify their own experience' (*Ms* 10318, fol. 492), and he intended that it should eschew a 'realist' (that is, physiological) perspective as well as 'poetic illusions'. But the novel comes across as a compensatory authorial fantasy of a virtuous woman seduced. Flaubert seems to have intuitively guessed as much: after finishing *Une page d'amour*, he complimented Zola on a display of 'maleness' which corresponded to his own overtly libidinous response to the portrait of its heroine, Hélène, in her hesitant erotic relationship with Dr Deberle. The novel was far from bland, he reassured Zola, to the extent that no young woman should be allowed to read it; 'Even at my advanced age', he wrote, 'the novel . . . *turned me on*. One's lust for Hélène is so overwhelming that one can well understand what your doctor wants.'[15] Shared fantasy or not, *Une page d'amour*'s exploration of the 'passion' between 'two perfectly decent people' (*Ms* 10318, fol. 493) cannot escape the physiological premise of Zola's understanding of the relationship between men and women, most intimately suggested in the heroine's vicarious arousal on glimpsing the caresses of an adulterous couple. Edmond de Goncourt's account of Zola's thinking about the novel confirms this: qualifying any conclusion to their 'gentlemanly' debate with the reservation that he, Flaubert and Zola had never been genuinely in love, he repeats the latter's assertion, which Turgenev argued against, that intensity of amorous feeling was inseparable from 'copulation'.[16]

Nana, as the next novel in the series after *Une page d'amour*, returns Zola to that premise, refusing to overlay it with emotional subtleties. With the exception of the utopian celibacy of *Le Rêve* and the sentimental idealism of *Le Docteur Pascal*, every novel of the *Rougon-Macquart* places what many contemporary critics considered an inordinate stress on carnal appetites, only rarely counterbalanced by instances of chastity, frigidity or impotence. *La Conquête de Plassans*, while already shifting Zola's focus from Second Empire politics to psychopathology, was also only the first of many of his novels to give expression to his anticlerical views; but here he links the religious irrationalism commonly imputed to women with sexual repression.

Bestial urges in Zola's fiction are stereotypically male: sexual assault and selfish gratification; predatory bachelors aping their philandering fathers in working their way through a succession of mistresses; the ogling of the immodest *décolleté* of glamorous ladies mentally undressed; deflowered virgins; idiosyncratic depravity; paedophilia and perversions; non-consensual impregnation; embraces as unwelcome as the pressured resumption of 'conjugal rights'; courtesans sharing their sensually ornate beds with the highest bidder; and casual, professionalized and figurative prostitution, whether on the street, behind closed doors or in the selling of women's bodies in the marriage market. But there is a wider lens to Zola's view of the moral bankruptcy of nineteenth-century France: it takes in the adultery of wives as well as husbands; prurient gossip enjoyed by women too about who is sleeping with whom; incestuous liaisons and pre-pubescent coupling.

Pot-Bouille, partly written in response to the outrage *Nana* had provoked, was designed to show that only bourgeois hypocrisy disguised a miasma of unlicensed desires no different from the promiscuity assumed to be the preserve of a morally deficient working class or demi-monde. Even *Son Excellence Eugène Rougon*, recording the banalities of political life, includes a secondary plot charting Clorinde Balbi's seductive prowess all the way up to her triumphant bedding of the notoriously libertine head of state. The novel also contains an almost gratuitous scene in which its otherwise clear-sighted hero is hypnotized, as Clorinde poses for a painting, by the display of her naked flesh. This is the point at which Henry James's admiration for the novel, cited earlier, is held in check by a 'prissy and priggish' moral revulsion at its 'indecency'.[17] But the awe provoked by the figure of Clorinde suggests James may have been as conflicted as her creator.

Zola's own ambivalence in respect of the human frailty to which Eugène Rougon is prey is most clearly identifiable in *Nana*'s amplification of such an episode. It opens with its eponymous heroine's entry on stage at the Théâtre des Variétés in the role of Venus. Her ensnaring of Mars, the god of war, is a transparent allegory, ignored by the spectators but all too clear for readers of the novel in 1880. On the one hand, Zola parodies the vulgarity and ineptitude of the whole performance. On the other, the collective lust of the audience directed at Nana's barely veiled voluptuousness elicits, after an initially tepid response, increasing sighs of pleasure before climaxing in frenzied applause:

> Every man there had been possessed by her. The rutting instinct she had awoken, like an animal in heat, had gradually spread through the theatre . . . tensing muscles, raising the hairs on necks . . . warmed by the irregular breathing of unseen women. (*RM*, II, 1119)

If Zola's insistence here is that these women are not 'respectable', it is only in anticipation of even the most virtuous eventually succumbing to a compulsion not amenable to rational control. His double focus, demystifying and yet engaging the reader in the spell cast by the third-rate actress, exactly corresponds to Flaubert's recognition that what his fellow novelist had done in *Nana* was to consecrate a mythology of sexual desire. Although not always as foregrounded, it is prevalent throughout Zola's work. In *Nana*, the spectre of the Fatal Woman, already discernible in his novels before the *Rougon-Macquart*, is conjured up explicitly as the devouring *mangeuse d'hommes* (man-eater) whose sexual rapacity is an all-consuming threat to the social order, irrespective of time or place.

Enlarged Perspectives

The major novels of the 1880s take this generalizing direction many a step further, starting with *Germinal*, composed in 1884–5. During the four years after the publication of *Nana* in March 1880, Zola's novels are in a minor key in the sense of his restricted focus not being integrated within a wider historical vision. However representative of different social worlds, their fictional contexts are both localized (the apartments of *Pot-Bouille*, the department store of *Au bonheur des dames* and the seaside village of *La Joie de vivre*) and only tangentially related to contemporary concerns beyond them. *Germinal* too is situated in a particular location, that of a coal mine in northern France. But Zola endows its setting and subject with a symbolic dimension responsible for the novel's power and far-reaching implications.

Germinal supposedly takes place in the closing years of the Second Empire. Zola was perfectly aware, however, that two particular miners' strikes in 1869 merely offered him justification for treating such a subject within the *Rougon-Macquart*, consistent with its historical constraints.

It had not been included in his original ten-volume outline for his series. The Commune was clearly decisive in persuading him that he would have to complement *L'Assommoir* with another study of the working class, but this time with politics at its centre. Industrial unrest in the coalfields close to the Belgian border in February 1884 provided him with the opportunity to do so, thanks to a fortuitous meeting with Alfred Giard, the socialist deputy for Valenciennes. When he went there, accompanied by Giard, in order to familiarize himself with the region, what he found was not just the terrible privation endured by a mining community: in the most graphic way, he was confronted by aspects of the human condition down the ages. Zola's achievement in *Germinal* was to reveal in unflinchingly granular detail a late nineteenth-century working-class experience characterized by inhuman misery. But the day-to-day lives of the miners, regulated by their labour underground, inspired what is in effect also a fable of the disinherited emerging from the bowels of the earth. And this is what gives the novel its universalizing resonance. It also explains why *Germinal* is widely recognized as Zola's masterpiece as well as being one of the finest novels ever written in French.

Rather than being circumscribed by its origins in particular events of 1869 or 1884, *Germinal* accommodates the repeated conflicts of the century as well as looking forward to the future. As the novel closes, there is a suggestion that its hero, Étienne Lantier (a composite portrait of militant union figures of the period), take his revolutionary ideas to Paris and the uprising of 1871, and, besides the associated violence of the mob, some of Zola's characterization bears traces of his attitude towards the Commune. But the novel's link to his portrayal of the Second Empire itself is tenuous. As Zola stressed in some of his earliest notes for *Germinal*, its wider relevance would lie in the depiction of the struggle between the forces of capitalism and a newly unionized, and thereby both emboldened and threatening, working class: 'the importance of the book will be its engagement with this most important issue of the twentieth century' (*Ms* 10307, fol. 402).

Germinal's enlarged perspectives, both spatial and temporal, can be accounted for by such authorial intentions as well as the imaginative dynamic of its writing. The title Zola chose refers to the seventh month (corresponding to 21 March–19 April) in the calendar recast in the immediate aftermath of the French Revolution by those convinced that 1789, as year I, marked a new beginning. More precisely, it was on '12 Germinal, year III' that starving Parisians had staged a famous uprising against the government of the Convention (1792–5), which had arrogated to itself the powers previously the remit of the National Assembly. If that title announces the paradigm, nowhere are the implied analogies more forcefully aligned than in the vision of revolution dramatized in Part v, Chapter Five. The collective demand for bread reminded the contemporary reader of a vanguard of women, with the same battle-cry, advancing on Versailles during the phase of the Revolution, in 1793–4, known as the Terror. And a supplementary conflation of time frames is effected by points of contact between, on the one hand, the rampaging miners and, on the other, the mindlessly destructive hordes roaming across the plains of France described by contemporary historians of 1789 – themselves writing in the equally terrifying shadow of the Commune.

It is not just such a historical perspective which Zola enlarges, nor the fact that its mining community is representative of others. More significant is that the archetypal is engendered from the same descriptive fabric which highlights the typical. A specific industrial landscape, no different from the somewhat featureless countryside of much of northern France, is transformed into the barren setting for the struggle, at the most basic level, for existence. There are certain repeated sequences – the descent into the pit, the miners, pickaxe in hand, at the coalface – which become recurrent textual motifs rather than simply indications of a routine: men are momentarily seized in the statuesque incarnation of their lives; their tasks are those of allegorical figures of toil and suffering.

The multiple connotations of the mine itself reinforce this sense of the perennial. While it is through Étienne's bewildered eyes that we are first alerted to the voracious appetite of the aptly named Le Voreux mine, what was introduced by Zola as a hallucinatory and possibly unreliable image is, for the rest of the novel up until its destruction, a substantive: the monstrous presence is an ever-present monster. Its labyrinthine corridors evoke the buried cities of legend; in it the miners are entombed as the living dead, vainly searching for an escape from a fate repeated from generation to generation. It is also a primeval world where bestiality breaks out in murder and lust, and it is a place of torture and eternal damnation, with its hellish conditions irresistibly associated with Hades and Tartarus. These are the eclectic comparisons to which Zola has recourse in explaining the intolerable temperature or the choking dust. In the process of detailing utterly factual determinants, his descriptive language generates associations which are the shared references of the (Western) cultural imagination.

A similar mythological enrichment of the text is a result of Zola's handling of his characters. Throughout the *Rougon-Macquart*, he tends to structure these antithetically, for the most part (as he had promised Lacroix) ranging 'heroes' against 'villains'. Less Manichean would be the pairing of Jean and Maurice in *La Débâcle*, symbolic of opposing forces in the civil war of the Commune. *Germinal* goes a step further: its central figures are organized into a pattern as old as literature itself. Étienne's progress through the novel is that of a traditional quest: the solitary hero's initiating meeting with Bonnemort, who voices the challenges ahead, gives to the novel a prologue in the manner of a classical fable; Maheu is a kind of king of the underworld who dispenses knowledge, work and food, as well as introducing Étienne to his daughter Catherine. Only once the filial bond is broken (by Maheu's death) can the prodigal son overcome a sexual longing kept in check by a taboo akin to incest. The narrative model is completed by Étienne's meeting with Chaval, the outsider who quits the leader's team, violates the family sanctuary, ravishes the daughter and removes her from the paternal hearth; Zola thereby plots a rivalry in both work and love which must, of dramatic necessity, be violently resolved. In such a scheme, it is inevitable that the ensuing duel should see Étienne heroically prevail. He does so in an extraordinary episode in the depths of the mine, in which Zola makes it clear that its destruction by Souvarine, the anarchist, creates the very conditions in which Étienne can kill Chaval and then make love to the dying Catherine. In an elemental space realistically mapped but resonant with mythological associations, Eros and Thanatos intertwine as precisely as consummation and corpse.

But that is instructive. At the close of *Germinal*, the defeat of the miners, forced to return to work in conditions even harsher than before the strike, is overlaid by a myth increasingly prevalent in the *Rougon-Macquart*: that of Eternal Return. As a title, *Germinal* has vernal associations beyond its gesturing towards political revolution. The emergence of Étienne from the wintry darkness of his experience into the April sunshine of a germinating nature may defy logic as well as plausibility. A great burst of light accompanies a concluding visionary prophecy of an army rising out of the darkness in the cause of social justice. That does not make of the novel a call to revolution rather than reform. For Zola, 'revolution' was less a definitive break in the narrative of human affairs, as the idealists of 1789, 1830, 1848 and the Commune had hoped, than integral to a conception of history and politics dictated by the more literal notions of cycle and circle, which the century's successive revolutions exemplified. At one point in *Germinal*, Étienne speaks of 'the Republic, which would provide bread for all'. To which his listener shakes her head, 'for she remembered the 1848 Revolution, a dreadful year which had left them stripped to the bone' (*RM*, III, 1330).

The end of *Germinal* opens up perspectives constrained by neither politics nor credibility. Although he hoped that the novel would scare bourgeois readers out of their wits, Zola's left-wing commentators ever since 1885 have been disappointed that *Germinal* failed to predicate a future in which capitalism would be overthrown by its victims. His own concern for balance extends the realities of suffering to the bourgeois figure of Hennebeau, the manager of the mine. Its exploitative owners are out of sight. By the time of *Germinal*'s writing, Zola was no longer concerned with the outcome of class conflict as such, nor with the vicissitudes of the Second Empire. Its catastrophic demise, together with the Commune, merely reinforced a historical world view which increasingly informs Zola's work. At the end of *Germinal*, Étienne and Souvarine play out the dialectical relationship between destruction and renewal which orders the seasons into cycle rather than sequence.

In respect of that regenerative structure, the discreetly positive implications of *Germinal*'s final pages remind us of an optimistic strain to Zola's writing often hidden from view. It is identifiable as far back as *La Confession de Claude*, in which the luminous endings of some of the *Rougon-Macquart* are prefigured: after Marie's death and the end of his affair with Laurence, Claude watches the sun rising on the horizon, filling his heart with renewed hope. Throughout his work, Zola is torn between the bleakness of *La Joie de vivre* and the dynamism of *Au bonheur des dames*. That the latter immediately precedes *La Joie de vivre*, temporarily laid aside, points to an instability which makes its title less ironic than ambivalent. Even there, the character of Pauline resists succumbing to the pain and death around her: while rejecting the idea that she should herself incarnate 'joie de vivre', Zola insisted in his notes that 'she has to be shown overcoming every catastrophe' (*Ms* 10311, fol. 147).

The forces of life remain equally triumphant at the end of *La Faute de l'Abbé Mouret*, as the birth of a calf immediately follows a funeral. Among the 59 possible titles for *L'Œuvre*, many of the figures of speech with which Zola played cluster around variations on parturition. This thematic matrix makes it less paradoxical than it may seem that even money, in *L'Argent*, is seen as potentially fertilizing, as it had been energizing in *Au bonheur des dames*. The prediction of France's rebirth at the end of *La Débâcle* is foretold in the scene in which peasants calmly ploughing their fields remain indifferent to the passing troops heading for yet another war. This perspective, thematizing unending fecundity at the expense of ephemeral circumstances, whether individual or collective, is most fully developed in *La Terre*: its horrific story is framed by the repeated cycle of the seasons and the suggestion that the remains of the dead will fertilize the harvests of the future. Right at the beginning of Zola's novel cycle, the cemetery of *La Fortune des Rougon* had been similarly regenerative. The ending of *Germinal* is more tentative in this respect. But its writing, one feels, gave Zola the impetus to modify the tonality of his series as he approached its completion.

Many such instances of regeneration are associated with female characters who are the antithesis of a Clorinde or a Nana. In *L'Argent*, after her despair, Mme Caroline contemplates with renewed hope, like the autobiographical hero of *La Confession de Claude*, the rising dawn of a spring day. *Le Docteur Pascal*'s closing image of a baby at Clotilde's breast, taking such a scenario of rebirth to its least subtle extension, undoubtedly reflects Zola's own parental joy after 1889. He had already inserted such a scene in *La Joie de vivre*, however, in which Pauline rocks a small child to sleep. The strength of these characters lies not in the perfection of the heroine of *Le Docteur Pascal* but rather in a dignity and resilience reminiscent of Zola's perception of his mother. In the final panorama of *Une page d'amour*, a residual optimism is filtered through the gaze of Hélène, whose sudden widowhood had been based on that of Zola's mother. Other exemplars of maternal fortitude include La Maheude (the matriarch of *Germinal*) and another widow, Henriette (in *La Débâcle*).

Au bonheur des dames is consistent with the above. The unruly early years of its hero Octave Mouret, whose entrepreneurial flair and fantasy, it has been suggested, remind one of Zola's father, had been glimpsed in *La Conquête de Plassans*: having twice failed the *baccalauréat* (as Zola had done), his eviction from the family hearth marks the start of his enjoying a promiscuous life in Marseilles (as Zola had not). *Pot-Bouille* shows him as the arch seducer, with his multiple sexual liaisons providing that novel's semblance of a plot. In *Au bonheur des dames*, he undergoes a conversion: having left behind his mistresses, he falls in love with Denise, the humble shop girl working in the small business subject to Darwinian elimination by the modern department store whose fabulous success he engineers. Throughout the novel, Denise resists Octave's advances. Only in its terminal paragraphs does he himself ask for her hand in marriage. Zola's 'heroine', as he calls Denise, is described as 'grounded, wise and practical'. And as he also wrote in his work-notes:

> that's what the book is about: Octave . . . having exploited women . . . is finally, in his triumph . . . conquered by a woman . . . not in a calculated way on her part, but simply as a result of her power as a woman. (*Ms* 10277, fol. 11)

This was to be the 'happy ending' (fol. 23) Zola had envisaged, giving to the novel's title another level of meaning. And that the couple 'live happily ever after' is confirmed in *Le Docteur Pascal*, in which we are told that Denise has just given birth to their second child. However confused its elements, it is tempting to locate here another version of Zola's idealized story of his parents. What is less speculative is that in the interpenetration of his interrupted work on *La Joie de vivre* and the fluency of *Au bonheur des dames*, both in the long shadow of Zola's mother's death, we have evidence of the personal dimension of the contradictions within his symbiosis of decomposition and renewal.

During the writing of *Nana*, Zola had been in his element: to Alexis, in the severe winter of 1879, he had reported from the isolation of Médan that 'you can't imagine how good it is to be cut off by all this snow. Never before I have been able to work in such tranquillity' (*Corr.*, III, 414). That quietude had been brought to an end by the multiple bereavements of 1880. But having worked through the morbid introspection occasioned by them and captured in a novel as prolonged in gestation as *La Joie de vivre*, *Germinal* is testimony to Zola's renewed energy. It would be as evident in the writing of the novels immediately after *Germinal*: *L'Œuvre* and *La Terre* both appeared in the space of the next two years. He penned the opening lines of *Germinal* on 2 April 1884, and had made such rapid progress that its serialization could begin a couple of months before he finished it on 23 January 1885. As suggested by such compression, Zola's correspondence during the composition of *Germinal* is marked by an unsurprising confidence in his creative powers. But it is also revealing that, in reporting to Huysmans in May that he was quietly working away on his text, he admitted that he was barely in control of what he was doing: 'the longer I go on, the more I am convinced that the actual writing of our works has a life of its own, irrespective of conscious intention' (*Corr.*, V, 108). This confirms, even belatedly, authorial awareness of the problematic dimension of his representation of the external world. It was not limited to *Germinal*: in the writing of *Nana*, as he intimated to Alexis, Zola's distance from his tawdry Parisian subject-matter was licensing. Whether sociologically or personally true, his fiction's qualities are inseparable from a formidable imagination being given free rein.

Zola's photograph of his country house at Médan.

4

Writing the *Rougon-Macquart* II: Naturalism and Beyond

Zola was aware of the potential contradiction between the representation of reality and his own increasingly inventive transcription of it. He could hardly deny that in *Germinal*, for example, imaginative reach transcended a documented subject. In a long response to Henry Céard's reservations about the novel's verisimilitude being subordinate to its poetic vision, Zola argued that these apparently ill-fitting dimensions of his fiction could be reconciled: his 'hypertrophie du vrai' (mania for exactitude) was 'the springboard . . . which makes possible the leap towards the stars'. While asserting that symbolic truths were the result of this cosmic 'flight', Zola had to admit that 'we all falsify more or less' (*Corr.*, V, 248–50).

Such an admission to a fellow writer could not be extended to his hostile critics, for whom the 'falsification' or 'distortion' of reality in Zola's novels was a consistent objection. Artistic licence is problematic for Zola only in relation to what he himself publicly declared were the underlying principles of his writing. These were articulated in response to the critical reception of the *Rougon-Macquart*. This had initially been muted. As it became increasingly clear that the focus of Zola's series was no longer restricted to a regime in the safely distant past, his novels were subject to ongoing controversy; this would mark the rest of his career, spilling over onto aspects of it beyond his creative and critical work. From the publication of *L'Assommoir* onwards, growing awareness that Zola was a writer to be reckoned with coincided with the beginning of what would be the regular denunciation of many of his novels, whether on aesthetic, moral or ideological grounds.

The ferocity of these attacks can be accounted for by the fact that such grounds were often not distinct from each other. *L'Assommoir* was initially serialized in *Le Bien public*, the left-leaning newspaper whose director Yves Guyot correctly predicted that the novel would increase its circulation. At the same time, in a further self-interested move to enhance the impact of Zola's name, he offered the novelist 500 francs a month to contribute drama reviews to the paper. Faced with the storm of *political* protest provoked by *L'Assommoir*'s portrayal of working-class deprivation, Guyot was pressured into abandoning its serialization in June 1876 after only six chapters had been printed; the rest of the novel appeared in the more literary *La République des lettres* between 9 July of that year and 7 January 1877. But its publication in volume form only intensified the polemical debate: critics with republican sympathies condemned its 'falsely ugly' depiction of the proletariat; right-wing commentators lambasted the novel as 'immoral' and, more insidiously, Zola himself as 'the leader of the literary Commune'. In the years ahead, he would be forced to confront this critical synthesis of 'pornography' and 'socialism', strategically calibrated by his political opponents.

The pre-emptive defensive stance adopted in the preface to *L'Assommoir*, stressing his 'bourgeois respectability', was to be of no avail. From then on, Zola was attacked for his depiction of physical appetites and social conditions. As his opponents insisted that obscenity, exaggeration and bias resulted from a perverse or politically motivated representation of reality, Zola found himself denying that any such distortion had taken place; quasi-scientific evidence, he argued, was at the heart of his objective realism. And to back this up, he claimed that the documents assembled by Naturalist novelists like himself were entirely responsible for the structure and content of their works: they both preceded the elaboration of character and plot and were transposed so directly that the creative imagination was virtually redundant.

Polemical pressures so vitiated Zola's accounts of his own achievement that his more dogmatic statements are misleading. His work-notes demonstrate that, in practice, the composition of each novel of the *Rougon-Macquart* is inspired by an idea, often dating from many years earlier, developed thematically through potential scenes and characters *before* he engaged in documentary research designed to assure the verisimilitude of his fiction. The prior formulation of a novel's focus is often metaphorical: *La Curée* would orchestrate the twin 'notes of flesh and gold'; *Le Ventre de Paris* would explore 'the belly of humanity, and by extension that of the bourgeoisie'; *Nana* would be '*the poem of male desire*' (Zola's emphasis); *Au bonheur des dames* would be 'the poem of modern [commercial] activity'; *La Terre* would be 'the poem of the earth, but on a human rather than symbolic level'.

Once he had sketched a novel's outline, including preliminary chapter plans, Zola undertook research of an almost scholarly kind: for *La Curée*, for example, he ploughed his way through dry-as-dust treatises on the legal framework of expropriation in the 1850s and extracted from press reports synopses of the fortunes and losses of contemporary speculators. Bibliographies listed in his work-notes for the *Rougon-Macquart* testify to extensive reading, often in the Bibliothèque impériale (in the rue de Richelieu, subsequently renamed the Bibliothèque nationale), where specialist works could be consulted: on medieval stained-glass windows for *Le Rêve*; in the preparation of *Le Ventre de Paris*, hygiene regulations for the central markets; tracts on alcoholism for *L'Assommoir*; studies of criminality for *La Bête humaine*; dozens of military memoirs for *La Débâcle*. *L'Assommoir*'s originality lies in allowing the reader to share a working-class perspective through Zola's handling of dialogue and interior monologue; he was able to do this convincingly by drawing from dictionaries of proletarian slang a vocabulary so colourful, vulgar and otherwise incomprehensible that modern editions of the novel have to provide a lexical appendix. Readers of *Germinal* are virtually saturated with prosaic information: about mineshafts, tunnelling techniques, the price of coal, wage levels, accidents, respiratory diseases, the sleeping and eating habits of miners; it ranges from the anecdotal details of their growing of vegetables to the organization of working-class associations, and from washtubs to syndicalist theory. In an exemplary way, to learn all this is to be forcibly reminded, not only of the integrity of Zola's documentation, but of the pedagogic aspirations of much nineteenth-century French fiction. In an era of educational enthusiasm, reflected in the publishing ventures in which Zola had been immersed at Hachette, his writing is driven by a commitment to teach his readers, in an age of steadily growing literacy, about realities behind appearances or beyond horizons.

When background information or his own experience were insufficient to fully master the subject of a novel, Zola set up personal meetings with officials or experts in the field: architects, station managers, engineers, geologists, agronomists, brokers, prosecutors and defence lawyers, to name but a few. During the preparation of *Le Ventre de Paris*, a supervisor gave him access to the cellars beneath the market stalls. He talked to the heads of the different departments of Le Bon Marché, the real department store on which his own fictional version in *Au bonheur des dames* is based: over a whole month, in the spring of 1881, he spent much time there, encouraged to do so by his wife, who was one its regular customers. Friends and colleagues made their own contribution to many of Zola's novels, alerting him to sources or filling in details he needed. For *Nana*, he was much enlightened, and possibly shocked, by those intimately familiar with the demi-monde, scrupulously making a note of their scabrous anecdotes. For *L'Œuvre*, Zola relied on Guillemet to add to what he had not really taken in while watching Cézanne and the early Impressionists at their easels: the minutiae of the craft of painting, from brushes to pigments and from framing to varnishing a canvas.

In order to animate his novels, Zola's 'site visits' were as crucial. It was also Guillemet who gave him a tour of the residence of one of the most high-profile courtesans of the period so that the novelist could describe the extravagant decor of Nana's own. And although Zola initially denied it, in *Le Voltaire* of 28 September 1879 (perhaps embarrassed by it being perceived as a bit 'tacky'), he did not delete Alexis' biography's subsequent confirmation of the visit to the address on the boulevard Malesherbes of 'one of those ladies' – necessitated by the fact that the author of *Nana* was of course chastely ignorant of their lifestyle. Zola returned with a sheaf of notes from all such excursions. For his series as a whole, they number in total several thousand. They are as exhaustive as the process of note-taking must have been exhausting: on the spot, he was scribbling furiously, either observing a scene or recording the often very technical discourse of his informants; when away from home, it involved working late into the night in hotel bedrooms so as to register what he had learnt during the day. They also tell us something about Zola himself: a determination to get it right, and over and beyond the garnering of information for the novel in hand, an insatiable curiosity about the world outside his study. But what he discovered sometimes shocked him to the core: whether in visiting *L'Assommoir*'s slums, *Germinal*'s coalfields or *La Terre*'s rural communities, he was overwhelmed by pity for those eking out their lives in material conditions many degrees more wretched than his own experience of poverty in the years immediately following his move to Paris in 1858.

In preparing *Le Ventre de Paris*, the several nights during which Zola observed the reprovisioning of Les Halles had a rather different effect on him, immersed in the riot of colours and smells which he would subsequently shape into a still-life sequence of memorable tableaux. For the horse-racing episode which occupies Chapter Eleven of *Nana*, he spent a whole Sunday (8 June 1879) as an unwilling spectator at the Longchamp track, and after what he had anticipated would be, as he confided to Flaubert, an extremely boring outing, he secured further information about fillies, jockeys and betting scams. During the writing of *Germinal*, he overcame his claustrophobia and was lowered in the cage into the Renard pit at Delain, one of the mines still working throughout the strike; crawling on all fours within its tunnels, in spite of his corpulent frame, Zola could experience at first hand the physical hardship of the novel's characters.

The privilege of gaining such insights was inseparable from a growing national reputation which 'opened doors', leading to various authorities being only too willing to help Zola understand the milieu in which they worked. The preparation of *L'Argent* saw him watching the frenetic dealings in the Paris stock exchange; for *La Bête humaine*, he got permission to travel on 15 April 1889 alongside the driver and fireman in the cab of a locomotive steaming between the Gare St-Lazare and Le Havre, stepping down on arrival covered in soot but generating for the novel visceral scenes based on his terrifying train ride; for *La Débâcle*, he retraced Napoleon III's movements across the battlefields of the Franco-Prussian War, delighted to note in April 1891 that the room in the inn where the emperor had sheltered still contained the engravings which had met his weary eyes, so historians had discovered, two decades before. Even relatively familiar contexts were revisited in the interests of accuracy. While drafting *Une page d'amour* in the Midi, he felt the need to go back up to Paris to remind himself of the panorama from the heights of the Trocadéro. Although, through working as a drama critic after 1873, Zola already knew the world of the theatre, its inner workings, as depicted in *Nana*, were detailed as a result of gaining access to dressing rooms and being put in touch with backstage staff responsible for make-up, costumes, lighting and props. For *L'Œuvre*, he returned to the annual Salon, this time (in May 1885) with notebook in hand, in order to convey, better than he had remembered from his earlier annual visits, the layout of exhibition spaces and the intricacies of ticketing arrangements. Notwithstanding his growing up there, *Le Docteur Pascal* necessitated a return to Provence to precisely depict the landscape of its setting.

It would be as much of a mistake to relegate such documentation to an entirely secondary position as it was to claim, as Zola did and as Alexis' biography complicitly underlined, that it was the starting point for the writing of his novels. Its insertion within plotlines and scenarios often results in modifications, sometimes of a radical kind, to what Zola had originally imagined. The documentation is creative in the sense that, through associative moves within and across his notes, a verifiable fact catalyses the invention of a new scene or character. What remains striking, however, is that Zola's publicly avowed dependence on its primacy as a guarantee of authorial neutrality hardly squares with his conception of literary representation as he had defined it at the very beginning of his writing career – let alone with his admission to Céard, cited at the start of this chapter in the context of *Germinal* – that imaginative distortion was the *sine qua non* of artistic representation.

In what is considered the foundational text of Zola's artistic principles, his 'Théorie des écrans' (Theory of Screens), explicated at length in a letter to Valabrègue as far back as 1864, he had reviewed the different kinds of metaphorical 'lens' or 'panes of glass' through which external reality could be viewed, and he recognized that, given the impossibility of absolute transparency or objectivity, artistic truth was inevitably subjective, if preferably minimally distorted (*Corr.*, I, 373–81). Zola's assessment of the Goncourts' 'distortion' in *Germinie Lacerteux* had similarly equated such subjectivity with creativity. He also applied this equation to Manet's pictorial originality, but he was forced to simultaneously defend the painter against charges of obscenity by paradoxically arguing that his canvases were so exactly a transcription of reality that they could not be accused of distortion of any kind. Zola thereby found himself mired in the contradictions discernible in the defence of his own work.

Naturalist Campaigns

That defence took many forms: in literary essays and political journalism; in Zola's drama criticism and through his own theatrical ventures. This writing was legitimized by his increasingly visible leadership of the Naturalist movement, recognized by his 'disciples' and acolytes drawn to the material evidence of his contemporary stature represented by his country house at Médan – as ever-expanding as the *Rougon-Macquart* themselves.

The most effective of these inter-related campaigning activities were mounted in the press, perpetuating a conviction arrived at during his journalistic apprenticeship in the 1860s that this was the most influential contemporary platform for the dissemination of ideas and opinions. That he sustained this activity throughout the first ten years he was engaged on the *Rougon-Macqart* is further testimony to an extraordinary work rate. It is also a measure of a financial insecurity that novels alone could not be guaranteed to overcome. The time he devoted to his writing for the press can be measured by the bare figures of his output: 109 articles in *La Cloche* in 1872; 21 in *L'Avenir national* the following year; some 250 in *Le Bien public* and *Le Voltaire* in 1876–7; 52 in *Le Figaro* in 1881. More occasional pieces were published elsewhere. To such figures has to be added the rejigging of dozens of these too for publication in volume form.

Only in September 1881 did Zola announce in *Le Figaro*, to general disbelief, that, in order to concentrate on his novels, he was withdrawing from journalistic activity once and for all: it had served him well; it had earnt him a living for over fifteen years and allowed him to fight his corner. It was time, he wrote, for others to take up the mantle. The Dreyfus Affair would in due course put paid to his expressed hope that he would never have to return to the fray, unsurprisingly 'tired' as he was by the 'battles' he had fought for so long over issues which had been so important to him. It was also true that the phenomenal success of *Nana* meant that in 1881 he no longer needed the money. But that hardly explains why, even before his direct involvement in the Affair in 1898, Zola published his *Nouvelle Campagne* (1896), bringing together another seventeen articles from *Le Figaro*. As he confessed in an 1888 interview, after seven years of self-imposed journalistic exile, he was chomping at the bit; he still had much to say.

Zola's writing in the Parisian press, itemized above, was only part of his journalistic labours. Between January 1871 and May 1877 he had contributed a virtually weekly 'Letter from Paris', even during his holidays, to *Le Sémaphore de Marseille*. With the tacit agreement of its editors, many of these 1,800 texts recycled for a provincial readership a digest of political, social and cultural events in the capital lifted from a column by Ernest d'Hervilly (1839–1911) in *Le Rappel*. There were exceptions, such as Zola's reviews of the 1874 and 1877 Impressionist exhibitions, and his second-hand information was seldom presented without Zola inserting his own point of view. All his articles in this paper, however, were published without his signature, at odds with his later condemnation of such anonymity (see his London speech discussed in Chapter Five). As he shamefacedly admitted to Flaubert, in a letter of 9 April 1874, this journalistic burden 'helps me to keep my pot boiling' (*Corr.*, II, 354). A further such enhancement of his income had been provided by the 64 essays he sent between 1875 and 1881 to *Le Messager de l'Europe*, the liberal

St Petersburg journal with whose directors Turgenev had put him in touch. Addressing Russian readers had the advantage of his lengthy explanations of cultural developments in France, including his own central positioning within them, being invulnerable to disagreement. When some of these pieces were translated back into French for the Parisian press, no such acquiescence was assured.

Zola's abandoning in 1877 his utilitarian contract with *Le Sémaphore de Marseille* coincided with the commercial success of *L'Assommoir*. From then on, his journalism was less driven by financial concerns than by literary ones. The sequence of articles in *Le Voltaire* of 17–21 May 1879, reprinted in the September issue of *Le Messager de l'Europe*, formed the basis of *Le Roman expérimental* the following year. In this best known of his theoretical works, Zola aligned his fiction with the methodology popularized by an influential treatise: *Introduction à l'étude de la médecine expérimentale* (1865) by the physiologist Dr Claude Bernard (1813–1878). In *Les Romanciers naturalistes* (1881), also a compendium of previously published articles, Zola traced the advent of his aesthetic through Balzac, the Goncourts and Flaubert, which had culminated in his own more systematic application of scientific principles. The articles in *Le Naturalisme au Salon* (1880) add up to a personal account of the evolution of French painting from Romanticism onwards. It prefigures his gradual disenchantment with Impressionism, reflected in *L'Œuvre*. This, it has recently been claimed, was a 'betrayal' of his early friendship with Monet in particular.[1] Zola was certainly unimpressed by Monet's hasty overproduction and increasingly blatant commercialism. More generally, however, the sketchy and pointillist technique of the Impressionists in the late 1870s was to Zola at odds with the mimetic ambitions which he had once assumed to correspond to his own. The landscapes of the Barbizon School seemed to him preferable because they were recognizable. They took him back, he added, to the excursions to the countryside southeast of Paris which he and Cézanne had enjoyed in the past. In all these texts, Zola's stance is uncompromisingly militant. Locked into its logic, many of his statements are at several removes from the inventiveness of the *Rougon-Macquart*.

Readers of Zola's theoretical disquisitions were left in no doubt about where he stood. His approval was lent to novelists, artists and dramatists to the extent of their affinities, either verifiable or superimposed, with his own practice and conceptual premises. His recruitment of so many of his contemporaries under the Naturalist banner was also provocative. In his diary entry for 19 February 1877, Edmond de Goncourt recorded that Zola had countered Flaubert's objections to such indiscriminate labelling by expatiating on the theme of his lifelong penury: because he did not have the older writer's private income, he was forced to 'give things a name . . . and my journalism is the means to hammer home the reputation on which I will be judged'; and, so he apparently said, 'I'm as contemptuous of the term *naturalism* as you are, but I shall go on repeating it . . . so that the reading public believes this is something innovative.'[2] Such cynicism may reflect Goncourt's own condescension towards any 'grubby' involvement in journalism from which he was protected by his own prosperity. But Zola's alleged remarks about terminology invalidate neither his artistic preferences nor his own approach to writing, let alone qualify his belief in the power of science. His overstatements, going beyond analogy, need not be taken at face value. The distinction, however, between realism in general and what Zola successfully branded as Naturalism remains pertinent – in the latter's 'experimental' focus on the 'mathematics' of cause and effect, and in its forensic attention to historical, social and biological determinants.

The 'battles' he fought in the press, while writing the *Rougon-Macquart*, were not those of a purely literary campaign. Under Thiers' presidency, in a reaction against the disorder of the Commune, the early years of the Third Republic had been dominated by conservative forces. When Thiers was succeeded by Marshal MacMahon in 1873, those were reinforced. The two-thirds majority in the National Assembly achieved by republican parties in the general election of 1875 only widened the fractures in French political life. The publication of *L'Assommoir*, and its hostile reception, coincided with a crisis seeping into cultural as well as ideological discourse: on 16 May 1877, the centre-left government of Jules Simon had been forced to resign, resulting in the National Assembly being dissolved. The electoral turmoil of the next six months was only the beginning of a long period in which the Third Republic was again riven by a factionalism opposing incompatible definitions of constitutional legitimacy. The republicans' ultimate triumph in 1879 over MacMahon's authoritarian conception of it hardly brought such arguments to a close. The heading of Zola's article in *Le Figaro* of 27 September 1880 – 'Les Trente-Six Républiques' – says it all, even if the notion of as many as 36 competing versions of democratic government was caricaturally 'over the top'.

But Zola's countless journalistic interventions in the debate raging since 1876 contextualize the most oft-cited of them: 'La République sera

Gustave Flaubert.

naturaliste ou elle ne sera pas', in *Le Figaro* of 20 April 1879. Thereby declaring that only on the basis of Naturalist principles could the Republic survive, Zola was playing on the statement made to parliament by Thiers in 1872 ('The Republic will be conservative or it won't exist'). Subsequently reprinting his own maxim in *Le Roman experimental*, under the title 'La République et la littérature', Zola stressed that the extension to the political domain of the theoretical tenets of his aesthetic was justified by what should be common to them both: the suppression of nostalgia for outdated formulae, freedom of expression and rational analysis substituted for emotionalism. In Zola's related positioning on secular education and the rights of women, Naturalism as a literary doctrine simultaneously revealed an ideological thrust impossible to ignore.

In one important respect, however, Zola's assimilation of republican ideas and Naturalist literary practice had its limits. At the elections of 1875, Gambetta had campaigned to extend the franchise to all males over the age of 21. It is one of the apparent oddities of his mostly left-leaning sympathies that Zola, by contrast, remained implacably opposed to universal suffrage. The French Revolution's ideal of *Égalité* cut no ice with him. Zola refused to accept the cherished nostrum that 'all men are equal.' Government 'by the people' seemed to him to lead directly to elective dictatorship. This was a view arrived at less as a result of having witnessed the democratic absolutism of the Commune, than of the successive plebiscites of the period he had lived through (starting with Louis-Napoleon's in 1852), exploited by autocrats legitimizing their power and policies by securing the approbation of a mostly ignorant population. From Napoleon Bonaparte to General Boulanger, Zola felt that his compatriots had time and again been in thrall to charismatic and demagogic leaders. This conviction is discernible in the *Rougon-Macquart*: in the sway held over their publics by Eugène Rougon's ministerial stature and Étienne's oratory in *Germinal*. In *L'Assommoir*, a more caricatural mode has M Madinier, the self-appointed head of the wedding party, delivering a comically faulty version of art history with which he bamboozles his uneducated charges as he leads them through the Louvre.

This negative conception is inverted, however, in Zola's own leadership of his literary school. If the 1880 publication of *Les Soirées de Médan* marked the moment when he publicly assumed it, the date itself is significant. On 30 November 1878 he had written to Flaubert, detained by family troubles in his Normandy retreat and unable to join Zola and their self-selected group of fellow writers for their monthly get-together in Paris: 'when you aren't with us, our centre is missing' (*Corr.*, III, 243). A further occasion when Flaubert was absent, in January 1879, was met with a similar lament: 'what will we do without you?' (*Corr.*, III, 279). Flaubert's sudden death (from either an epileptic fit or a massive heart attack) on Saturday, 8 May 1880, plunging his friends into mourning, had given such sentiments, in retrospect, a sadly premonitory resonance. On hearing the news in a telegram from Maupassant the next day, Zola wrote to Céard that he was 'insane with grief' (*Corr.*, III, 461).

As the letters cited above underline, Flaubert had been a revered figure as well as a focal point in the lives of the group of writers of which Zola had been a part since 1874. His disappearance created the need for a successor to fill the void. That it had to be Zola was not a sign of his self-importance. He was qualified to assume the role by dint of his enhanced profile as the author of *L'Assommoir*. It was also a duty motivated by his gratitude to Flaubert, whose encouragement of his work Zola would repay in a sequence of long essays in the 1880s giving expression to his enormous debt to him, both personally and aesthetically. In one of them he recounted that no other death had affected him as much: between trying to get his head around it on the Sunday and attending the funeral on the Tuesday, he had lain awake at night 'haunted' by Flaubert's spectral presence (*OC*, XI, 121).

Zola had briefly met Flaubert in 1869, but throughout the 1870s, during his writing of the first half of the *Rougon-Macquart*, the older man (his sobriquet was 'Le Vieux') had been a mentor to him, mixing praise with corrective advice. In Zola's first known letter to him, in October 1871, he was respectfully addressed as 'Dear Sir'; by 12 March 1874, it was the disciple's 'Cher maître'; a month later it was 'My dear friend' (*Corr.*, II, 354). His relationship with him was almost filial. Flaubert's premature death at the age of 58 had once again robbed Zola of a paternal imago. In taking his place, there was no compensatory imperative as there had been in the case of François Zola's failure. But there is a sense in which Zola's novels composed after 1880, as well as his studies of Flaubert which are complementary to the completion of the *Rougon-Macquart*, are a kind of homage: they bear witness to the pioneering foundations on which Zola had built; Flaubert was positioned in a literary genealogy as his immediate predecessor; and Zola could posthumously enhance the reputation of the 'father of the modern novel' in acknowledging his seminal influence on his own work.

That overlaying of destinies is both literal and metaphorical. As one of the pall-bearers at Flaubert's funeral outside Rouen on 11 May, Zola was unbearably close to the horse-drawn hearse. He also had a close-up view of the procession made up mostly of dignitaries and colleagues: the coffin was followed along the country road, he remembered, by a mere smattering of local inhabitants. He added that the vast majority of the citizens of Rouen had never heard of the deceased. Flaubert's greatness was thus as little recognized by his native city as that of Zola's father had been by Aix-en-Provence. Memories of both funerals contribute to the desolate one at the end of *L'Œuvre* at which Zola's potentially great fictional artist is laid anonymously to rest. It is one of the most moving scenes he ever wrote. The bereavement with which I began this story of Zola's life had been in a childhood recollected, if not in tranquillity, at least at half a century's distance. The funeral in his novel of 1886 is infused with the emotion of being at Flaubert's graveside only a few years earlier. Its final words, however, voiced by Sandoz (Zola's mouthpiece), are 'Let's get back to work' (*RM*, IV, 363). This was how Zola remembered his trying to overcome the depression caused by all the bereavements of 1880. The words also reflect Zola's determination to sustain the Flaubertian legacy. His house at Médan would become what Flaubert's in Croisset had been for so long: the hospitable destination of a literary pilgrimage; a place of life-affirming pleasures marked by ardent discussion over fraternal meals.

Brought out by Charpentier, the group's supportive publisher, *Les Soirées de Médan* was more than a declaration of avant-garde solidarity: its title also speaks of long companionable evenings (*soirées*) of storytelling.

My next chapters will recount what his Médan domain meant for Zola's private life. In the context of this one, his country property is indissociably linked to the writing of the *Rougon-Macquart*. If Flaubert's death marked the symbolic end of an era, Zola's future centrality had earlier been assured by his purchase of the house in May 1878, following the commercial success of *L'Assommoir*. As that was followed by an ever-increasing income, so he progressively enlarged over the next eight years what he called his 'rabbit hutch', taking over adjoining outhouses and tracts of land to transform a garden into a large estate. At the bottom of it were the thundering trains of the Paris–Le Havre line, which were the constant sonic backdrop to his drafting of *La Bête humaine* in 1889–90.

Construction of what would be called the 'Tour Nana', at the top of which Zola had his study, began in October 1878. It would in due course be followed, in 1885–6, by the tower known as the 'Tour Germinal'. Another building would be the 'Charpentier pavillion'. Internally, stained-glass windows also indexed Zola's fiction: one, for example, represented the character of *L'Assommoir*'s Mes-Bottes. The property is visitable today as the Maison Zola–Musée Dreyfus, and its stunning catalogue is testimony to its owner's attention to detail, which must have tried the patience of architects, masons, decorators and craftsmen subject to his unremittingly intrusive involvement.[3] In its definitive form, the house is often cited as an example of Art Nouveau. The extensions to, and remodelling of, a house were more than a series of domestic concerns: they were symptomatic of those of Zola's reputation. From his 'court' at Médan, he busily extended it outside France, summoning literary correspondents from abroad. It was also the engine room of a massive administrative operation negotiating serial and translation rights of his novels, reinforcing European culture's dominant aesthetic mode and his own status, increasingly recognized as the greatest novelist of his generation. And younger writers seeking advice and encouragement generously conveyed by letter would trek out from Paris to pay homage to 'Le Maître'.

Zola's status as 'Le Maître de Médan' goes a long way towards accounting for the substance and tenor of his Naturalist campaigns. His leadership attracted a like-minded generation of writers and artists. The relatively minor ones risked being listed in 'la queue de Zola', literally his 'tail' but also a term with more vulgar connotations. If any of Zola's followers betrayed signs of diverging from his magisterial example, he would reproach them in person or in print. In the unequal democracy of Médan, Zola was a benign and welcoming dictator. Those outside his circle, opposing his principles and values, were treated more brutally. Those within it considered themselves the most committed of contemporary elites, ranged against the prejudices, philistinism and political mediocrity of the age. They were the vanguard of modernism, with a belief in science rather than religion; they were the men of the future, as Zola had predicted to Alexis and Cézanne in 1871. That future was now: it was manifest in the cultural hegemony Naturalism had established during the decade since that prediction, save for a few traditional pockets of resistance which Zola was determined to silence. His presiding role was an essentially Romantic one, grounded in the immodest certainty that, in Percy Bysshe Shelley's hallowed phrase, writers were the 'unacknowledged legislators of the world'.

For that reason alone, Zola's advocacy of republican virtues does not extend to universal suffrage. Such a levelling (down) was incompatible with a hierarchical structure at the heart of cultural politics. The most ironic legacy of the era's 'democratization of art' was the creation of an aristocracy of taste. Proliferating literary 'groups' and artistic 'circles' privilege the influence of the informed and enlightened, seeking out their own publics. This elitist model is visible in Zola's art criticism: in his rehearsal of the inequity of elections to the Salon admissions jury which excluded pictorial innovation at odds with popularity. Such prioritizing of individual talent over the crowd had already been voiced in Zola's articles of the late 1860s, in which his contempt for the mass of ignorant spectators at the Salon is indicative. It also informs his support, between 1874 and 1879, for the first four exhibitions of the Impressionists, termed 'the Independents' by allies and detractors alike in their secessionist revolt against the authority of the state. The later internecine strife tearing this group of painters apart and going their separate ways represented, in Zola's view, a surrender to the values of the common herd and a failure of leadership he himself was determined to avoid.

In republican papers such as *Le Bien public* and *Le Voltaire*, Zola had been preaching to the converted. His taking up the offer to contribute to the more right-wing *Le Figaro* was prompted by the hope that he would be able to move a recalcitrant audience towards his conjoined artistic and political views. Instead, he was simply subject to more personalized hostility. It seems not by chance that it was in this newspaper, on 22 September 1881, that Zola should announce his retirement from journalism under the heading 'Adieux' (Farewell); among his stated reasons for doing so was his sense that 'je m'encanaillais' ('I was forfeiting my dignity'), increasingly revolted by his futile involvement in a demeaning activity (*OC*, XIV, 663–9).

Zola's journalistic incursions into the political arena after 1876 had done nothing to temper the cynicism only recently reflected in *Son Excellence Eugène Rougon*; if anything, the stark oppositions of the Second Empire had been more amenable to polemical writing than those of the Third Republic, blurred by abstraction, equivocation and fanaticism. For the most part, Zola's battles were conducted on the fertile terrain in which he was more personally invested: the acrimonious debate generated by his novels. In a final article (*EsA*, 401–9) on the visual arts, in 1896, he claimed that his interest in French painting, for example, had not been sustained over the years – not least because its post-Impressionist directions were even more at odds with Naturalist criteria than those against which he had judged Monet's development. The theatre, he recalled, had in any case offered him a more productive arena in which to fight the critical battles surrounding the *Rougon-Macquart*. Both appearing in 1881, *Le Naturalisme au théâtre* and its sequel, *Nos auteurs dramatiques*, were further collections of articles which had appeared between 1876 and 1880. As the first of those titles indicates, Zola's militancy was again on display. As he had written when accepting *Le Voltaire*'s invitation to do so, he was only too happy to place his drama reviews in its columns, thus enabling him to continue the 'campaign' on behalf of Naturalism he had waged for the two years previously in the now-defunct *Bien public*.

These pieces targeted playwrights whose melodramas, comedies of manners and light-hearted musicals (known as *opéras comiques*) seemed to him to be devoid of human truths. Those as prominent as Octave Feuillet (1821–1890), Alexandre Dumas *fils* (1824–1895) and Victorien Sardou (1831–1908) were more or less rubbished; too many of the plays of Eugène Labiche (1815–1888), however amusing, failed to prioritize 'analysis' over caricature; *Les Fourchambault* (1878), by Émile Augier (1820–1889), was 'sadly lacking' in physiological detail. As in the case of Zola's judgement of the work of most novelists past and present, there were familiar exceptions: he welcomed the plays of Edmond de Goncourt, rejecting as they did the conventions of both classical and Romantic theatre; Daudet's also passed muster for the same reason. But, less obviously, in the staging of *L'Ami Fritz* by Erckmann-Chatrian (as its two dramatists were hyphenated) at the Comédie-Française in 1876, Zola discerned in its realistic sets 'the first example of Naturalism' (*OC*, XI, 795) gaining entry to the prestigious stronghold of outdated productions. A few other dramatists were partially reprieved: in praising only the first acts of *Le Prince* (1876) and *La Cigale* (1877), by Henri Meilhac (1831–1897) and Ludovic Halévy (1834–1908), Zola urged them to make a greater effort to sustain for the full length of their plays their talent for 'observation' and 'exactitude'. Some of the novels of the *Rougon-Macquart* bear the imprint of these drama reviews. To cite but one example, Zola reserved some of his most acidic critical bile for the extravagantly costumed operettas of Jacques Offenbach (1819–1880): *La Blonde Vénus*, sung so wonderfully badly by the heroine of *Nana*, is an incisive parody of the immensely popular comic opera (*opéra bouffe*) *La Belle Hélène*, authored by Meilhac and Halévy and set to music by Offenbach in 1864.

It was, as much as his journalism, Zola's own practice as a dramatist which afforded him, at least in theory, the space to performatively demonstrate the applicability of his aesthetic principles. Their staging might persuade large and socially elite audiences, hopefully night after night, to subscribe to them. In a March 1880 article, he compared the paltry sum needed to buy a book with over double such an amount people were prepared to spend on a seat in the stalls, thereby rehearsing his conviction that the theatre was the most important cultural location in which to challenge contemporary assumptions. In 'fevered' anticipation of the future stage adaptation of *L'Assommoir*, as he had written in a letter of 2 September 1877, he believed it to be in the theatre that 'we must make the decisive blow' (*Corr.*, III, 114).

But long before the militant Naturalist campaigns of 1880–81, Zola's theatrical ambitions had existed alongside his literary ones. That they were important to him is underlined by Alexis, in his authorized biography, devoting a whole chapter to their realization, from Zola's juvenile efforts onwards. What is not mentioned is the extent to which his plays occasionally have a function beyond provoking publicity: the 1873 stage version of *Thérèse Raquin*, even if truncated to satisfy the stringency of the Théâtre de la Renaissance, had been reviewed with enough moral outrage to convince Zola that he had found another genre in which to bring his name to public attention, and the prefaces he subsequently affixed to the texts of his plays, as he would do for his novels, countered critical 'misunderstandings' by spelling out authorial intentions. But in the plays themselves there are also themes which feed into the writing of the *Rougon-Macquart*.

These different dimensions of Zola's work as a dramatist are exemplified by *Les Héritiers Rabourdin*, put on over seventeen nights at the Théâtre de Cluny in November 1874. Zola had distributed complimentary tickets to supportive colleagues who had also been summoned to the dress rehearsal. But the play was, as he put it in a letter to Daudet, 'massacred' by the critics (*Corr.*, II, 373), and, in his preface to the published text of it, he accordingly responded by arguing that they had attacked 'the Naturalist formula' rather than the play. This was indebted to Ben Jonson's *Volpone* (1605/6), later the subject of Zola's very first drama review in *Le Voltaire* of 9 July 1878; here he explained that what had inspired him for *Les Héritiers Rabourdin* were Jonson's 'violent truths' and his portrayal, no less relevant than more than two and a half centuries earlier, of 'the unbridled appetites of the beast in man' (*OC*, XII, 165). While this picks up a notion first invoked in 1866, *La Bête humaine* was still fifteen years away. But *La Terre* was also far into the future and, as Kate Griffiths has shown, Zola's reworking of the inheritance plot in *Volpone*, as well as that of *King Lear*, prefigures its elaboration in his novel of 1887.[4]

In spite of the kind words in letters from sympathetic friends, Zola was perfectly aware that *Les Héritiers Rabourdin* had not been, to put it mildly, a success. Solace and solidarity were found at the occasion shortly afterwards, christened 'Le Dîner des auteurs sifflés' in bringing together fellow novelists whose plays had provoked a cacophony of whistles (*sifflets*) or been booed off the stage: the Goncourts' *Henriette Maréchal* (1865), Daudet's *Lise Tavernier* and *L'Arlésienne* (1872) and Flaubert's *Le Candidat* (1874). Turgenev joined them by claiming, perhaps speciously, that he too had experienced something similar in Russia. Such private dinners had been instigated by Flaubert, the first being held on 14 April 1874. They continued until his death. That of 1877 known as the 'Dîner Trapp' (after the name of the restaurateur) was organized by the poet Catulle Mendès (1841–1909), who had taken on the serialization of *L'Assommoir* in his journal. It was there that six younger writers (Alexis, Céard, Huysmans, Maupassant, Léon Hennique and Octave Mirbeau) had gathered to honour their elders: Flaubert, Edmond de Goncourt and Zola. Allegiance had been virtually pledged to the last by baptizing their movement as Naturalism, publicly consecrated, as I mentioned earlier, by the publication three years later of *Les Soirées de Médan*.

Zola's next play, *Le Bouton de rose*, was an even more resounding failure: premiered on 6 May 1878, its run was cut short after only seven dismal performances greeted by minimal audiences with mocking incredulity. Based on one of Balzac's *Contes drolatiques*, it was less droll than ridiculous. Its variations on the theme of adultery, actual or assumed, anticipate the more burlesque episodes of *Pot-Bouille*. But its plot was as farcical as the anatomical double entendre of its title (playing on the name of its improbably unfaithful young bride) was puerile. Its contrived 'happy ending' was precisely the kind of reassuring denouement which Zola continued to castigate in reviews of 'entertaining' contemporary drama.

Les Héritiers Rabourdin had at least been a serious take on Ben Jonson's satire. To counter perception that both that play and the theatrical version of *Thérèse Raquin* were too gloomy, Zola intended that *Le Bouton de rose* should provide a 'lighter note', for the same reason, and in the same year, as the insertion of *Une page d'amour* within the *Rougon-Macquart*. In his diary entry following his attendance at its first night, Edmond de Goncourt recorded his astonishment that a writer with pretensions to lead a literary school should have abased himself with such a humourless work. Zola himself knew it was no good but blamed the mediocrity of the acting. He was loath to admit that comic writing was not his forte. But he insisted he was not discouraged. In the preface to the volume of his three plays published by Charpentier soon after the fiasco of the most recent of them, a confidence boosted by the success of *L'Assommoir* was misplaced: he declared that he was patiently determined to ensure that 'as my novels are finally being read, so one day my plays will be listened to' (OC, XII, 413). In fact, Zola was to write only two more plays himself: *Renée* in 1887, adapting *La Curée* at the behest of Sarah Bernhardt, who finally turned down the leading role in it which she had supposedly coveted, and *Madeleine* two years later, reprising the 1865 drama on which *Madeleine Férat* had originally been based, but slightly modified in the light of the novel itself. Neither play generated critical enthusiasm.

More pragmatically, while struggling with *Le Bouton de rose* and in order to enhance the quality of his work as a dramatist, Zola had turned to a theatre professional: the gifted impresario William Busnach (1832–1907), who had himself written many successful plays and librettos. Their collaboration would last for most of the ten years after their adaptation of *L'Assommoir*. First staged at the Théâtre de l'Ambigu on 18 January 1879, its 250 performances testified to a theatrical triumph which Zola had at last secured; such was its draw that it continued to be put on by various other theatres over the next two decades. The adaptation of *Nana* in 1881 was equally well received, as was that of *Le Ventre de Paris* in 1887. Zola's interest and enthusiasm in jointly producing these with Busnach was only matched by his excitement as each 'first night' approached, and then revelling in the noisy acclaim of the other spectators around him. An unintended consequence of the collaboration was that it tended to deflect critical hostility towards Zola himself: reviewers unsure exactly how much the novelist had contributed instead singled out for praise Busnach's marvellously realistic stage settings.

The theatrical version of *Pot-Bouille*, however, barely survived for seven weeks in the winter of 1883–4: for a bourgeois audience of the day, it was too uncomfortable a reminder of Zola's savaging, in the novel on which the play was of course based, of the priapic obsessions and moral turpitude of a hypocritical middle class. And the adaptation of *Germinal* similarly returned Zola to the challenges besetting his whole career: it was banned by the censors in October 1885, citing the potentially seditious inclusion of Étienne Lantier's call for a socialist revolution and the scene in which troops fire on the unarmed miners. When it finally appeared on 21 April 1888 with these contentious aspects of the play deleted, not even its spectacular visual effects (such as the flooding of the mine) served to prolong its staging for more than seventeen performances. Controversy crippled it from the start: Zola withdrew his cooperation on learning that the Théâtre du Châtelet was cutting short rehearsals; published in the press was his demand that its directors should allow members of the working class to see the play free of charge; and when 3,500 spectators were admitted to the performance of 27 April, it required some three hundred police to maintain order in the midst of cries of 'Long Live the Republic'. Zola's creative work had once again come up against the political realities of his time.

The Critical Turn

Later in life, Zola half-jokingly told an interviewer that the attacks he had endured had been so voluminous that he was contemplating publishing a whole volume of them. Seldom has any writer before or since been the target of such consistent vituperation over an entire adult lifetime and, indeed, after it. During the years of the *Rougon-Macquart*, however, and in respect of his other writing simultaneous to producing his series, one detects a shift from his earlier response to criticism of his work. Even the most aggressive objections to his first novels were grist to the mill of a desired publicity. As he progressed the *Rougon-Macquart*, by contrast, he revealed a concern to pre-emptively satisfy, rather than provoke, critical reservations: in frustrating expectations, avoiding anachronisms and double-checking the exactitude of descriptions. In planning *Le Rêve*, Zola consciously addressed reviews of his previous work which had lamented his failure to give his characters an inner life: 'as I'm accused of not engaging in psychological analysis, I want to force people to admit that I am indeed a psychologist. So let's give them some psychology, or whatever that means (!)' (*Ms* 10323, fols 217–18).

To be sure, Zola's combative prefaces and theoretical essays continued to confront his critics. But apparently thick-skinned indifference to their barbs is sometimes deceptive. In *L'Œuvre*, Claude Lantier's despair in the face of the reception of his work has an autobiographical edge to it. After the first night of *Les Héritiers Rabourdin*, for example, Zola wrote to friends that this time the critics had 'gone too far', his depression modulating into fury that they had torpedoed the success he thought the play might have enjoyed. In Alexis' supportive account of the critical disaster of *Le Bouton de rose*, Zola had taken it on the chin, heading for a restaurant after its first performance with undiminished appetite and regaling his thirty dining companions with derision aimed at both the play's actors and audience. Edmond de Goncourt, on the other hand, described a 'lugubrious' gathering with Zola 'utterly depressed, letting his wife order his supper, not engaging in conversation, pale and hunched over his plate, mechanically twirling the blade of his knife in his clenched fist'.[5]

More distressing was the fact that, rather than being purely literary or political, attacks on Zola became increasingly personal. Knowing no English, he was of course unaware of derogatory remarks abroad such as that of Henry James decrying 'the singular foulness of his imagination'. In the French press, however, this kind of comment was taken to extreme lengths. In critical elaboration of the 'obscenity' of episodes in the *Rougon-Macquart*, Zola was the subject of disgusting innuendo relating to his private life. This reached its most shameful peak in an open letter on the front page of *Le Figaro* of 18 August 1887, dubbed 'Le Manifeste des Cinq'. On the pretext that the publication of *La Terre* had finally exhausted their tolerance of Zola's 'scatalogical' novels, its five sanctimonious signatories went further than simply condemning, 'in the name of Art', the graphic nature of his descriptions: the writer himself was depraved; his 'pornographic aberrations' were sensationalist in intent or, more likely, symptoms of 'a disease of the lower organs' afflicting an onanistic 'solitary monk'.

Zola characteristically brushed off this 'stupid and undignified' impugning of his artistic integrity as well as rumours that a bitterly envious Edmond de Goncourt had encouraged it. His letter of 14 October to the latter, professing his utter disbelief that so senior a colleague could have been involved, is quite masterly. Asked in an 1888 interview (published in *Le Figaro* on 22 March) for his reaction to the vitriolic attack on him, Zola insisted that he was familiar with none of these young writers who claimed to be part of the Naturalist school (Paul Bonnetain, J.-H. Rosny, Lucien Descaves, Paul Margueritte and Gustave Guiches); if those of his inner circle had expressed such views, he would have been more concerned. He did admit to Jacques van Santen Kolff (1848–1896), the Dutch critic with whom he shared many literary confidences during the writing of the *Rougon-Macquart*, that the affair had 'rather ruined' his return from holidaying in Royan. He assured him, however, that he was on good form: 'I'm suntanned, and I've never been as calm or as cheerful as during this imbecilic uproar' (*Corr.*, VI, 200). It seemed to Zola that, together with its subsequent echoes in the wider press, this inconsequential 'incident' was further evidence of the trivializing of contemporary journalism: it now entertained readers with anecdotes and tittle-tattle rather than providing a forum for considered debate, and it had lost sight of its investigative mission, which had once been akin to his own. His correspondence generally reflects a man who carefully guarded his privacy, but in the late summer of 1887, a flurry of letters, best considered as an exercise in damage limitation, do obliquely suggest how wounding it was to see headlined this most public and insulting catalogue of his assumed perversions.

In relation to the writing of the *Rougon-Macquart*, there is a more illuminating aspect of Zola's interchanges with his critical readers. The most perceptive of them focused less on contradictions between Naturalist theory and Zola's practice than on his fiction in its own right. In so doing, they also provided a mirror in which the novelist himself could acknowledge the widening perspectives of his series that I have outlined. Jules Lemaître (1853–1914), in his review of *Germinal* on 14 March 1885, had extended his praise to the 'epic' grandeur of the novel cycle as a whole, differentiated from Homeric wisdom only in its negation of nobility and hope, but with the same narrative rhythms as those of ancient myths. Recognizing in Lemaître one of the most acute and influential literary commentators of the period, Zola never failed to respond to this critic's insights into each of his novels with courtesy and appreciation: so impressed was he by the review of *Germinal* that he hastened to respond on the same day it appeared in the *Revue politique et littéraire*. In relation to its characterization of the *Rougon-Macquart* as 'a pessimistic epic of human animality', Zola's only misgiving concerned the term 'animality': it reflected, he suggested, the 'philosophical' disagreement between Lemaître and himself about whether human motivation was physiological or psychological. But he also thanked him 'for one of the most penetrating texts that has ever been written about me' (*Corr.*, V, 244). Lemaître was not the first critic to underline the mythopoetic power of Zola's writing, but none had articulated it in such detail or with such authority.

Another of Lemaître's commentaries also struck a chord: on 17 April 1886, in the same literary review as his earlier one devoted to *Germinal*, he likened Zola's achievement in *L'Œuvre* to that of Michelangelo. Flaubert had done as much in privately hailing the end of *Nana* as positively 'michelangeslesque'. 'His figures', Lemaître wrote, 'make one think of *The Last Judgement*', and in singling out Zola's gift for creating a 'material and extravagant vision', he prefigured what the novelist would find in the self-reflecting mirror of Michelangelo's decoration of the Sistine Chapel when he visited it during his stay in Rome in 1894. With the *Rougon-Macquart* now behind him, Zola was offered there the opportunity to engage in a retrospective assessment of the distinguishing qualities of a life's work. In his travel journal, after surveying with awe the Chapel's frescoes and ceiling, Zola wrote of Michelangelo's 'totalizing synthesis and colossal symbolism': 'there's no possible real-life model for such enormous enlargement. Everything is generated by the imagination.' Little wonder that he should complete the identification with this supreme artist: 'A gigantic work, moving me beyond measure, of which I've been inwardly dreaming all my life' (*OC*, VII, 1071).

If never quite as explicitly, such affinities had been discernible long before 1894: Zola had found Taine's enthusiasm for Michelangelo, in his *Voyage en Italie*, contagious, celebrating it in his 1866 reviews of the book. Flaubert's praise for the end of *Nana* was no cliché: he had been as overwhelmed as Zola by the glories of the Sistine Chapel, in his view relativizing all other human achievements. Zola's conversations with Cézanne, equally convinced that Michelangelo represented the apotheosis of painting, complemented his reading of art-history books and visits to the Louvre; the scene there in *L'Assommoir* underlines his familiarity with 'the splendour of the Venetians' (*RM*, II, 445). Leaving aside instances of a specific debt to Taine, some of Zola's earliest writing testifies to the place Michelangelo occupies in his imaginative frame of reference, whether obliquely or allusively: in the figure of Goujet, the 'colossus' at his anvil, also in *L'Assommoir* and prefigured in his 1868 text 'Le Forgeron', with its blacksmith 'naked to the waist, with his tensely bulging muscles, like one of Michelangelo's gigantic figures' (*OC*, IX, 396); in his 1875 obituary piece devoted to Jean-Baptiste Carpeaux (1827–1875), where Zola refers to the sculptor's 'passion for Michelangelo who he worshipped all his life' (*EsA*, 660); and in *L'Œuvre*, where a conversation about Wagner's originality generates a euphoric critical conflation – 'Ah! Beethoven, the power, the serene fortitude in the midst of suffering, Michelangelo and the tomb of the Medicis!' (*RM*, IV, 200).

For Zola, the pictorial achievements of the quattrocento represented an ideal against which contemporary painters could be judged. The associated criteria inform his assessment of the Impressionists up until their third exhibition, in 1877, differentiated from the sketchiness to which he felt they later succumbed. Pissarro, with his 'solid workmanship', contextualized in an article of 1868 by prefatory remarks on 'the masters of the Renaissance', was positioned by Zola in an artistic lineage going back to colourists like Velázquez and Veronese. This valorization of solidity and structure explains his recognition, once he had forgiven him for his 'stupid' involvement in the Commune, of Courbet's greatness. His technical ability and facture, as Zola would increasingly stress, 'were unequalled by any practitioners today. You have to go back to the Renaissance to find anything as grand and as truthful': 'a magnificent classical artist inscribed in the great tradition of the paintings of Titian, Veronese and Rembrandt' (*EsA*, 373); in other words, an 'Old Master' for modern times. Zola's appreciation of the Old Masters is long-standing, however disguised it once had to remain within the critical discourse of a self-appointed opponent of officially sanctioned pictorial tradition. Situated at the mid-point between the symbolic enrichment of *Nana* and the cosmic enlargement of *Germinal*, the ambitions he confided to Huysmans in 1883 confirm his awareness of the direction of his own work: 'the longer I go on, the less my writing is motivated by representing a corner of reality and the more I'm attracted by the great creative artists who construct a world' (*Corr.*, IV, 388).

Authorial Reflections

In an 1897 interview, Zola admitted his propensity, 'like the painters of the Renaissance' (*EsA*, 703), to include in the margins of his novels a self-portrait of the artist at work. In the *Rougon-Macquart*, there are numerous such examples. Some are ironically aimed at potentially hostile readers: in *Pot-Bouille*, the unnamed writer on the second floor of the apartment building is condemned by its lubricious residents, one of whom reports that he is being pursued by the police for his 'filthy' novel about them. And likewise in *Nana*, in the passage in which the heroine assumes the unlikely role of conservative literary critic, Zola has her reading a 'scandalous novel about a courtesan' and ranting against the idea that any such immoral book should claim to 'give a true picture of life', arguing that a writer's responsibility was instead 'to entertain . . . to make you dream' (*RM*, II, 1369).

At other moments, however, Zola angles the self-portrait towards his own practice as a novelist, reflecting its more problematic dimensions. At one level, this is not surprising. His preparatory notes for the *Rougon-Macquart* are more telling than the projected image of the writer's effortless outpouring of language at the rate of 125 lines per morning: hesitations, about-turns, crossings-out, fragmented notes and abandoned drafts pasted over, and last-minute decisions squeezed into virtually indecipherable script. As well as registering instances of writer's block, these notes include reminders to avoid repetition: by not making a character too similar to one in an earlier novel, or too closely modelling Muffat in *Nana* on Baron Hulot in Balzac's *La Cousine Bette*. Even Alexis admitted that *La Faute de l'Abbé Mouret*, for example, had caused him 'difficulties', confirming what Zola had written to Turgenev in a letter of June 1874 (*Corr.*, II, 357). While composing *Pot-Bouille*, Zola realized he had arrived at a dead end: 'it has no main idea running through it. Perhaps I should introduce a worker to provide some sort of comparison . . . No. That won't work' (*Ms* 10320, fol. 386). Zola's correspondence during the writing of each novel of the *Rougon-Macquart* mostly gives the impression that everything was going well, especially when it wasn't.

More significant than moments of frustration in the throes of composition are doubts about his creative methodology. These are discernible in the definitive texts of the novels themselves. In Vabre, the minor character of *Pot-Bouille*, self-deprecation directed towards filing information in the interests of a passion for completeness is not far off: described as a *roman* (a novel), the history of the building in which he lives is the saga of Vabre's entire existence, and his sole hobby is obsessive classification akin to that of Zola's surrogate in *Le Docteur Pascal*.

More generally such self-awareness on Zola's part is opened up by the recognition of analogies between less caricatural figures and their creator. Even if grounded in verifiable parallels, it is often in these analogies that Zola's reflections on his art can be identified. Analysis of the rhetorical strategies employed by both the novelist and his more articulate protagonists, for example, has allowed Naomi Schor to conclude that 'Zola's leaders are all variants on the writer, a writer profoundly dissatisfied with the inadequacies of (his own) writing.'[6] The last part of that insight is far from being confirmed by Zola's satisfying exchanges with Céard, Lemâitre and Huysmans about the qualities of the later *Rougon-Macquart*. It would be more accurate to detect in autobiographical threads an authorial distancing which falls short of disavowal of his achievement, while remaining testimony to an artistic integrity at several removes from the certainties rehearsed in Zola's Naturalist campaigns.

Germinal is a case in point. At the simplest level, Zola seems to have projected on to Étienne Lantier aspects of his own life and personality. Always allowing for differences of context, there are coincidences it is difficult to ignore. As in *L'Assommoir*, Zola refers to Étienne sending back money to his mother, as he himself had done when he had first left his home in Aix-en-Provence. A whole career is evoked: the thrill of earning fees from his early writing, the beginnings of popularity, the hopes of playing a major role in the shaping of the future, becoming the uncontested head of a militant group and gradually listened to and increasingly admired. As in *L'Œuvre*, this mirroring process by no means precludes self-irony, whether at the expense of inflated vanity or messianic pretensions, and a bitterness about the progressive disaffection of disciples, inseparable from the fact that in 1884–5 Zola's own (literary) grouping was starting to disintegrate. Étienne and the novelist certainly have more in common than just their southern accents. The character shares, for example, Zola's long-held fear of being buried alive, as well as a repressed sexuality.

This kind of unconscious projection was catalysed by the actual preparation of *Germinal*. In his notes, Zola identifies so closely with Étienne that he often substitutes a first-person pronoun in his vivid imagining of the character's actions or feelings. When Étienne first goes down the mine, his intense anguish is exactly that felt by Zola himself during the exploratory descent recorded within 'My Notes on Anzin'. If it is Étienne's responsibility to distribute within the text Zola's information assembled in these 103 pages of notes, the novel also ascribes to him the very process of documentation which had been the writer's own. Étienne's evening conversations with Souvarine are those Zola had with Turgenev about anarchist movements in Russia. And Étienne has to work through much of Zola's bibliography, including 'treatises on political economy . . . full of arid and incomprehensible technical detail' (*RM*, III, 1275). Both of them undertake an ill-digested education in socialist theory, prior to the repudiation of the naive idealism with which they had set off.

Étienne's linguistic gifts take such mirroring a stage further. Zola's distrust of verbal facility had been sharpened by his experience as a parliamentary correspondent in 1871. In the case of masterful characters in the *Rougon-Macquart* with whom he partially identifies, Saccard's 'creative inventions' in *La Curée* or the politician's 'fictions' in *Son Excellence Eugène Rougon* do not in themselves pose fundamental questions about Zola's own. In *Germinal*, however, Zola's scepticism is more specifically focused on the relationship between imaginative language and the reality his novel was seeking to represent. Étienne and Zola's visions exploit a common fund of images challenged from within. The character's role as surrogate novelist is at its most explicit when his talent as a wordsmith is mocked. Zola continually uses the term 'novelistic' in likening his eloquence to that of a storyteller. As Étienne expands Zola's metaphors into a dazzling version of the future, his listeners are entranced, as carried away as he is himself (and indeed the reader) by the power of his construction. Even La Maheude's pragmatism ('Can't you see he's telling us fairy tales' (*RM*, III, 1279)) yields to Étienne's rhetorical talents. The most damning critique of them is Souvarine's: he 'intelligently' warns Étienne that verbal skills will serve no purpose whatsoever, and that revolution involves action rather than 'phrases lifted from literature' (*RM*, III, 1330).

One of Souvarine's functions is to act as a counterpoint to the novel's own textual fabric, so poetically charged that Zola was aware of the risk of *Germinal* leaving behind his original intention to 'study' the social conflicts of his time. Its critical reception is thereby anticipated. Only at the moment we put the book down does our reading of *Germinal* in terms of the thematic signposting of its title appear to be confirmed. What the readers of 1885 found most confusing was that, within the novel, there was no evidence whatsoever to justify its lyrical conclusion. Zola's admission to Céard of the 'lyrical' qualities of his fiction and that within him was a 'poet' underlines what is implicit in *Germinal*: that its political contradictions can only be reconciled in a poetic coherence.

L'Œuvre takes this self-questioning further. Coming as it does immediately next in the series, it is as if the writing and reception of *Germinal* prompted Zola to explore more directly the competing dimensions of his creativity. As mentioned in the Introduction, Zola was usually at pains to discourage presumed parallels between himself and his characters. *L'Œuvre*, however, remains the most overtly autobiographical of all the *Rougon-Macquart*. It is not just in the figure of the novelist Sandoz, whose name is a partial anagram of Zola's own, that this is evident. His surrogate's calm and methodical progression of his series finds its obverse in Claude Lantier's frustrations, intermittent artistic impotence and crises. Cézanne is undoubtedly one model in this respect. It is as clear that it is through the indirections of the novel's fictional painter that Impressionism is held up for critical inspection. But the composite portrait also draws on Zola's reflections on his own life and work.

The parallels with Zola's own biography are of two kinds. Most obviously, they include Claude's nostalgia for the Provençal years of his youth and memories of invigorating interludes with friends at riverside hamlets which Zola had enjoyed in the 1860s. Signalled in the contrast between celebratory initial gatherings and progressively fractious occasions, the novel also charts the splintering of Médan solidarity. The confidence generated by the success of *Germinal* seems not to have mitigated Zola's worries in this respect. With their leadership under threat, both Claude and Sandoz register a disappointment on Zola's part more bitter than in the case of Étienne Lantier's loss of authority in *Germinal*, by virtue of the specifically aesthetic focus of *L'Œuvre*. A personal concern less near the surface of the novel, perhaps even subconsciously confessional, is the suffering of Claude's lifelong partner, Christine, whose conjugal happiness is sacrificed on the altar of a creative single-mindedness subject to only the most fleeting instances of guilt or remorse.

Claude also displays artistic traits which are Zola's own. He tracks the character's failed attempts to overcome the legacy of Romanticism, in spite of spirited declarations to the contrary. Consistent with his increasingly militant Naturalist principles, Zola had publicly asserted his own liberation from that legacy in an essay in the July issue of *Le Messager de l'Europe* devoted to George Sand, prompted by her death only a month earlier, on 8 June 1876. His homage to her 'creative flair' barely masks the definitive liquidation of his juvenile enchantment with her work. In her distortion of the real, Zola wrote, she represented a formula so outdated as to be beyond resurrection (*OC*, XII, 389–413). Claude, however, shares with Zola the curse of having been born, as the fictional painter laments, under the sign of Balzac *and* Hugo, the contrary poles of prosaic realism and imaginative excess, objective representation and subjective expression. Such an abiding tension was given a supplementary acuteness by Hugo's return to public acclamation at this very moment: his immense state funeral on 1 June 1885, consecrating the poet and novelist as a secular saint by taking his remains to the Panthéon, put at risk, Zola wrongly felt, the impact of the serialization of *Germinal* that summer.

Claude's ultimate failure is not, of course, Zola's own. In accounting for it, however, he focuses on aspects of his own predilections and practices. In particular, he highlights Claude's losing sight of reality, increasingly at odds with an ambition, as overarching as Zola's own, to represent the modern world in its entirety. In his beautiful descriptions of segments of it, Claude is incapable of distinguishing between the material and the picturesque. Above all, his talents are compromised by the temptation of symbolic modes.

Nowhere in the novel is this clearer than in Claude's final canvas: it depicts, against the accurately observed heart of the capital (the Île de la Cité), a boat on the river with three women in it, the central one of whom is implausibly naked. As Zola had confided to Huysmans, in a May 1884 letter about his writing escaping 'conscious intention' (*Corr.*, V, 108), so Claude is unable to fathom the creative motivation of his picture. But the narrator explains that it was a product of 'some tormenting secret symbolism, the old streak of romanticism in him that made him think of his nude figure as the incarnation of Paris, the city of passion captured in the resplendent beauty of a naked woman'. Sandoz is appalled by a picture defying logic to such a degree: 'How could a modern painter, determined to represent nothing but reality, bastardize a work by introducing such imaginings?' (*RM*, IV, 236). The 'abâtadir' of the original French (which translates as 'bastardizing') points to the *illegitimacy* of the coupling of the prosaic and the symbolic. Claude ignores Zola's critical voice: he persists in his personal rendering of 'Venus rising in triumph from the waters of the Seine' (*RM*, IV, 236), and as he endlessly embellishes this figure, 'painting . . . like some insane visionary, driven by the torments of the real to the exaltation of the unreal' (*RM*, IV, 343), the urban context loses definition and the central figure's two supposed bathing companions are no longer of interest. His is a vision of Woman (that is, as capitalized in the text, the Fatal Woman of Zola's fiction, from his earliest novels to *Nana* and beyond). Taken to extremes which make it a cautionary tale for the novelist, Claude's painting exemplifies the 'hypertrophie du vrai' (mania for exactitude) that Zola had ascribed to *Germinal*, when he confirmed to Céard that his lyrical and poetic flights of fancy were responsible for his novels' avowed 'enlargement' of reality.

It is also often the case that Zola's thinking about his novels refers to the actual mechanics of plotting. This is visible, for example, in the preparation of *Pot-Bouille*. To Céard, in a letter of 24 August 1881 from his holiday address on the Normandy coast, he wrote that, while he was not much enthused by the novel, he was nevertheless enjoying its likeness to 'a machine whose complicated inner workings need to be perfectly regulated for it to function correctly' (*Corr.*, IV, 217). The most extended such metaphor is applied by Zola to *La Bête humaine*. Looking forward to his future novel about the railways, he had told Alexis many years before,

> I would like the book itself to resemble the journey of a great train, from its departure at the head of the line to its arrival at its terminus, occasionally slowing down and with stops at every station, in other words at each chapter.[7]

That he conceived as a train a novel about a train endows *La Bête humaine* with the most all-encompassing self-reflexivity of any of the *Rougon-Macquart*.

Other novels overlay on autobiographical insertions Zola's reflections about his own writing. In its structure and themes, *La Bête humaine* enacts such reflections. Zola also told Alexis that he wanted to make the train itself, and thus the novel, the location of all human experience: eating, sleeping, love and death, and even, he mused, perhaps a woman giving birth in a compartment! He was aware that this might leave him open to the charge that he was an 'old Romantic', as indeed the Claude of *L'Œuvre* confirms. But these totalizing perspectives would be recognized by Lemaître, in yet another review which Zola appreciated (*Corr.*, VI, 455), when the critic suggested that *La Bête humaine* represented the thematic *summa* of the *Rougon-Macquart* as a whole. Its title alone represents the culmination of preoccupations which can be traced as far back as *Thérèse Raquin* over twenty years earlier.

It is also a concluding mirror of Zola's writing itself. It is more revealing in that respect than in *La Débâcle*'s completing his historical panorama of the Second Empire or the apologia of *Le Docteur Pascal* bringing a formal close to his novel cycle. The composition of *La Bête humaine* in 1889 is testimony to a writer in full creative flow. As a result, it is the most compelling of the *Rougon-Macquart*. And its liberation from Naturalist dogma is so self-evident that it problematizes both a related mode of enquiry and its assumptions of quasi-scientific intelligibility. Zola's ambition had been that, in its scope and modalities, his novel cycle would shed an all-seeing light on the modern world. *La Bête humaine* retrospectively places a question mark over his entire series, insofar as elucidation is frustrated and omniscience denied.

As is evident from both his literary and art criticism, Zola prioritizes coherence, clarity and 'solidity'. These traditional aesthetic values are given renewed urgency in his fiction. The historical, political, social and cultural disorder which he was living through is countered by the ordering principles of his work: cyclical superstructures and microcosmic cycles, topographical categories and taxonomical frames, narrative 'blocs superposés' (structured masses) and the calculated distribution of combinatory effects. The writer as craftsman can be metaphorically related to other pragmatic professions. If that of the engineer seems the most apposite, it is less as – yet another example of – a paternal shadow than because mastery of the world's complexity presupposes an understanding of its inner workings. In *La Bête humaine*, that mastery comes up against its limits: in plotting spun out in self-generating imbrications leading nowhere and in the allegorization of the creative tension between fictional structuring and the imaginative transposition of an external reality characterized by dissolving structures.

The inner workings of *La Bête humaine* oscillate between two models of writing in the *Rougon-Macquart*: on the one hand, the integrating design of Zola's attention to narrative logic, and on the other, an imaginative elaboration visible in *Nana* and *Germinal*. In the same way as *L'Œuvre* accommodates in Sandoz and Claude alternative conceptions of creativity, *L'Assommoir* also offers such a doubling: Goujet seems to be implicitly related to Zola himself; but shadowing the euphoric staging of the consummate craftsman at work, the labour of the Lorilleux couple results not in a pragmatic shape wrought from impure material (described as 'black metal'), but rather in a refined abstraction devoid of both purpose and significance – 'Continually and mechanically' (*RM*, II, 430), and with technical precision, Lorilleux's gold chain is extended in interminable repetitions, compelling rhymes without reason, totally beyond the watching Gervaise's comprehension. The episode is antithetically juxtaposed with her admiration for Goujet's productive skills in another forge, which makes that of the Lorilleux's chain its inverted correlative. But this is also to be reminded of Zola's stress, in the preliminary notes for his series as well as in the plotting of its individual novels, on the 'enchaînement' (chaining together) of episodes. To do so is to superimpose on the heroic version of craftsmanship, projected by Goujet, the possibly ironic mirror held up by Lorilleux, the 'chaîniste' (the chain-maker), in which we can see reflected a more problematic self-representation of the Zola who had once planned 'La Chaîne des êtres' (the Great Chain of Being).

As his 1881 thinking, cited earlier, about the plotting of *Pot-Bouille* suggests, Zola's literary procedures correspond as much to those of the mechanical as to the natural(ist) sciences. The terminology is pervasive: informing the very heading of his 'Notes générales sur la marche de l'œuvre', with *marche* equated with the series' workings and forward drive; his translation of biological heredity into 'the organizing mechanism'; and his ambition to study 'the internal mechanism' of a family. The functionality of Zola's characters and scenes underlies Michel Serres' thermodynamic model, in which the entire *Rougon-Macquart* series is cast as a gigantic machine, emblematic of the nineteenth century's utilitarian experience and collective imagination.[8] In both literal and figurative terms, Lorilleux's 'mechanical' (artistic) activities have to be situated in this wider context: as does the Goujet ultimately unable to resist the efficiency of 'mechanical production' (*RM*, II, 535). Central to *La Bête humaine* is, precisely, a machine (La Lison, the anthropomorphized locomotive). Grafted onto Zola's family tree, because the original intention to use Étienne again would have required the union leader to be transformed into a homicidal maniac, its hero (or anti-hero) is Jacques Lantier. His belated invention is neither the first nor the last of the fictions of *La Bête humaine*. But as the 'mécanicien', the engine driver, Jacques is another suggestive variant on the novelist as craftsman.

Further justification for considering him in this perspective can be found in those elements of his characterization which, like Étienne's in *Germinal*, point to an oblique self-portrait of his creator. Living in the Batignolles district, as Zola had once done, Jacques also has something of his moral rectitude, 'imprisoned like a monk in his cell', 'neither drinking nor chasing women, teased by his party-going companions for his excessively good behaviour' (*RM*, IV, 1045). And he is endowed with a properly novelistic talent. In imagining Roubaud's murder, 'this scenario of a drama he was organizing' (*RM*, IV, 1235), Jacques thereby appropriates the very directions adopted (if eventually discarded) by Zola himself during the preparation of the novel. Losing his equilibrium and relinquishing control of his machine as *La Bête humaine* progresses, he also reflects Zola's own compositional disorder as he drives the novel forward.

Edmond de Goncourt found in *La Bête humaine* only the 'imaginative exaggeration and fabulations . . . secreted by an adled brain',[9] personalizing the latter by ascribing its impurities to Zola's, but not far off the mark in detecting in the novel an extravagant inventiveness beyond mere artistic design. Through indiscretion on the part of Alexis in November 1889, Goncourt had had the rumour confirmed that Zola now had a double life. At the time of writing *La Bête humaine*, he was going through his most acute personal crisis since 1880. Some modern commentators have been puzzled that the novel's dark plotting – combining atavistic violence, criminal insanity, judicial corruption and collective catastrophe – should have coincided with the happiest turning points in Zola's life: his falling in love with Jeanne Rozerot and the successive births of his two children, the first of them on 20 September 1889, four months after he started drafting *La Bête humaine*. In letters that summer, Zola reported from Médan that he was making good progress: he was in a fine state of 'physical and literary health' (*Corr.*, VI, 401), not least, as he explained to one correspondent, because he had given up drinking alcohol two years earlier; the only blip, as he sadly told Charpentier on 12 June, was that his ailing dog Fanfan had finally died (to which his publisher replied that it was a merciful release).

Such a characteristic disjunction between his public and private selves hides what the text of the novel reveals: that its raging excesses draw on, and give expression to, some of the most deep-rooted of Zola's intimate concerns. As Dr Toulouse would later reveal, one of the most morbid of them was that, when travelling in a train, Zola was terrified of it being forced to stop in a tunnel both ends of which had collapsed. The novel dramatizes a variant on the recurrent evidence of such claustrophobia throughout his life and work. More specifically related to his personal circumstances during the preparation of *La Bête humaine* may be its intertwined themes of secrecy and erotic obsession, and murderous jealousy of the kind he feared his wife, on eventually discovering his infidelity, might wreak on his mistress. The novel can be read as a private catharsis. Only one thing is certain: *La Bête humaine* is a novel of exceptional emotional intensity which leaves an indelible mark on its textual fabric.

In the same way as there are, in effect, two locomotives within the anthropomorphized La Lison – successively in and beyond its driver's control – so *La Bête humaine* contains two kinds of novel, the one obeying generic rules and the other outside its conventions. There is much evidence of an authorial shaping which sits uneasily with Zola's ambition to write *La Bête humaine* without recourse to 'conscious artistry' (*Ms* 10316, fol. 338). But it also largely masks the self-absorbed uncertainty of the novel's composition, at odds with Zola's determination to write it 'd'une plume courante' (with uninterrupted flow). His work-notes reveal the fractured rhythms of its preparation, stops and starts, a four-month gap between November 1888 and February 1889, and changes of pace from regressive procrastination to vertiginous acceleration.

The text itself brings into ironic relief its own melodramatic procedures by lending them to the characters who tell each other equally reduplicative stories. But *La Bête humaine* also embeds reflections on the *Rougon-Macquart* as a whole. The original 'destination' of the series too had been to 'tout voir' (to see everything). In marked contrast, the symptomatic optical experience of *La Bête humaine* is to peer vainly into the murk of a winter evening and political corruption, or to be blinded by driving snow and hallucinatory impulses. Even the locomotive's headlamp, its 'œil vivant de cyclope' (with the encyclopedic connotations of the all-seeing eye), pierces the darkness only to enlarge it. From train compartments to marital sanctity, the novel thematizes the adulteration and blurring of delineated boundaries. In the same way, the classificatory systems of scientific observation are ultimately unable to accommodate a reality subject to forces undermining the very processes of differentiation.

Zola's awareness, in *La Bête humaine*, of the fallacy at the heart of his totalizing project is reflected in the deconstruction of the mode of enquiry exemplified by Denizet, the examining magistrate. In reversing the conventions of the detective novel (the criminal is identified at the beginning and apprehended at the end only by his own confession), Zola frames with dramatic irony attempts to elucidate the murder of Grandmorin at the hands of Roubaud seeking revenge for the politician's paedophilic seduction of his wife-to-be. To this end, Denizet assembles 'an enormous dossier' supporting deductive practices which override its inner contradictions. 'Above all', Zola had written in the preliminary notes for his series, 'ensure a deductive logic', and his own dossiers constantly invoke this imperative. Denizet, preoccupied by 'verisimilitude' and bringing to his scientific methodology 'his passion for truth', is the most devastating of self-portraits of a Zola who had promised himself in his preliminary notes for the *Rougon-Macquart*, 'my books will be simple *procès-verbaux* (judicial enquiries)' (*RM*, V, 1744).

The various hypotheses developed by Denizet not only rehearse, but are drawn from, those adumbrated to no avail in Zola's speculative plotting of *La Bête humaine*. His proceeding 'mathematically' directly echoes Zola's repeated injunctions to that effect in the planning of his novels. What Denizet constructs, with the aid of his own 'documents' and their technical vocabulary, is nothing less than a Naturalist edifice: 'a masterpiece of analysis . . . a logical reconstitution of the truth, a truly creative work' (*RM*, IV, 1307). Creative it is, but the real truth it is not. That truth he dismisses as a mere 'fiction', making it doubly paradoxical that 'this work of creative intelligence' should become, in the public domain, 'a terrifying novel'. His 'mathematical' accretions are negated: his reasoning equations cannot quantify the irrational. Denizet's confidence, however, that 'the truth itself would have been less credible if it had been stained by fantasy and illogicality' (*RM*, IV, 1311) is instructively misplaced – for these are the fracturing agents of a novel which points to predetermined craftsmanship as an equally fallible instrument with which to explain the indeterminacy of human experience.

In Denizet's 'certainties' are implicated not only a literary methodology but that of contemporary scientific discourse. In the recognition of such a dead end, Zola's novel posits an alternative creativity. He had intended that, after *Le Rêve*, *La Bête humaine* would return to the real. But it was equally his initial intention to give it 'an element of mystery, of the beyond, of something leaving reality behind' (*Ms* 10316, fol. 339). A parenthesis within this work-note ('must find something') reveals his uncertainty as to how an 'unknown force' might be accommodated. It also speaks of a lacuna, both epistemological and inventive, which haunts the composition of *La Bête humaine* from the beginning. The 'mystery' is not only unamenable to the dictates of reality, but beyond a dictation which would record the all-seeing diagnosis of the 'experimental novelist'. The novel testifies instead to the free play of Zola's imagination, 'almost beyond his own control'.[10] Its wildly proliferating plots are monstrously (in the sense of taxonomical perversion) at odds with Naturalist subordination of *inventio* to mimesis. *La Bête humaine* is a novel unconstrained by logic and plausibility. In its endless re-enactment of 'l'homme au fond des cavernes' (the primeval caveman) as the sole explanation of human motivation, there is no resolution of its enigmas. It thereby rewrites a mythical, rather than a scientifically verifiable, version of reality.

In an extension of Zola's own analogy between his work and 'the journey of a train', his textual machine is brought to a shuddering halt when confronted by bestial drives which block its progress. A number of the titles Zola considered for the novel are only compatible with the omniscience of the novelist-as-scientist if they anticipate understanding *in the end*; many do not: 'En route pour' (heading towards), 'le meurtre incompréhensible' (incomprehensible murder), 'sans cause' and 'sans raison' (for no reason), 'ce qu'on ne voit pas' (what remains invisible), 'd'où vient le crime?' (what motivates criminality?). As the repetitive return journeys of the trains preclude any glimpse of a terminal destination, so none of these questions posed by alternative titles receives a definitive answer. But another, 'l'obscure origine' (the unknowable origin), suggests the extent to which *La Bête humaine* brings Zola's series, by association, full circle.

Denizet's dead end conjures up the Saint-Mitre cemetery of *La Fortune des Rougon* ('bounded on three sides and leading nowhere' (*RM*, I, 5)) where Zola's mythical imaginings of origins had begun. *La Bête humaine* only arrives at an inversion of Zola's own certainties. As the provisional title of 'sans cause' underlines, causality is no longer the guiding principle of his explanatory project. The mechanics of *La Bête humaine* depend on chance, accidents and coincidence. Zola investigated how far a locomotive would run under its own steam if, as he envisaged for the final chapter of the novel, its two-man crew had somehow fallen overboard and been crushed by the wheels of the engine. Not far enough, he discovered, to meet the symbolic meaning of the climax of *La Bête humaine*. He decided that the facts would have to be ignored: the driverless train of the novel's final pages is endlessly hurtling not so much in the direction of the historically specific Franco-Prussian War as towards an irrecuperably distant unknown. This, Zola had admitted to Dr Toulouse, was his greatest fear. Authorial reflections in *La Bête humaine* challenge his own presuppositions but also those of readers too readily categorizing the nature of Zola's fiction.

The End of the *Rougon-Macquart*

Le Docteur Pascal, the final volume of the *Rougon-Macquart*, appeared on 19 June 1893. Zola's completion of his series had been impatiently awaited by many contemporary critics of the view that it had become wearingly long. Sensing the mood, the journalist Jules Huret (1863–1915) had published in 1891, originally in *L'Écho de Paris*, his *Enquête sur l'évolution littéraire*, an enquiry into the future directions of French literature, implicitly in the aftermath of Zola's novel cycle. To this end, Huret canvassed the views of 64 writers representative of every recognizable aesthetic tendency. The vast majority of them were agreed that Zola's formula had had its day. This was the context for the ever-loyal Alexis, away from Paris when he was meant to be interviewed, to send Huret a famous telegram: 'Naturalism not dead. Letter follows.' Others were less naive. Stressing that the *Rougon-Macquart* cycle was an unforgettably marvellous achievement, Mallarmé was nevertheless in no doubt that the completion of the series would mark the moment when Zola's literary principles and practice disappeared once and for all.

Zola himself, asked by Huret about the consensus that Naturalism was in terminal decline, reiterated his conviction that a new avant-garde, notably that of Symbolism, was merely building on the 'search for truth' exemplified by his own. Privately, he was less certain. Some of Zola's correspondence of the 1880s devoted to strictly literary concerns fills the gap left by his withdrawal from the public platform afforded by his uncompromising contributions to the press: 'I'm in Flaubert's lineage,' he wrote in a letter of 29 July 1886, 'committed to solidity, clarity and perfection; I can't tolerate the messing about with sentences, faulty grammar and neologisms. I'm disgusted by the gobbledegook of young writers of the so-called decadent movement' (*Corr.*, V, 421). But he was not unaware that the disintegration of his own literary movement was gathering pace. The disaffected envy which would surface in 'Le Manifeste des Cinq' was itself symptomatic of a shifting cultural climate discernible only in retrospect. In March 1890, one of the contributors to *Les Soirées de Médan* and a consistent champion of Naturalism, Léon Hennique (1850–1935), had told Zola, in all frankness, that his younger 'disciples' were all so intimidated by his monumental work that they needed to develop their own literary ambitions independently of his guidance.[11]

More significant than such self-interested detachment from Zola's leadership was indeed the shifting cultural climate. It is evident in the preparatory notes for *Le Rêve*, in which Zola's ironic inclusion of 'psychology' was intended to satisfy critics lamenting his exclusively physiological explanation of human behaviour. The widely acclaimed novels of Paul Bourget (1852–1935) offered the most striking alternative: his *Cruelle énigme* (1885) and *Le Disciple* (1889) explored affective vicissitudes in unprecedented detail. His influential *Essais de psychologie contemporaine*, followed by a related volume of essays, had attracted Zola's attention from the moment of their initial publication in the press, from November 1881 onwards. His letters to Bourget almost admit that his erstwhile admirer was on to something, qualifying his respect by adding that psychological complications subject to such painstakingly intricate analysis must be a consequence of the collective anxiety of the age (*Corr.*, IV, 435).

For Zola, its manifestation takes many forms. That anxiety was registered in the preliminary notes for the *Rougon-Macquart*. It intensifies thereafter. Its social and political dimensions underlie Zola's sense that *Germinal* pointed to the alarming conflicts of the future. But, in the cultural domain, *L'Œuvre* is equally predictive, dramatizing artistic struggles and theoretical contradictions in anticipation of the next century. In its preparation, Zola interpolates an addition to why his fictional painter is incapable of realizing his ambitions: 'I want to include the fact that our modern art is also responsible for it . . . our impatient rejection of tradition, in a word the *instabilities* of our time' (*Ms* 10316, fol. 265). The underlining of the original 'déséquilibrement' is Zola's own. While the novel's chronology situates it in the late 1860s, that of its composition in 1885–6 is reflected in Zola's note: '*Fin de siècle*, the troubling indirections of art, the beginning of something else' (fol. 214). This cross-references the unconvincing hope, to be voiced in a conversation about the art of the future by Sandoz and the painter Bongrand: 'we'll have to await the twentieth century for our Romantic neuroses to abate, for education to spread and democracy to be established, so that we can finally emerge from this period of transition' (fol. 294). 'But all that', Zola added, 'perhaps', as provisional as an indeterminate 'something else'. It is not beside the point that here he conflates political, pedagogic, physiological and pictorial ideals, for the corresponding 'instabilities' in the artistic world are not sufficiently metaphorical to be disassociated from the wider dismantling of certainties.

The most germane of those instabilities for a novelist committed to observing and representing external reality is a new conception of visuality, in the context of an astonishing range of contemporary inventions in the field of optical instrumentation. Scientific research had established the fact that colour was not an innate feature radiating out of an object but rather the marker of the light bouncing off it. The associated theorizing of Impressionism legitimized the transposition of the world in different lights and at different times of day. Zola's art criticism of the 1880s shows him trying to grapple with this disconcerting phenomenology. His resistance to it implicitly revalidates the mimetic imperatives of his fiction. In *L'Œuvre*, the evangelical advocate of theories of complementary colours is parodied. Claude Lantier's enthusiastic embrace of them is a catastrophic harbinger of artistic impotence. In his 1864 letter to Valabrègue, cited earlier, Zola had resorted to the ophthalmic analogy of different kinds of distorting lenses in his own theorizing of realism. The limits of this acknowledgement of the subjectivity of representation are discernible, however, in the conviction that what remains invariable is external reality itself; based on Zola's premise that 'the world is the same for all of us' (*Corr.*, I, 376), it is the accuracy of representation which should be the sole concern of artistic endeavour and critical judgement. In his irritated response to a minor Neo-Impressionist painter accusing him, in *L'Œuvre*, of not giving the theoretical consensus its due, Zola unwittingly provided a succinct summary of his unreconstructed approach to representation: 'Two good eyes are sufficient. I have more confidence in direct observation than in theory.'[12]

L'Œuvre also contains a more oblique self-portrait than those of Sandoz and Claude. In the figure of Bongrand, who is conscious of the decline of his creative powers, Zola is already contemplating the judgement of posterity. He admitted in an 1897 interview (*EsA*, 702) that the character was inspired by Flaubert as the model for this elderly painter so generous to younger colleagues. His naming was consistent with Zola's evocation of Flaubert's personality over the years, as both *Bon* (Good) and *Grand* (large in frame but also in spirit). But in underlining Bongrand's fear that his best work was behind him, this identification is reinforced by the allusion, in the course of Zola's interview, to the anxiety haunting the author of *Madame Bovary*. Of that novel, Zola had written in his *Les Romanciers naturalistes* that Flaubert had felt that all his work subsequent to *Madame Bovary* had been found wanting by comparison. At one point, Zola had had the idea that Bongrand should perhaps be an established writer, allowing him to develop the general idea that it was more difficult to sustain a reputation than to make one. Bongrand's creative frustrations relativize his future immortality, but when the character is imagined embarking on a new work with the 'energy of a beginner', Zola's evocation of 'the excitement of the written page and the pleasure of correcting proofs' (*Ms* 103216, fols 274–5) is so unmistakeably personal that it is at this exact point in his work-notes that an autobiographical step too far leads to Bongrand's assimilation with Courbet instead.

Such a substitution is no less revealing. Whether ascribed to real painters or fictional characters, the challenge of maintaining a reputation as opposed to establishing one was certainly Zola's. An obsessive preoccupation in this respect was not exclusive to Flaubert, judging by Edmond de Goncourt's record of Zola's own anxiety in 1882: 'The crushing success of the past poisons his literary future. As he depressingly admits: "Deep-down, I know that I will never again write a novel with such an impact as *L'Assommoir* or generating such enormous sales as *Nana.*"'[13] By the time he was working on *L'Œuvre* in 1885–6, it was not only the phenomenal success of *Germinal* which exacerbated such a concern. Zola's novel about the artistic instabilities of the period also reflects an awareness of the growing reaction against the aesthetic hegemony he had hoped would be permanent. Jules Huret's evidence of a quasi-Darwinian 'evolution' putting paid to such optimism was doubtless deflating. It was not a surprise. In sanguine moments in due course, and in keeping with his historical vision, Zola claimed to be reconciled to the fact that literary 'empires' too were fated to eventual extinction, to be succeeded by the advent of a new generation of writers.

When Huret called upon Zola to interview him for his 1891 survey, however, he reported that he had been welcomed with a cheery smile by the novelist: 'You've come to see whether I'm dead! Well, on the contrary, as you can see, I'm in excellent health in body and mind, and I've never felt as inwardly calm.'[14] The future of Naturalism might be under scrutiny. Zola himself was not finished yet.

Zola at his desk in his Paris apartment, 1894. Photograph by Félix Nadar.

5
The Last Chapters of a Writing Life

Le Docteur Pascal went on sale on 19 June 1893. Planned to coincide with this completion of Zola's novel cycle, a banquet was held two days later at the Chalet des Îles, a restaurant (still 'high-end' today) on the island within the Bois de Boulogne. It was organized by his two publishers, Charpentier and Fasquelle. Marquees were spread across its lawns to accommodate some two hundred guests who had been invited to celebrate Zola's monumental achievement. These included both friends and leading figures of the Parisian cultural world.

The French state was also seen to be acknowledging Zola's formidable contribution to its glory: the Minister of Education, Raymond Poincaré (1860–1934) (a future president of France, 1913–20, and one of the few politicians to have backed the call for the revision of Alfred Dreyfus' indictment), was in attendance; it was Poincaré who formalized on 14 July Zola's elevation within the hierarchy of the Légion d'honneur. This was of more than anecdotal significance. He had been passed over for even the bottom rank in 1878 after *L'Assommoir* had been thought ideologically suspect. With some reluctance, he had been made an *officier* a decade later. His next putative promotion had been frustrated by objections that *La Débâcle* was embarrassing to the French army. Zola confided to friends that he had been persuaded to accept the honour of being made a *Chevalier* not out of vanity but because it belatedly marked official recognition of the importance of the literary developments he had pioneered. But the award on the completion of the *Rougon-Macquart* was not the end of the story: Zola was suspended from the Order in July 1898 as a result of his attack on the military authorities during the Dreyfus Affair; although reinstated after it, there was some debate in relation to his funeral in 1902 as to whether there should be the traditional guard of honour to which members of the Légion d'honneur were entitled. Poincaré's presence at the 1893 banquet was neither incidental nor the final instalment of Zola's career-long and troubled relationship with the politics of his times.

There were, however, notable absentees from this great banquet: representatives of the Académie Française, that august body determined never to open its doors to so scandalous a writer; Edmond de Goncourt, as envious of Zola's fame as ever; and a number of the Médan circle, with the exception, of course, of the ever-loyal Alexis, reinforcing the sense that its members were no longer in thrall to its leader. Some of these absences were unavoidable: Daudet was ill, and Maupassant was locked in a mental asylum, since attempting to commit suicide eighteen months earlier, where he would die from tertiary syphilis a fortnight after the banquet. Huysmans' absence merely underlined a distancing from Naturalism evident since the publication of *À rebours* in 1884 and his exploration of spirituality in subsequent novels. Another absentee was Hennique, who had signalled in his March 1890 letter to Zola his intention to go his own way. Céard's declining to attend, on the other hand, was symptomatic less of literary currents and feuds than of the ways in which Zola's public and private lives would uncomfortably intersect in the years ahead: as one of the Zola couple's oldest friends, he felt he would have had to give a speech paying tribute to Alexandrine's unwavering support during her husband's dazzling career, but, still unreconciled to Zola's betrayal of her with Jeanne Rozerot, he told Amélie Laborde (the wife of Alexandrine's second cousin and her close friend at the time) that to do so might be too painful for all concerned. Reports of the occasion in the press, some equally knowing but in a less personally intrusive age, merely noted that Alexandrine appeared 'subdued'.

The next indication of Zola's public status was the invitation he received that July from the Royal Institute of Journalists (subsumed within the National Union of Journalists in 1946) to attend its annual conference in London from 21 to 26 September 1893. He and his wife arrived there on the eve of its opening, having survived the choppy cross-Channel leg of the trip with some trepidation, this being their first-ever journey by ship. During the following ten days, both of them were hugely impressed by what they saw of the great Victorian metropolis: the immensity of the buildings, the width of the avenues around Hyde Park, the majesty of the Thames viewed from their rooms at the Savoy, the sheer size of the Liberal Club, the dynamism of the imperial capital at the height of its power and pomp. They were taken in an open carriage to tourist sites: Westminster Abbey, St Paul's Cathedral, the British Museum. They were invited to Hatfield House and taken to Greenwich to see the Observatory and the naval college. By comparison with London, Paris seemed to Zola almost provincial. Even an excursion to the East End brought home to him that Whitechapel's working-class slums were less awful than those he had depicted in *L'Assommoir*. Zola's notes on his ten-day visit, staying on after the end of the conference, are so characteristically detailed that he might have had in mind another novel to add to the trilogy of *Les Trois Villes* (The Three Cities). Even the legendary London fog appeared on cue, enhancing his appreciation of the city's beauty: 'by the light of a watery sun', he wrote, 'I had a vision of a dream-like city with its evanescent spires and domes and rows of enormous dark palaces coming into view before fading away into the mist.'[1]

Zola was overwhelmed by the extraordinary warmth of his welcome: greeted by enthusiastic crowds, standing ovations at every formal engagement and a firework display at the Crystal Palace, climaxing in an illuminated portrait of him in the sky. From banquet to banquet, he was treated with the ceremony normally accorded to a visiting monarch. Zola described a 'royal procession' into a reception at the Guildhall, to the fanfare of heraldic trumpets and the applause of 2,000 spectators. Alexandrine too, for a change, shared the limelight, escorted into the great building like a queen consort by the Lord Mayor himself. Zola was equally touched by less magnificent gestures, such as the basket of flowers sent to her at their hotel by Oscar Wilde before an evening at the theatre together. As he wrote to Jeanne on 25 September, 'the English are charming, I have been acclaimed as I never have been in France' (*LR*, 138).

Zola was also relieved on a more personal level: Alexandrine had been in such a distressed state before the trip that Céard had travelled with them to provide the moral support which, in the event, proved unnecessary. The visit to London was not without its more laughable moments: on yet another occasion when Zola was seated next to the Lord Mayor, the fact that neither of them knew a word of the other's language left both host and guest waiting for a toast to put an end to hours of baleful silence; Zola noted that the 'poor man' seemed somewhat bored. But from morning till night, whether inspecting the new extension to the Underground, seeing the Turners in the National Gallery, or being hosted amid the splendours of the Athenaeum (where Zola was given obligatory temporary club membership), the red carpet was rolled out.

Every formal speech Zola made or off-the-cuff response to journalists was reported in both London and Paris. His 1893 welcome would not be forgotten. During the Dreyfus Affair, rather than face incarceration he left for England on 18 July 1898. His decision to spend his enforced exile there was a direct consequence of this first triumphant visit.

Zola had initially hesitated to accept the invitation to London in the knowledge that his *Rougon-Macquart* novels, even abridged, bowdlerized and expurgated with his tacit approval, had been attacked in England for their alleged obscenity. As he wrote to Ernest Vizetelly (1853–1922) about *Le Docteur Pascal*: 'In your translation of it, you have the right to modify any passages which seem worrying to you' (*Corr.*, VII, 341). This led to the absurdity, in that novel, of Clotilde, Pascal's niece and mistress, announcing a conception rendered immaculate as a result of the cutting of two erotic scenes deemed to be potentially offensive to Victorian sensibilities. Not even such a mangling of Zola's texts could save the publishers from prosecution. Since 1884, the London-based publishing house of Vizetelly & Co. had been bringing out translations of Zola's novels. Henry Vizetelly (1820–1894), Ernest's father, had been sentenced by the Central Criminal Court to three months in prison in 1888–9, marking the success of the National Vigilance Association's campaign against his son's translation of *La Terre* (as *Soil*). On the same charge of corrupting public morals, Ernest too had been heavily fined.

Zola, hopeful that the visit might do something to assuage such resistance to his writing, was ultimately reassured: Ernest's contacts in the London press had made it clear that he had nothing to fear. But the novelist's worries were not unfounded: the translation of *La Terre* had been the pretext for a debate in the House of Commons on 8 May 1888, invoking the Contagious Diseases Act and condemning the 'inartistic garbage' (as per Hansard, the parliamentary record) of Zola's work more generally. It is thus perhaps surprising that he was introduced to the daughters of the Leader of the House. It is more ironic, doubtless to the Vizetellys' satisfaction and the kind of incredulity expressed in a letter to *The Times* of 27 September 1893, that the welcoming address at the conference, with special mention of its honoured plenary speaker from France, should have been delivered by the Attorney General in William Gladstone's government, Sir Charles Russell (1832–1900), a Liberal MP since 1880 and shortly to become, in 1894, Lord Chief Justice.

While the completion of the *Rougon-Macquart* made the timing of Zola's visit to London opportune, it was not only on account of his unequalled eminence as a foreign writer, or at least as the most prestigious living one (Hugo having died in 1885), that he had been invited to the Royal Institute's conference. This had been primarily motivated by his prominence as a journalist. Every tribute and toast evoked that crucial apprenticeship for his future career. On his arrival at Victoria station, the welcome party was headed by Sir Edward Levy-Lawson (1833–1916), the owner and editor of the *Daily Telegraph*, which took the unique step of publishing in French Zola's first words on alighting from his train. He was accompanied by a bevy of distinguished French journalists who reported on every aspect of his visit, whether serious or social.

The subject of Zola's address on the afternoon of 22 September at Lincoln's Inn Hall was anonymity in the press, at that time standard practice in British broadsheets. His arguments against it, as his own 'shameful' unsigned contributions to the *Sémaphore de Marseille* twenty years earlier had implicitly suggested, sparked a lively debate. Its text had been distributed in advance in both English and French, so that *Le Figaro* printed it on the same day. Many of Zola's meetings in London were with newspaper editors, either privately over lunch or collectively at the Press Club in Fleet Street. There, less constrained by protocol, he spoke from the heart, rehearsing for the assembled journalists his lifelong conviction, underlined in his 1881 valedictory article in *Le Figaro* and again in his response to the uproar created by the 'Manifeste des Cinq': their professional calling, he stressed, was the essential instrument for a deeper understanding of the modern world. This cultivation of the British press would prove to be a fortuitously good investment of his time and solidarity: during the Dreyfus Affair, the London newspapers were the most unequivocally committed of Zola's supporters outside France.

But perhaps the most compelling reason for Zola choosing to take up the invitation to London was what he saw as his duty as president of the Société des gens de lettres (Society of Men of Letters). The invitation had been initiated by its representative in Great Britain. Founded in 1838 in the golden age of newspaper serialization of fiction, this association's *raison d'être* was to protect the commercial rights of authors. Zola's support for it was inseparable from his repeated assertions, based on his own experience and his time at Hachette, that writing was not a pastime but a way of earning a living. He had first been elected to its presidency for a one-year term in April 1891; he was subsequently re-elected on an annual basis until 1895–6, at which point he devoted two long essays in *Le Figaro*, included in his *Nouvelle Campagne*, to the association's history and ongoing activities. As head of it, Zola was a public voice, whether at funerals and memorial services for well-known writers or in lobbying for tighter copyright legislation in the interests of his 'constituency'. Zola used his presidential years to advance his own literary agenda. Some occasions at which he spoke were also justified, however, on altruistic grounds, such as his reading passages of his latest novel, *Lourdes*, in April 1894 to an audience of 4,000 at the Trocadéro in order to raise funds for the poor.

Zola's most energetic campaign in this role, launched only a couple of months after his election in 1891, was in commissioning Auguste Rodin (1840–1917) to create a sculpture of Balzac. Only the finest sculptor of his generation, Zola argued, could produce a statue worthy of the society's first president and, no less significantly, the predecessor of Naturalism. He also recognized in Rodin's art, with its proportions akin to Michelangelo's, another reflection of his own. Zola's essays of the 1880s had already proposed that the author of *La Comédie humaine* should be immortalized in a material incarnation of the portrait of Balzac he had repeatedly penned. And he went to great lengths to bring this project to fruition: he followed up his invitation to Rodin, whom he had first met in 1885, with an attention to detail hardly justified by the formalities of his presidential instigation of the project, and he secured, in anticipation of the agreed completion of Rodin's work by 1 May 1893, the municipal authority's agreement that the statue should be positioned in the square giving onto the Palais-Royal. Zola's efforts were ultimately frustrated by a mixture of Rodin's procrastination (not until 1898 would his definitive model be ready) and fury when his first design was found so unacceptably ugly by the society as to be insulting to the iconic literary figure he was meant to be celebrating. The relationship with Zola had already been so strained by Rodin's resistance to being coaxed into meeting his contractual commitment that the sculptor returned the society's advance. This attritional situation would have consequences when the time came to erect a statue memorializing Zola himself.

As president of the society, Zola also assumed a quasi-diplomatic role: involved in negotiating a Franco-Russian literary treaty and representing France at various formal occasions to celebrate European alliances and friendships. It was in such an ambassadorial capacity that he decided that his visit to London should take precedence over his holiday in Brittany, originally planned for the summer of 1893. He was not too unhappy to cancel the latter, rather dreading having to cope at close quarters with

Alexandrine's state of mind and related health complaints. Zola's overseas mission cast him as the representative of contemporary French literature. His remorseless schedule of engagements notwithstanding, this manifested itself in meetings other than as a fellow journalist: with the cultural attaché at the French Embassy, with the association of teachers of French and the Alliance française, and even in his charitable donation to the French hospital in London. His speeches, whether to the Authors Club on 28 September or elsewhere before that, had a common theme: in less militant tones than those of his Naturalist campaigns in the French press, Zola invoked a literary evolution (from Rabelais, Racine and Corneille through to Lamartine being overtaken by Balzac) culminating, implicitly, in the *Rougon-Macquart*. In its subtle way, it was his own answer to Huret's 'Enquiry' into literary trends published in 1891 (detailed in the previous chapter), the year in which he had joined the executive committee of the Société des gens de lettres.

Zola also had a meeting with Chatto & Windus, the publishing firm which had taken over the translation of his work after the bankruptcy of Vizetelly & Co. as a result of his 'obscene' novels being taken out of circulation. But when Zola returned to France on 1 October, his public pronouncements on what his visit to London had achieved made it clear that he was not suffering from the illusion that Anglo-Saxon attitudes to his work had been completely overturned. What he stressed was more personal: that he hoped that his public demeanour had laid to rest an image of him as a human being as monstrously repugnant as his fiction. Neither Alexis' biography nor Huysmans' earlier essays (notably those brought together in his *Émile Zola et L'Assommoir'* (1877)) had succeeded in correcting a grotesque stereotype. Zola's renewed effort to project an altogether more sympathetic personality suggests that, even at the age of 53 and with his reputation internationally established, he was not invulnerable to the invective he continued to endure. His reflections on his London visit were a reminder to his hostile critics in Paris of the commentary in newspapers on both sides of the Channel which had praised his courtesy, modesty and humility.

New Projects

What remained undiminished after his return from London was a creative energy which did nothing to assuage the controversy around his public profile. Following on from using the theatre to reinforce the Naturalist hegemony, Zola sought to exploit to the same end another genre: that of the *drame lyrique*, setting some of his texts to music. His new collaborator was the composer Alfred Bruneau (1857–1934) (much influenced by the better-known Jules Massenet (1842–1912)), whom he had first met in 1888. Zola's own musical talents had not progressed since briefly taking up the clarinet at the age of fifteen. Nor did he have a particularly good 'ear'. Having sat through a performance of one of Bruneau's works, he admitted to Alexandrine, in a letter of 27 October 1901 (having a few days previously nostalgically reminded her of their happiness at a performance of *La Traviata* in their early years together), that listening to music for two hours without an interval was more than he could tolerate (*LA*, 710). He did his best to convince Bruneau (a fervent 'Wagnerian') otherwise, telling him that Wagner's *Meistersingers* was the piece he loved best. His admiration for the composer, after hearing excerpts from *Lohengrin* at a concert in 1868, was less to do with the music than with the booing which greeted it, confirming the irruptive advent of another artist at odds with cultural orthodoxy. Such a frame of reference explains Wagner's positive referencing in *L'Œuvre*. What Zola derived from the composer, as Céard was the first to point out, was an analogous orchestration of literary techniques: variations on a theme and structured repetitions. For adaptations of his texts, Bruneau was entirely responsible for the score. But Zola himself wrote many of the libretti and took a keen interest in production values and rehearsals.

The first of his texts to be staged after his return to Paris was *L'Attaque du moulin*, his contribution to *Les Soirées de Médan*. An earlier such adaptation had been *Le Rêve* in 1891, met with a mixture of astonishment and critical support for its innovatory qualities. By contrast, the response to the 39 performances of *L'Attaque du moulin* between 23 November 1893 and 17 March 1894, while appreciative of Bruneau's originality, distinguished between the latter and Zola's contribution. Huret headed his review of the opening night 'Un regard en arrière' (A Backward Look), wondering how embarrassed Zola's erstwhile 'disciples' might have been by such a travesty of Naturalist principles, and he questioned both his presidency of the Société des gens de lettres and the legitimacy of his ambition to be admitted to the Académie Française. That Huret's question was merely rhetorical was confirmed by the appended views, in *Le Figaro* of 24 November 1893, of members of the Médan circle: Alexis remained supportive; Céard was not; Zola refused to get embroiled. He was no more discouraged by such a critical reception than that provoked by his plays. In 1897 he and Bruneau put on *Messidor*, reworking aspects of *Germinal*; this was followed by *L'Ouragan* in 1901, the melodramatic plot of which received such tepid reviews that the Opéra-Comique abandoned the production in short order. What did survive until the end of Zola's life was a friendship with Bruneau so warm that, and as some two hundred of the composer's letters to the novelist also testify, he and his wife became part of the extended 'family' Zola habitually welcomed to his country home.

The Last Novel Cycles (1894–1902)

There is a sense in which all Zola's theatrical incursions were essentially strategic or at best a diversion. His priority remained his novels. Over lunch with Henry James on 29 September 1893, on the eve of his departure from London, he was asked what he intended to do next. James was left 'gaping' by Zola's response that he was about to get going on a new novel cycle: *Les Trois Villes* (*Lourdes*, *Rome* and *Paris*). James had wrongly supposed, as previously mentioned, that the *Rougon-Macquart* alone represented a life's work. Zola finished the last part of his trilogy in August 1897. In the summer of 1898 he was engaged on the first volume of yet another novel cycle, *Les Quatre Évangiles* (The Four Gospels). Lodged between those two dates was Zola's direct involvement in the Dreyfus Affair.

This was an interlude, if more personally traumatic, akin to the break in his writing of the *Rougon-Macquart* caused by the Franco-Prussian War. A strictly chronological account of Zola's life and work during the years 1894–1902 would have to insert his role in the Dreyfus Affair and his related exile in England *within* the composition of the two series which occupied the rest of Zola's career as a novelist. Teasing out of such temporal overlapping the various strands of biographical narrative and fictional projects is further complicated by Zola's death in 1902. He had conveyed to Alexandrine in October 1897 his worry, at the point when he began work on *Les Quatre Évangiles*, that it would take him three or four years to complete, he thought, and it would be so 'particular and serious' and such a large endeavour that 'at my age, I'm nervous about embarking on it' (*LA*, 211). In the event, *Vérité*, the third part, was published posthumously in February 1903. *Justice* was to be the final volume of this series; only the preliminary notes for it indicate what the conclusion of this great project might have been.

The fact that the two series are thematically continuous and similarly differentiated from the *Rougon-Macquart* is not sufficient to consider them together. *Vérité*, the penultimate of *Les Quatre Évangiles*, poses a particular problem in that it is the only one of these late novels visibly marked by Zola's experience of the Dreyfus Affair between 1897 and 1899: it is a personal rethinking of his role in it, but by virtue of being written in 1901–2, his reflections are extended to later stages of the Affair. If this had been the sole focus of *Vérité*, it would form a coda to Zola's involvement in it, and it still partly does. But in this, his very last novel, Zola also obliquely inserts a retrospective *summa* of his life and work. For that reason, it can be sectioned off from the first two of *Les Quatre Évangiles* and positioned accordingly in my final chapter.

The differences between these last two novel cycles and the *Rougon-Macquart* are the result of an authorial stance barely disguising didactic intentions. That had been visible in the increasingly apocalyptic tenor of the later novels of the *Rougon-Macquart*, from *Germinal* onwards. Zola was determined to develop his role as the prophetic spokesman of his generation most qualified to reach a wide audience. Nadar's 1894 photographic portrait of him reflects Zola's own conception of his contemporary status. In these new series, the implicit pedagogic dimension of his earlier one, imparting acquired knowledge about the workings of the modern world, would now be in full view, justified by the commitment to alert his readers to urgent challenges of the next century already emerging in the *fin de siècle*.

For contemporaries, the interest of Zola's writing remained, for a while at least, acute: *Lourdes* (1894), for example, sold as many copies as *La Débâcle* two years before. The popularity of these late novels inevitably faded, however, as their overt political, social and philosophical concerns gradually lost their topicality. The continuities with, or thematic reversals of, the *Rougon-Macquart* alert us to aspects of Zola's thinking after the completion of his twenty-volume series. Posterity's efforts to rehabilitate the value of *Les Trois Villes* and *Les Quatre Évangiles* most often rely on their importance for historians, not least in the fierce ideological debates of the period that their critical reception illuminates.

They are massive works, half of them well over seven hundred pages in length in the original 18-centimetre (7 in.) published editions (the shortest, *Lourdes*, fills 598 pages). Their reach is reflected not only in their scale and the number of characters but, in the case of *Vérité*, in a fictional time span of over fifty years. They are testimony to Zola's characteristic need to impose an overarching structure. Their focus on a single family is more rigorous than the occasionally tenuous link, in his earlier series, between a plot and the twin branches of the Rougons and Macquarts. The central protagonists of both Zola's new cycles are members of the Froment family, and liberated from the temporal constraints of the Second Empire which Zola had sometimes found so awkward in writing the *Rougon-Macquart*, the narratives can accommodate the family's descendants all the way to grandchildren. In a letter of 16 November 1899, however exaggerated, Zola revels in his newfound freedom: '*Les Quatres Évangiles* will extend from 1900 to the year 2000. It's my right as a poet' (*Corr.*, x, 95).

Les Trois Villes are anchored in a present determined by the past. *Les Quatre Évangiles* look to the distant future, and the names of the four heroes of the latter (Matthew, Mark, Luke and John) point to the template of the New Testament. What is also common to the two novel cycles is their own evangelical discourse: in *Travail*, the second of the *Évangiles* series, Zola wrote in his notes that he wanted to conjure up the 'utopia of the twentieth century . . . with science triumphant . . . and the resolution of conflict . . . humanity reunited in a single family . . . to finally ensure universal peace and harmony' (*Ms* 10333, fol. 348). For *Les Quatres Évangiles*, Zola was determined that the series as a whole would be 'resoundingly optimistic'. He looked forward, he confessed in his preliminary notes for the project, to adopting a perspective deliberately contrary to that of the *Rougon-Macquart* by being able to put his imagination to the service of a vision of 'goodness and tenderness'. It would be, he insisted, 'the logical conclusion of my entire work' (*OC*, VIII, 506).

Only in retrospect, whether in their fragile dawns or regenerative offspring, can one just about glimpse in the *Rougon-Macquart* the seeds of that 'logical conclusion'. *Le Docteur Pascal* most clearly anticipates it. And as the optimism therein is inseparable from Zola's personal circumstances at the time, so his last two novel series are coloured by the renewed happiness of his private life. For many of Zola's readers, *Les Trois Villes* and *Les Quatre Évangiles* mark the sad decline of his creative powers. Although they display a novelistic imagination sustained over thousands of pages, Zola has recourse to familiar character types and scenarios. And their narrative drive is impeded by precisely those kinds of didactic interpolations which he had sworn to himself he would avoid in differentiating himself from Balzac before starting the *Rougon-Macquart*. As if aware of the risks thereby involved, Zola almost self-consciously foregrounds social context and elaborates convoluted plots in mitigation.

If his late novels serve as a reminder that Zola's most compelling fiction is grounded in personal tensions subsequently resolved, less remarked upon is the extent to which these late novels are shaped, paradoxically, by the very success of the *Rougon-Macquart*. During the writing of that novel cycle, Zola had assumed an increasingly public profile. With its completion, his status as the most important literary figure of the age was assured. He was what is now called a 'celebrity'. It remains unimaginable, in our own time, that a *writer* would receive the kind of official welcome in European capitals which Zola enjoyed in London and Rome. As a result of his prominence, he was interviewed time and again on a range of topical subjects. His views were sought on this and that, from political developments to cultural trends. He was granted personal audiences with the president of the Republic and with government ministers. His interventions in the press, such as his 'À la jeunesse' (addressed to the next generation, in *Le Figaro* of 7 February 1896), were those of a sage dispensing advice. *Les Trois Villes* and *Les Quatre Évangiles* provided Zola with another public platform. In their assertions and arguments, they are more unambiguously subjective than any of the statements ascribed to authorial surrogates in his earlier fiction. The heroes of all these late novels function as his mouthpiece, as is equally evident from Zola's *Nouvelle Campagne* articles in *Le Figaro*, which simultaneously rehearse their protagonists' points of view, sometimes verbatim, over his own signature.

Les Trois Villes (1894–8)

Long before divulging his plans to Henry James, Zola had been turning these over in his mind. He first started thinking of the future *Lourdes*, the opening frame of *Les Trois Villes*, in 1891. That September, during a month-long trip to the southwest, he made a detour to the market town of its title, in the foothills of the Pyrenees, still synonymous today with the destination of the sick and the infirm hoping to be miraculously healed there. The draw of Lourdes dates from 1858, when a fourteen-year-old shepherdess, Bernadette Soubirous (subsequently canonized), was allegedly granted eighteen Marian visions in the Grotto of Massabielle. This legend is rehearsed in Zola's novel. These apparitions having been recognized by the Church in 1862, the first national pilgrimage a decade later, facilitated by the opening of a railway line, would in due course establish Lourdes as the most visited Christian site in the world: the inaugural pilgrimage attracted some 30,000; today the figure is between 5 and 6 million.

The nine pages of notes from Zola's three-day visit there in 1891 record his astonishment at both the religious phenomenon and its naked commercialization: a proliferation of hotels (so fully booked that in none of them was he able to find a room, forcing him to stay in nearby Tarbes), guided tours and commemorative merchandise at prices to match. Only once before had Zola ever mentioned Lourdes: in an article in the anti-clerical *La Cloche*, on 6 June 1872, coinciding with the first pilgrimage validated by the government, he saw its 'national' character exemplifying a right-wing alliance of Church and State (*OC*, XIV, 74–7). It was less as a polemicist than as a novelist that his brief visit twenty years later had piqued his interest. In March 1892, when asked about his future projects, Zola confessed that he was tired of writing for the theatre and that his fortuitous stop in Lourdes was tempting him to devote a novel to what he had seen. It suggests that he was also beginning to tire at the prospect of how much more labour it would take to complete the *Rougon-Macquart*, and that, already at that stage, he was looking ahead to new literary horizons. On a personal level, another aspect of the future fell into place while he was in Lourdes: in *Le Figaro* of 27 September 1891, Céard placed a coded announcement of the uncomplicated birth two days earlier of Zola and Jeanne's son Jacques.

By July 1892 his impatience was such that Zola announced in the press his intention to go to Lourdes to research a new novel. He was there between 19 August and 1 September, shortly after the publication of *La Débâcle* but prior to embarking on the manuscript of *Le Docteur Pascal*. Only once that final novel of his series had appeared, however, did Zola start drafting *Lourdes*, on 5 October 1893, a few days after his return from London. These specific dates do not alter the fact that *Lourdes* brings into focus authorial preoccupations with a longer history. In planning the *Rougon-Macquart* in 1868–9, Zola had wanted to devote at least one novel to religion. *La Conquête de Plassans* fulfilled this ambition to only a limited extent: the spiritual role of the Abbé Faujas is subordinate to that of his political machinations, and *La Faute de l'Abbé Mouret*, the next year, is essentially a meditation on Original Sin overcoming abnegation. The mysticism of *Le Rêve*, situated in the shadow of a great cathedral, is less questioned than functional in a further reworking of the Fall, the temptations of which are this time resisted. Other novels of the *Rougon-Macquart* include priests as minor characters, usually so unscrupulous and hypocritical as to leave readers in no doubt about Zola's views of organized religion.

Bypassed in earlier texts was an exploration of religious beliefs in their own right. What made it propitious to do in the 1890s was the so-called 'Catholic Revival': the last two decades of the century saw a reaction, articulated in both literary texts and intellectual debate, against the secular and materialist understanding of human behaviour enlarged by scientific progress and reflected in Zola's Naturalism. In an explanatory letter to Van Santen Kolff, in March 1894, he underlined this context of his intentions in *Lourdes*:

> My starting point is the examination of the temptations of blind faith in our exhausted *fin de siècle*. The reaction against science is returning us to the beliefs of the tenth century . . . an infantile dependence on prayer . . . instead of on the powers of medicine. (*Corr.*, VIII, 125)

The symbolic meaning of his 'complex' novel, he went on, was based on the premise that humanity itself was a sickly patient looking to the miraculous in the face of the apparently terminal diagnosis offered by science.

More than twenty years earlier, in the 1872 article in *La Cloche* mentioned above, devoted to the reportedly miraculous cure of a sick child, Zola had made it clear that the only 'miracles' he believed in were the engineering kind which resulted in the piercing of a railway tunnel. In order to realize what he intended to explore in *Lourdes*, he decided that the central protagonist of the entire trilogy of *Les Trois Villes* should be a priest undergoing an undeclared crisis of faith. Through Pierre Froment, the father-to-be of the four sons of *Les Quatre Évangiles*, Zola also channels his own thinking about the religious currents and contradictions of the time, all of which seemed to him to be incompatible with modernity. Protestants as well as Catholics, he had written in *Le Figaro* of 17 May 1881, were both members of anachronistic 'sects' which would vanish, he confidently predicted, long before scientific progress had run its course.

In its expert structuring (five parts, each with five chapters), *Lourdes* returns to the internal organization of *Une page d'amour*, with its narrative across five days overlapping the duration of the national pilgrimage.

Zola had chosen the dates of his stay accordingly, although he extended it for another ten days in order to fill in the background to the annual rituals. Much of this information is accommodated in the 245 pages of notes he assembled during his visit. But they also form a travel journal (*Mon voyage à Lourdes*) recording his daily movements, starting with his departure from Paris on 18 August. That itself had been a media event, ensuring that journalists would dog his footsteps in Lourdes. While Zola begins his novel by having Pierre Froment accompany the pilgrims on their journey, he and his wife travelled separately from them on a regular service, getting to Lourdes exhausted late on the 19th but in time to witness at its station the next day the successive arrival of fourteen special trains. That it was by this means of transport that the pilgrims had set off was central to the paradox Zola was exploring. In the nineteenth century, the train, in its practical application of scientific principles, was an icon of progress and modernity. In *La Bête humaine*, Zola set it against atavistic regression. In *Lourdes*, the train is not contrasted with an innate irrationality within his vision of man. It was simply at the root of his 'stupefaction' that the hallucinatory beliefs of its passengers should revert to those of the age of horse and cart.[2]

Contemporary critics concerned only with *Lourdes*' literary qualities, the latter occasionally conceded by even its ideological detractors, could not deny that Zola had transformed his meticulous notes into a novel of truly epic force: in the spectacle of vast crowds as powerfully drawn as in any of the *Rougon-Macquart*; in that of pilgrims wending, or hobbling, their way to the hospital and thence to the Grotto site of collective incantation summoning the intercession of the Virgin Mary; in panoramic visions of the city relativizing individual suffering; in descriptions of human misery as pitiable as that evoked in *Germinal*, but here more medically determined as the deformed, the paralysed and the blind struggle along the *via dolorosa* of time immemorial towards a hoped-for salvation. The novel's flimsy plot is almost beside the point. Its ideas, however, are transparently staged in conversations between sceptical doctors and delusional believers. Unsurprisingly, neither Zola nor Pierre Froment is converted by their experience, however profoundly moved by what they have seen. And, equally unsurprisingly, not only was *Lourdes* condemned by outraged Catholic critics as soon as its serialization began in April 1894, it was also placed on the Index of Prohibited Books by papal decree on 19 September, barely six weeks after its appearance in volume form.

That Zola continued to be exercised by the questions he had raised is evident in the fact that he immediately embarked on a sequel to *Lourdes*, with Pierre Froment again the central figure and still doubting his religious vocation. *Lourdes* had explored Catholic rituals beyond historical specificity. *Rome*, the second part of *Les Trois Villes*, is more topical: it takes place between 1890 and 1894, and it is inseparable from the vigorous debate surrounding Pope Leo XIII's 1891 encyclical (*Rerum novarum*), which had tentatively suggested reforms to the Church's treatment of the poor. Such a perspective is endorsed by Pierre, Zola's surrogate, who is the author of a book optimistically entitled *La Rome nouvelle*. A synopsis of it is the mirroring prelude to Zola's novel. And in a pre-emptively (if vain) self-reflexive move on Zola's part, Pierre arrives in the Eternal City to save his book from interdiction. In spite of its serious reforming intent and historical documentation, *La Rome nouvelle* is scornfully dismissed by the representative of conservative Catholicism as 'de la littérature' (*OC*, VII, 852) and thereby condemned to the papal Index as surely as Zola knew in advance that *Rome* itself would be. Like Zola, Pierre leaves Rome equally unconvinced that Catholicism will undergo a much-needed renewal. But, more generally, the novel is far more subversive than *Lourdes*: in evoking the morbid terror inspired by the Jesuits, in the unremitting criticism of a self-serving priesthood, in Zola's trailing his protagonist through labyrinthine corridors of the Pontiff's sub-contracted influence, and in the vanity of ambitious cardinals furtively eyeing the papal throne. The Vatican duly confirmed Zola's expectations of proscription on 27 August 1896, even before the final instalments of *Rome* had appeared in Paris in *La Revue hebdomadaire*.

Zola had originally conceived his project on the model of that of his fictional author. *Rome* too was to be primarily an exploration of the ideological infrastructure and conflictual tensions of contemporary Catholicism. To educate himself on a subject he knew little about, he travelled to Rome on 29 October 1894. Zola had a crowded schedule there: meetings with ecclesiastical dignitaries, political grandees and distinguished art historians, as well as with journalists and newspaper editors; he was entertained in the best social circles and was treated with the deference which had been accorded to him in London. Appended to toasts in his honour were expressions of national pride in welcoming back to the land of his forefathers one of Italy's most famous sons. Several steps up the hierarchy from the mere Lord Mayor of London, and accompanied by the French ambassador, he was received by King Humbold and his queen, Zola's request for an audience with the pope being deemed inappropriate in the light of the reception of *Lourdes*. The sympathetic portrait of Leo XIII in the compensatory fictional audience secretly accorded to Pierre underlined the character's support for the kind of social Catholicism the pope was advancing. Zola himself was under no illusions about any such reformist agenda. In an article in *Le Figaro* of 1 December 1895, he argued that the obstacles in its path would ensure that the Church itself was fated to disappear (*OC*, XIV, 710).

Well beyond the documentary needs of the novel in hand, he extended his stay in Italy until mid-December, including a five-day excursion to Naples. These six weeks became in effect a working holiday which for Zola was personally and aesthetically transformative; his *Journal de voyage*, written on a daily basis, is testimony to it. Over and above the brilliantly recorded impressions of the Italian capital he would transcribe in *Rome*, these notes are, and unlike in those for *Lourdes* or indeed for any of his novels except *L'Œuvre*, punctuated by autobiographical reflections. These are activated by the fact this was the first time in his life that Zola experienced a prolonged immersion in a foreign culture. To orient himself, comparisons with Aix-en-Provence were reassuringly familiar as memories came flooding back: in the Roman *campagna*, the yellow roof tiles in the midst of a dusty landscape and the roads on the approach to the city were likened to those of 'my Provence . . . my Aix, but much bigger' (*OC*, VII, 1032). He noted that passing boats on the Tiber were threatened by brattish boys hurling bricks down from the bridges: 'another reminder of Aix, the kids of my childhood' (p. 1075). In the search for a viable subplot for his novel, involving his heroine refusing to submit to an arranged marriage, Zola's notes on the mores of Italian womanhood also have assimilating parentheses: from men, young women 'between the ages of twelve and twenty, are kept apart. Exactly like in Aix' (p. 1062), their prospective suitors 'rewarded only with a flirtatious message (Aix)' (p. 1090); their virginity 'only surrendered to males from the same social class (Aix)' (p. 1050); their families 'resistant to marriage with outsiders (Aix again)' (p. 1062).

Like many before and since, the traveller's dislocation also reinforced a love of home. Zola responded to public evocations of his Italian provenance with less than wholehearted enthusiasm. He had been flattered by the welcome received during his brief visit to Genoa two years earlier. The opportunity to contemplate at greater leisure the country of his father's birth allowed him to elaborate a more equivocal picture of it. The anti-monarchist in him was relieved to find the king an unpretentious 'kindly fellow', and he was charmed by the queen, as unencumbered by airs and graces, and impressed by her intelligent interest in literary matters. On the other hand, his social whirl was more trying. In public, he was unfailingly polite. In his private notes, he wrote of his evening engagements that these were 'tedious', and Roman high society struck him as stilted, introspective and backward-looking. The city itself, with its squalid alleyways beneath the walls of silent palaces, seemed to Zola to be equally frozen in its glorious history, closed to a modernity exemplified by the dynamism of Paris. He later told Alexandrine that he feared that his representation of Italy's decay meant that he could never go there again. At many of his meetings, he was invited to give his views on the 1882 Triple Alliance in which Italy, Germany and the Austro-Hungarian Empire were joined in their opposition to France. Thereby reminded of European conflicts held in check by such fragile treaties, he determined to end *Rome* with a restatement of his hopes for universal peace established by scientific progress bringing religions and nations together. But Zola was also somewhat irritated to be thought of as a privileged intermediary by virtue of his Franco-Italian credentials. In his own mind, he was as exclusively French as his father had become.

In other respects, Zola's Roman sojourn was far from negative. In documenting himself for his novel *in situ*, he was brought face to face with a Rome insufficiently understood if limited to the kind of narrative which antithetically juxtaposes, as in Pierre Froment's *La Rome nouvelle*, the past and the future. The hero of *Rome* is taken along the same itinerary through the city's streets, squares, churches, galleries, museums, famous ruins and other tourist sites as (with his Baedeker in hand) Zola himself, which he intended would allow him to 'evoke all my own feelings . . . as an artist' (*OC*, VII, 1028). For both Zola and his protagonist, Rome is an extraordinary visual experience. Both are introduced to the work of a wide range of artists, making of the novel a text saturated with pictorial references. In looking at centuries-old statuary, Zola transferred directly to Pierre his own sense of 'an extraordinary lifelike intensity' and a necessary reappraisal, totally at odds with the antipathy he had displayed in the 1860s towards the Neoclassical sculptural ideal of the Académie des beaux-arts: 'How it grabs one differently from a classical history responsible for our dismissal of the works of Antiquity, now that they can be understood and appreciated' (*OC*, VII, 1033). Pierre's preconceived view of Roman architecture, in the opening pages of the novel ('devoid of charm . . . and not even externally grand') undergoes a proleptic shift: 'It was clearly beautiful in its own way, as he would end up acknowledging once he had thought about it' (*OC*, VII, 517). And there is no mistaking the autobiographical weight of Pierre's definitive revaluation of the art of the past: 'He returned having had revealed to him the whole of classical art which, until then, he had found distasteful' (*OC*, VII, 770).

It was mentioned earlier that the climax of this educational journey is reached in the Sistine Chapel and Zola's euphoric identification with Michelangelo's achievement. This is preceded by a disagreement between Pierre and Narcisse Habert on the respective merits of Michelangelo and Botticelli. Habert is modelled on the near-homonym of Ernest Hébert (1817–1908), the director at the time of the French art institute, the 'École de Rome', where winners of the prestigious Prix de Rome were rewarded with two-year scholarships in order to copy the Old Masters. Hébert seemed not to hold it against him that, in the novelist's art criticism in the 1860s and 1870s, his paintings had not been spared Zola's contempt: he acted as his amicable guide through the artistic treasures of Rome. But in the discursive confrontation of the radically different aesthetics of Botticelli and Michelangelo, Zola was staging the tensions within his own work: between epic grandeur and the latent sentimental idealism surfacing at the end of *Le Docteur Pascal* and relatedly manifest in his including Botticelli's *La Primavera* among the images decorating the apartment he had secured in 1889 for Jeanne Rozerot.

The judgement of posterity is one of the recurrent themes of Zola's art criticism, particularly in relation to Delacroix and Manet. His literary criticism too distinguishes between writers whose reputations had evaporated and those destined to be forever remembered. But it is clearly a question also hanging over his own work, evident in his thinking about the character of Bongrand in *L'Œuvre*. It becomes more pressing towards the end of his writing career, both for personal reasons and in his awareness of the shifting cultural climate. Zola put the question to himself in his notes for *Rome*: he wondered whether or not Michelangelo's genius had been recognized in the artist's own time. That question had been posed in a distant city. Writing the novel in Paris between April 1895 and March 1896, Zola was returned to a less speculative critical context. In accounting for Habert's refusal to subscribe to Pierre's insistence on Michelangelo's qualities, due to 'his undeclared and subconscious hatred . . . of simplicity and strength' (*OC*, VII, 672), Zola associates the point of view of this 'modern mindset . . . corrupted by the search for something new' with writers of the *fin de siècle* differentiating themselves from his achievement in the *Rougon-Macquart*.

Zola's references to writer and critic Anatole France (1844–1924) and Paul Bourget, at this point in the notes for *Rome*, make it clear that Renaissance painting was not Zola's main concern. Even his contemplation of Raphael is a pretext for addressing yet again the accusation that his novels ignored psychology. Habert's expressed antipathy towards Michelangelo is an abbreviated transposition of the charges levelled at Zola himself by hostile critics: 'a man with no sense of mystery or of the unknown, whose crude and ugly masses of flesh likened the bodies of men to tree trunks and those of women to gigantic butchers' wives' (*OC*, VII, 667). To which Pierre responds, on Zola's behalf, that it was Michelangelo's unmatched creative powers which were responsible for animating the materiality of the human body 'which so offends your delicate sensitivities'. The topicality of the overt subject of *Rome* would inevitably not endure. Less ephemeral were Zola's preoccupations with his own legacy: for such are the affinities with Michelangelo revealed to him in the Sistine Chapel that his description of its pictorial splendours becomes an *apologia pro mea sua*.

No sooner had Zola sent off to his publishers the completed manuscript of *Rome* in the spring of 1896 than he embarked on the final part of *Les Trois Villes*. *Paris* is another novel anchored in the present of its writing. Its internal chronology, calculated in relation to the three years elapsed since Pierre Froment's departure from Rome to take up his new responsibilities at the Sacré-Cœur in Montmartre, places it in 1897, the year Zola finished the novel. But its narrative is based on events of 1892–4 symptomatic of a deep-seated national malaise which would shortly erupt in the Dreyfus Affair: parliamentary subterfuge, irreconcilable ideological divides and a series of anarchist atrocities culminating in the assassination of President Carnot in June 1894.

The novel's models are transparent. That of the invented but equally fraudulent 'Chemins de fer africains' is the Panama Scandal: in this, nearly a million French citizens lost investments pocketed by financiers and politicians, many of the latter (including six ministers) having been bribed to conceal the bankruptcy of the company contracted to construct a canal from the Atlantic Ocean to the Pacific. The figure of Salvat is primarily based on Auguste Vaillant, guillotined in February 1894 for having hurled a home-made bomb into the Chamber of Deputies from its public gallery three months earlier; Zola's character's analogous gesture is as ineffective – its only victim is an impoverished young milliner. Behind Sanier's newspaper in the novel, *La Voix du peuple*, is *La Libre Parole*, directed by the rabidly antisemitic journalist Édouard Drumont (1844–1917), who had also been implicated in the Panama Scandal. *Paris* was a novel which needed little documentation beyond what was continuing to be reported in a 'media frenzy' sustaining both public interest and collective panic inspired by the apparently accelerating disintegration of the Third Republic.

That Zola had temporarily left behind his focus on religion is underlined by the fact that, in this third incarnation, his fictional priest has now definitively lost his faith, legitimizing his appointment only by his charitable work with the poor. This signals his commitment to the social Catholicism he had failed to have endorsed in Rome. But it is also the dead end of his spiritual quest: whereas the Parisian panorama in Zola's novels habitually opens up horizons, when Pierre steps out of his basilica at the beginning of *Paris*, his gaze from Montmartre cannot penetrate the mist shrouding the city. Zola's wider purview in this novel makes of it a reworking of some of the major themes of the *Rougon-Macquart*: political corruption, financial criminality and sexual depravity. In denouncing these, *La Voix du peuple*'s investigative journalism is, for its targets, as 'odious' (*OC*, VII, 1193) as Zola's in the pages of *Le Figaro* at the same time as he was writing *Paris*. The novel's own denunciation of interlinked scandals has much of the ferocity of Zola's depiction of the Second Empire. His return to such subjects also marks a return to his most powerful writing while testifying to a sustained moral positioning.

Unlike the *Rougon-Macquart*, however, *Paris* as a novel does not speak for itself. It displays Zola's characteristic structuring, again in five parts. But instead of the disembodied narrative voice of his great series, here Zola's authorial spokesmen are far from invisible. Although he attempts to delegate his point of view in plausible dialogues, Zola's own discursive energy is palpable. Between the alternative fictional principles of 'showing and telling', Zola appends to demonstration both analysis and, above all, hypothetical solutions to the modern problems he dramatizes. The result is a novel which articulates multiple debates: on ideal political structures, on the tensions between individual rapacity and the collective good, on socialist remedies to inequality, on the competing theoretical presuppositions of thinkers from Auguste Comte to Karl Marx. These foregrounded discussions are set against marvellous panoramic descriptions of Paris itself. As in much of Zola's fiction, and indeed in the comforting backdrop of his early poverty, these put into a wider perspective the imperfections of individual and social experience. In *Paris*, however, the city's symbolic role is extended into the future. In an article Zola wrote immediately prior to the novel's serialization in the autumn of 1897, the city, 'as the centre of the world', had a civilizing mission: 'Over Paris as it is today, with all its ignominies and the feverish symptoms of its forward march, there will arise the great dawn of the next century.'[3]

Les Quatre Évangiles (1899–1902)

If *Les Trois Villes* had prepared the ground for such optimism, *Les Quatre Évangiles* would substantiate it. This second series is indeed evangelical in tone and intent. The compositional dynamic of the *Rougon-Macquart* moves by associative indirection from originating idea to definitive text. Each of *Les Quatre Évangiles*, by contrast, allegorizes a message. At first sight, it is delivered as unproblematically as Étienne Lantier's messianic one in *Germinal*. But even Zola's commitment to the radiant future the series proposes is not quite the 'blind faith' of the religious beliefs to which he refused to subscribe. Both *Travail* and *Vérité* are almost rescued from utopian fantasy by a residual lucidity.

This is less true of *Fécondité*, the first of the series' projected four novels. Zola started work on it in December 1897, only for its planning to be interrupted by his involvement in the Dreyfus Affair during the first half of 1898. But it remains not the least revealing, and remarkable, feature of Zola's writing life that, during his exile in England, which lasted until June 1899, he continued to progress it. Alexandrine had sent him, in a trunk, his preliminary notes so that he could do so. This undoubtedly provided a daily structure during eleven months of relative isolation and as an antidote to boredom and distress. It also confirmed both a personal and intellectual investment in the novel's subject. Intensified by his own belated paternity, and as its very title indicates, *Fécondité* substantiates the regenerative themes of the *Rougon-Macquart*. Like *Paris*, the novel accommodates a wide-angled vision of *fin de siècle* France. Its central focus, however, is depopulation as a social pathology which also reflects nationalist anxieties about the demographic growth of Germany.

There was nothing subtle about Zola's intentions: 'What I want to do', he wrote in his preparatory notes for *Fécondité*, 'is to picture a family whose fertility . . . will be the source of prosperity and happiness' (*Ms* 10301, fol. 42). The antithesis of such joy is indexed in the despair of infant mortality, perhaps poignantly referencing once again the haunting fate of Alexandrine's baby three decades earlier. The novel's plot is little more than the scaffolding supporting debates aimed at Malthusian advocates of restricting population growth, and it largely consists of a series of fictional illustrations of opposing arguments, often aimed at any deviation of Zola's long-held view of human sexuality and procreation. This is taken to such lengths that the final pages of the novel bring together nearly three hundred descendants of Mathieu Froment and his wife, consecrated by an authorial vision of a genetic inheritance extended to populating the French colonies overseas. What Zola had gone through during the Dreyfus Affair leaves no shadow on the natalist exuberance of the text. This was not true of reviews of *Fécondité*. Almost provocatively, it was in *L'Aurore*, in which 'J'accuse' had appeared, that the serialization of the novel began on 15 May 1899. Zola's opponents maliciously suggested that no other newspaper was willing to publish it. The anti-Dreyfusard reviewers had another field day. *Paris* had been published in volume form on 1 March 1898, a week after the ending of the trial in which he was prosecuted for the defamatory aspects of 'J'accuse'. The critical reception of *Paris* exactly anticipated the ideological subtext of that of *Fécondité*.

The next of *Les Quatre Évangiles*, *Travail*, would be written after Zola's return from his exile in England on 5 June 1899. Started towards the end of that year, it was serialized, again in *L'Aurore*, between 3 December 1900 and 11 April 1901. Unlike *Fécondité*, it does bear the discreet trace of the Dreyfus Affair: in the urgency of Zola's call for an end to internecine strife, and, more personally, in Luc Froment's being subjected to the kind of vilification and incipient violence which Zola himself had experienced on the streets of Rennes in August 1899 on the occasion of Alfred Dreyfus' second court martial (political pressure having succeeded in having him brought back from Devil's Island so that incriminating evidence could be considered anew, he was again found guilty, but with 'extenuating circumstances'). The novel never amplifies such an oblique allusion. With its title gesturing towards its author's own productivity, *Travail* was to be devoted to 'work as the progenitor . . . of the world . . . with manual labour ennobled . . . building the ideal city of the future' (*Ms* 10333, fols 349–50). Zola's inspiration was the social model proposed by Charles Fourier (1772–1837), who had dreamt of a working community organized to overcome social divisions, and who had already been cited by the novelist in *Paris* and *Fécondité*.

Travail is as discursively structured as *Fécondité*: its conclusions are reached only after consideration of the pros and cons of alternative models to Fourier's, from collectivism to revolutionary syndicalism. In respect of the latter, the novel testifies to how far Zola's thinking had come since 1885. *Travail* is set in an industrial landscape as imaginatively pictured as that of *Germinal*. Its fictional workers are also divided between the good, the bad and the ugly, notably in the repurposing of the triangular rivalry of Étienne–Catherine–Chaval in that of Luc–Josine–Ragu. But it so radically inverts the plotting of Zola's earlier novel that it has justifiably been seen as an 'anti-*Germinal*'.[4] At its centre is a metallurgy works, previously an armaments factory now devoted to making useful products. Recalcitrant workers are converted to contribute to the common endeavour. Rich and poor collaborate. Women are valued on the shop floor as well as in the home. Instead of the conflictual violence which had torn miners and managers apart, there is cooperation and harmony. Whereas *Germinal* had predicted that the struggle between capitalism and the working class would pose the most critical question for the twentieth century, its sequel in *Travail* offers admirable solutions. These are pronounced by Luc, as authorial alter ego. But embedded in the novel is also an awareness both of the cynicism it might elicit and of the paternalist thrust of Zola's own utopian discourse. It is a further indication of the state of France at the time that *Travail* was welcomed by leading socialists as well as social scientists in its genuine attempt, however idealist, to propose a national future guided by a spirit of reconciliation.

6
Public and Private Lives

Innumerable books have been devoted to the Dreyfus Affair, in recognition of its traumatic significance for the history of modern France. Zola's own role in it hardly needs retelling. The most focused account is that of Alain Pagès, published in 1991.[1] The most detailed fills much of the third volume (2002) of Henri Mitterand's compendious biography frequently cited in this book. The subsequent publication of Zola's letters to Alexandrine in 2014, however, affords a more nuanced view of his progressive involvement in the Affair than is habitually gleaned by recourse to Zola's correspondence with its participants and to his declarations in the press. In both those cases, he adopts a public persona consistent with the heroic stature later ascribed to him by sympathetic historians of it: a selfless and unwavering determination to right the scandalous miscarriage of justice by which Captain Alfred Dreyfus had been convicted of treason. That is not to deny the extraordinary courage he displayed, nor what this cost him personally, by intervening in the Affair. But these private letters to his wife, during her stay in Italy in the autumn of 1897, provide unprecedented insight into Zola's motivation at the time while also allowing us to relate his intervention to different aspects of his life and work.

The Dreyfus Affair had in effect begun three years earlier. In September 1894, in the wastepaper basket of the military attaché to the German Embassy, a memorandum was discovered by a cleaning lady working for the French secret service; this made explicit the four kinds of highly confidential information about France's defences that the author of the document was party to. That such secrets could be handed to the Germans left the French high command in no doubt that they were faced with a case of potentially dangerous espionage. Suspicion that the spy concerned was Dreyfus, a Jewish artillery officer with possible access to such sensitive material, was reinforced by the fact that he was a German-speaker (as a native of the province of Alsace annexed in 1871). This fed into both a revanchist and antisemitic discourse peddled by nationalists. These suspicions were confirmed by the testimony of handwriting experts, resulting in his arrest on 15 October. Prolonged interrogations of Dreyfus himself culminated in his court martial behind closed doors, between 19 and 22 December. This concluded with him being found guilty and sentenced to incarceration for life in the gruesome prison facility in French Guyana to which the State had dispatched its 'traitors' since the beginning of the Second Empire.

Zola and his wife had been in Italy during most of these months, and the few French newspapers which they were able to read in Rome hardly mentioned the above sequence of events. Nor was Zola apparently much interested when Dreyfus' case did become very public: on 5 January 1895, in the forecourt of the École militaire, Dreyfus was subjected to the humiliation of having his officer's stripes torn from his uniform and his sabre broken in two; he was then paraded around the courtyard while a huge crowd of onlookers shook their fists and hurled verbal abuse. Some of Zola's more inventive biographers recounted that at a dinner party that same day, on listening to an eyewitness account of this degrading spectacle, he was appalled, and so moved by the report of Dreyfus' voiced protestations of innocence during it (countered by right-wing dining companions claiming that he had confessed his guilt) that this was the moment when he decided that he was determined, even if he alone took on this thankless role, to prove it. There is no evidence to support this suitably dramatic entry on his part into the political arena. But in due course Zola could not but refer to the most notorious moment in the Dreyfus Affair: in a set of notes written in February 1898, he admitted that a second-hand report of the 1895 ritual (perhaps in one of the multiple newspaper accounts of it), evoking 'the ferocity of the crowd' and its solitary scapegoat, had sufficed to revolt him from 'a human point of view' (*OC*, XIV, 1108).

The timeline of Zola's involvement in the Dreyfus Affair is altogether different from any claim that it coincided with Dreyfus's public degradation. There is no record of Zola's awareness that Dreyfus was shipped to Guyana in March 1895 and thence to Devil's Island on 13 April. When it did finally come to his close attention over two years later, the case had been so lost from view that Zola's mentions of it to correspondents start off by wondering if they vaguely remembered it. His own interest was sparked by other people's. But his decision to get involved is preceded by hesitation prior to thinking through how his own strategies might be most effective.

On 5 November 1897, for example, Zola was visited at his Paris address by Bernard Lazare (1865–1903), the author of a history of antisemitism in 1894 who, the following year, had agreed to help Mathieu Dreyfus (1857–1930) in his efforts to overturn his younger brother's conviction. Bernard-Lazare (hyphenated, by his own volition) was seminal in the gradual transformation of Dreyfus' individual case into a capitalized 'Affair' – with the far-reaching ramifications which Zola's own writing about it would in due course underline. Bernard-Lazare's three eye-opening publications, brought out between 1896 and 1898, vary in length but all bear titles highlighting Alfred's innocence.[2] He had come to see Zola on 20 November 1896 in the context of the first of these; his 1897 meeting with him coincided with the appearance of a much fuller second version of what he called 'A Judicial Error', now including an appendix accommodating the conclusions of graphologists refuting the evidence so instrumental in Dreyfus' indictment. Zola was not yet entirely convinced. Or rather, as he wrote to Alexandrine the day after Bernard-Lazare's visit, he preferred to remain distanced from the enormity of 'the poisoned wound' (*LA*, 228) which the Dreyfus Affair was rapidly becoming, cautioning her not to breathe a word, even in Italy, which might be construed as a shared belief in Dreyfus' innocence.

Already, however, Zola was being harassed by journalists trying to ascertain where he stood. And this was for the same reason that he had initially been approached by Bernard-Lazare and as he would shortly be by others seeking justice for Dreyfus. Zola was not just the most famous novelist of the period, he was a public figure whose views mattered. On more than one occasion, he had been asked whether he would stand for election to the Chamber of Deputies or be willing to be appointed to the Senate. His response had been that his writing was a more effective means of steering political debate. And so it was to prove.

Of all those soliciting his support in the Dreyfus Affair, the most important was Auguste Scheurer-Kestner (1833–1899), vice president of the Senate since 1895. Zola's lunch meeting with him on Saturday, 13 November 1897, had been set in train by the lawyer Louis Leblois (1854–1928), who had also prepared the ground for it by coming to see Zola on two occasions during the previous week. Leblois had conveyed to Scheurer-Kestner what he had learnt in confidence from his old friend

Colonel Georges Picquart (1854–1914), the head of French counter-intelligence. Picquart had been posted to North Africa by the military authorities, intent on supressing his incontrovertible claim that the real spy handing over secrets to the Germans was an infantry commander by the name of Ferdinand Esterhazy (1847–1923) (in Zola's *Vérité*, his equally dissolute incarnation is the *abbé* Gorgias). Picquart remained so resistant to keeping quiet that he would be arrested and imprisoned in July 1898 on the grounds that he had betrayed his oath of loyalty to the French army.

So credible was Leblois' account of what Picquart had discovered in an Esterhazy telegram of March 1896 that, even before meeting Scheurer-Kestner at his home on 13 November, Zola was now certain of Dreyfus' innocence. As he wrote to Alexandrine on the 10th, the Affair would be a military version of the Panama Scandal which would bring down the Minister of War at the very least. By comparison with what he now knew, she could ignore the excerpts of Bernard-Lazare's arguments appearing in the newspapers ('he knows nothing and is incapable of revealing the real truth'). He tried to reassure her that his marital and paternal responsibilities meant he would proceed very carefully in what was likely to prove explosive. 'But I must admit', he added, 'that such a drama is overwhelming, for I don't know anything finer' (*LA*, 232).

That the Affair had seized, in the first instance, his *imagination* is confirmed in the letter Zola sent Alexandrine on the evening immediately following his meeting with Scheurer-Kestner, at which three other guests were present, including Leblois. Zola was mightily impressed by his host: the innate goodness and nobility of the 64-year-old widower, the purity of his motives and his old-fashioned demeanour ('he smokes a pipe like Flaubert'). Zola was so enervated by the discussion that, uncharacteristically, he ate little of an excellent lunch. But he emerged from it feeling unsure whether conflicts of interest made it problematic for the cautious vice president of the Senate and, like Dreyfus, a native of Alsace, to actually lead what was now an incipient 'campaign': 'one can only take this further with a passion for truth, the energy and the lightning strike that it needs' (*LA*, 243). Scheurer-Kestner had achieved nothing by raising the case with President Faure (personally and constitutionally determined to remain aloof from party politics) on 29 October. The setting up of his meeting with Zola suggests that he didn't quite know what to do next.

It has been argued that Scheurer-Kestner later felt that Zola had 'hijacked' the Dreyfus Affair in a characteristically self-promoting move which, according to Ruth Harris, 'destroyed all possibility of compromise'.[3] But the senator's knowingly warm handshake as Zola departed from their meeting suggested that he too was thinking that the writer could play a more effective role in it than himself. Zola was aware that his wife would have misgivings were he to assume it: he had no intention of intervening, or so he had reportedly told Leblois during his second visit earlier in the week, 'being totally unqualified' (*LA*, 236) to do so. This modesty was disingenuous at best. What becomes ever clearer during the following days is the growing intensity of Zola's emotional response to what he was learning: that ministers had known for over a year that Dreyfus was not the author of the memorandum, and the fact that not a single member of the government had resigned was absolutely 'monstrous' (*LA*, 244).

Even after his meeting with Scheurer-Kestner, Zola was insisting to Alexandrine on 15 November that he would remain distant from the 'frightful mess . . . but don't worry, I have no intention of getting in any way involved, even though my indignation is heartfelt' (*LA*, 249). He was, however, clearly tempted to do so: as he had written to her after returning from his lunch, 'it's a superb drama . . . of tragic grandeur.' It was so compelling and 'haunting' (*LA*, 269) that he gave up his writing habits and instead spent entire mornings reading the newspapers.

In the addendum to the 1901 preface of *La Vérité en marche* (Truth on the March, 1901), (a volume reprinting his articles during the Affair), Zola admitted that it was the novelist in him who had initially been inspired by Dreyfus' story; his commitment to the cause of justice had been a consequence rather than the origin of his involvement. His letters to Alexandrine in the dying days of 1897 confirm as much. He thought the facts he was learning at the time were 'extraordinary' (*LA*, 236). And he continued to envisage his possible 'noble' role in the Affair as that of a writer. He was perfectly aware that his strengths lay in writing rather than oratory. His long experience of giving speeches had not overcome his innate timidity and nervousness when required to do so. But, above all, this was consistent with his long-held view of a writer's relationship with society; his entire career testified to the power of the press, more influential than any role a politician could play. Zola's decisive entry into the maelstrom of the Dreyfus Affair is seen as inaugurating the French tradition of the committed intellectual's contribution to public debate – in which writing is less abstracted commentary than a form of direct action.

Zola's first such tentative step was to publish three articles in *Le Figaro*, starting with one on 25 November 1897 supporting Scheurer-Kestner. After the second of them, appearing on 1 December, he told his wife, 'I am now engaged in writing the finest pages of my whole life. This is both joyful and glorious' (*LA*, 289). Such elation in his emergence from the sidelines is explained by agreeable surprise at the ('80% favourable') reaction to his *Figaro* articles: the second, even more than the first (concluded by his 'Truth will out' formula), had generated hundreds of congratulatory letters and been sympathetically endorsed by all sections of the press except those on the nationalist right. Among the literary fraternity, to Zola's particular pleasure, even his aesthetic adversaries joined in the chorus of approval. Although immodestly confident that he was 'always right' (*LA*, 281), Zola had often been concerned that the 'lessons' of his late novel cycles might be ignored: in relation to *Paris*, for example, he told Alexandrine that a 'half-success' wouldn't do, worrying lest his reading public 'abandon' him (*LA*, 174). But the reception of his *Figaro* articles was so radically different from his habitually being 'dragged through the mud' (*LA*, 285) that, just for a moment, Zola was under the illusion that at last his own positioning on contemporary issues was validated by a wider public. As he wrote to Alexandrine on 29 November, he was thereby convinced of the 'usefulness and beauty' (*LA*, 281) of his role.

Although he had predicted it, Zola had not quite taken on board the extent to which Scheurer-Kestner would come under vicious attack both in the Senate and in the press. And Zola himself would soon be disabused of his newfound expectation that he spoke for France. As the anti-revisionist camp became more vociferous, the panicked management of *Le Figaro* withdrew Zola's public platform. He found another in the recently founded *L'Aurore*; of the left-wing members of its editorial staff none was more radical than Georges Clemenceau (1841–1929), who would go on to successive premierships, notably during the First World War.

It was Clemenceau who thought up the provocative title of Zola's 'J'accuse', perhaps the most famous journalistic text in the history of modern France. Zola himself had originally cast it as simply 'A Letter to M. Félix Faure, President of the Republic', consistent with the tradition of open letters published in newspapers. The catalyst for it was the Esterhazy case: he had been publicly denounced as the real culprit by Mathieu Dreyfus in a letter written to the Minister of War on 15 November and published in the morning newspapers the next day; as Zola wrote to Alexandrine, 'the bomb has gone off' (*LA*, 251). Zola hoped that the military authorities would have no choice but to investigate, and that confirmation of Esterhazy's guilt would lead, as a consequence, to the recognition of Alfred Dreyfus' innocence. But he was not certain that there would not be a whitewash. And so it proved: Esterhazy was indicted on 2 January 1898, but, on the 11th, at the end of his two-day court martial, the unanimous verdict of acquittal was greeted by cries of 'Long live the army!'

On that same day, Zola began to write, under the deliberately punctuated heading of 'J'accuse . . .!', his historic 39-page manuscript (some 4,500 words). It was ready for final amendments by the evening of the 12th. Typesetters and rotary presses worked through most of that night to produce 300,000 copies of *L'Aurore* (ten times its usual circulation), its imminent publication advertised on billboards and an army of paperboys recruited to sell it on the streets. Even the formatting of Zola's open letter was designed to command attention, with its heading in bold culminating in an exclamation mark. This was reinforced by the entire front page of *L'Aurore* being devoted to it, compelling the reader onwards to two additional columns overleaf where the text climaxed: a litany of accusations substantiating the implied continuum of the title's ellipsis, and this merely provisional list was so wide-ranging that the charges both ironically invoked and virtually outweighed what Alfred Dreyfus had been accused of.

Zola's text is prefaced by a flattering reminder of the concern for justice which President Faure had displayed during his political career. It then provides a detailed recapitulation of each and every phase of the Dreyfus Affair since 1894. Dreyfus' original court martial is subject to a forensic exposition of illegalities of process amounting to a 'judicial crime'. And the handling of the Esterhazy case is reviewed with a barely concealed anger which receives its fullest expression in Zola's final paragraph: an ad hominem inventory of the generals involved in collusion and cover-up, each of them portrayed in the eviscerating prose characteristic of Zola's polemical writing over the decades. His first texts devoted to the Dreyfus Affair, in the articles in *Le Figaro* on behalf of Scheurer-Kestner, have been described as evidence of spontaneity bordering on 'recklessness'.[4] This is not true of 'J'accuse'. Zola knew exactly what he was doing and what the consequences of his concluding diatribe would be. He referred explicitly to the specific clauses in the 1881 press laws on libel which he was consciously transgressing, and he dared the authorities to prosecute him.

Deuxième Année. — Numéro 87 | Cinq Centimes | JEUDI 13 JANVIER 1898

Directeur ERNEST VAUGHAN

L'AURORE

Littéraire, Artistique, Sociale

Directeur ERNEST VAUGHAN

Les annonces sont reçues : 142 — Rue Montmartre — 142

J'Accuse...!

LETTRE AU PRÉSIDENT DE LA RÉPUBLIQUE

Par ÉMILE ZOLA

LETTRE A M. FÉLIX FAURE

Président de la République

Monsieur le Président,

Me permettez-vous, dans ma gratitude pour le bienveillant accueil que vous m'avez fait un jour, d'avoir le souci de votre juste gloire et de vous dire que votre étoile, si heureuse jusqu'ici, est menacée de la plus honteuse, de la plus ineffaçable des taches?

'J'accuse', front page of *L'Aurore*, 13 January 1898.

The government was initially hesitant as to whether to do so might give further 'oxygen' to the Dreyfusard campaign. Pressure from the right-wing press and nationalist parliamentarians resulted, however, in the decision to put Zola on trial. This opened on 7 February. As the prosecution had intended, Zola's brilliant young lawyer Fernand Labori (1860–1917) was unable to divert the attention of the court to the Dreyfus Affair itself. It was only for the defamatory dimension of 'J'accuse' that Zola was found guilty on 23 February and given the maximum sentence of a year's imprisonment and a fine of 3,000 francs. On appeal, this was confirmed at court hearings in May and July. Nor was this the only judicial imbroglio in which Zola was enmeshed: he was simultaneously suing Judet for libelling his father, and the three handwriting experts he had somewhat gratuitously impugned in 'J'accuse' had accused him, independently of the original February prosecution, of harming their professional reputations. On this further charge of defamation, Zola was also found guilty, resulting on 9 July in his being given a suspended two-week prison sentence and a 2,000-franc fine and having to pay each of his 'victims' 5,000 francs in damages. Subject to a further appeal, this verdict (with much harsher penalties) would only be confirmed on 10 August. But, by then, Zola had already left France.

Zola in England

Zola's taking the boat-train to England on the evening of 18 July 1898 marked a moment more significant for him personally than for the ongoing vicissitudes of the Dreyfus Affair itself. A month later he tried to explain to Alexandrine, 'I had to remove myself from the fray in order to remain master of the Affair' (*LA*, 315). He had done so, he added, so that he could strategically plan his next move. But, far from mastering them, he was already distant from events: the progressive unravelling of the case against Dreyfus had begun with Esterhazy's renewed arrest on 12 July; this was taken a stage further when a vital witness (Colonel Joseph Henry) committed suicide on 31 August, having confessed that he had been the author of a text (supposedly between the allied Italian and German military attachés) falsely corroborating the flimsy prima facie evidence of Dreyfus' guilt. Zola's decision to leave Paris was questioned by some of his supporters, who felt he should have stayed in France to sustain his campaign, reinforced by an imprisonment equated with martyrdom. But he was not unaware that leaving Paris was itself a symbolic public act akin to Hugo's exiling himself in the Channel Islands after Napoleon III's *coup d'état* of 1851 and returning only when his regime collapsed.

As he had been on his 1893 visit to England, Zola was given crucial practical assistance from Ernest Vizetelly. After a first night at the Grosvenor Hotel, Zola was found accommodation near London: initially at the Oatlands Park Hotel, between Weybridge and Walton-on-Thames, then a detached villa ('Penn') in the vicinity and more permanently at the Queen's Hotel in the outer suburb of Upper Norwood. A memorializing 'Blue Plaque' today marks the spot. Alexandrine joined him there between 25 October and 5 December; she returned for a second visit on 22 December, staying this time for over two months – until 27 February 1899. Before her first visit (and with her blessing and practical help), Zola had organized for Jeanne, Denise and Jacques to come over to spend the 11 August–15 October period with him at 'Penn' (and then in another house, 'Summerfield', with a bigger garden for the children), dates which allowed them to go back to Paris ten days before Alexandrine arrived; they would do so again for the following Easter holidays (29 March–11 April 1899), decamping with him on this occasion to a hotel near the Crystal Palace. To detail these various movements is

Queen's Hotel, Upper Norwood, in the south London suburbs, June 1898.

to put into perspective all the letters written during these eleven months of exile in which Zola wrote of his loneliness.

A stream of high-profile visitors further relativized this much-lamented isolation as well as problematizing the very notion of the 'escapee' being out of sight of the French and British authorities: Desmoulin came on the day following Zola's arrival in England; the director of *Le Siècle*, Yves Guyot, who had published the first part of *L'Assommoir*, saw him on 22 October; Duret came often (8, 10 and 17 November); in 1899, Clemenceau came on 3 January and again in May; the writer Octave Mirbeau (1848–1917) and his wife at the beginning of February; Fasquelle, on the 11th of that month, taking back with him eight new chapters of *Fécondité* and returning for more of the same in May and on 1 June. Well might Zola ask, as early as 28 August 1898: 'Has anybody actually looked for me? I doubt it. Everybody is delighted that I'm out of the way' (*LA*, 324). He had been advised by his supporters that, from now on, he should avoid diverting attention from Dreyfus' own conviction. In a letter of 4 October, he admitted that 'everybody must know I'm in England, but nobody really wants me to return . . . not even bothering to look for me' (*LA*, 364).

Zola's major role in the Dreyfus Affair was effectively over. He was loath to acknowledge it. Immersing himself in the drafting of *Fécondité*, he nevertheless continued to brood on developments in Paris. Undercutting his thinking about developing his role, there is almost a sense of disappointment. But the latter is also tinged with a sense of relief. He would later nostalgically recall his year of exile as one when his work was not interrupted by other concerns. In fact, judging by his correspondence during it, Zola did not enjoy this second visit to England: its climate and food were equally depressing. He couldn't speak English and its grammar was beyond him: he could just about cope with the gist of articles in the London newspapers. Unlike his father, Zola was monoglot to the point of obstinacy: the English nanny briefly employed for Denise in 1895 had taught him nothing; friends visiting him in Upper Norwood tried in vain to interest him in learning the language with the aid of illustrated storybooks for children which he knew his daughter had so enjoyed. Instead, he asked Vizetelly, who had hoped he might read Oliver Goldsmith's *The Vicar of Wakefield*, to lend him four novels by Balzac (*Corr.*, IX, 252), a copy of *Les Caractères* (1688–94) by La Bruyère and Stendhal's *La Chartreuse de Parme* (1839) (*Corr.*, IX, 231).

The delicate strategies involved in organizing the alternating visits to London of Alexandrine and Jeanne took their toll. And this double life was emotionally exhausting by virtue of the duplicity involved: a mere three days before the arrival of Jeanne and his children in August 1898, Zola told Alexandrine that such was his 'appalling solitude' that he was thinking of sneaking back to Paris so they could resume their 'peaceful life together' (*LA*, 307). No less draining was his obsessive focus on the most prosaic of arrangements necessitated by his being away from home: in the lists of clothes and money which were to be sent from Paris; in asking Jeanne to bring with her his complete cycling outfit but (with characteristic seriousness) *not* her 'cook or chambermaid' (*Corr.*, IX, 242). On 7 May 1899 a weary Zola again talks about disappearing, this time to Médan: 'how happy I would be to find refuge there' (*LA*, 482). But the end of his disorientating experience was in sight. Once again, his movements were determined by events: one of the key figures confirming Dreyfus' supposed guilt, Armand du Paty de Clam (1853–1916), was arrested on 1 June, and on the 3rd, the government quashed Dreyfus' original 1894 conviction, thereby reinforcing Zola's sense that it was now safe to leave England. His delight was undisguised: he announced his return to France in a series of virtually identical letters on that day, to Desmoulin, Duret, Labori, Bruneau, Charpentier and Anatole France. To the last of these correspondents, he admitted that his exile had been 'hard' on him (*Corr.*, IX, 498).

Private Lives

On his return from England on 5 June 1899, Zola appeared to resume the existence he had led before the Dreyfus Affair. As far as the latter was concerned, Zola's judicial travails could be consigned to the background: served a writ on the day of his return to Paris, in relation to his July 1898 sentence, Zola's appeal against its implementation was followed on 23 November by the court's decision to indefinitely postpone it. Zola's house at Médan, so much missed during his exile, was even more central to his life than it had been before. He and his wife sustained the habit of living in the capital only during the winter, but this was less attractive than it had been. At the end of each summer, leaving Médan behind was rather dreaded. Stays there were increasingly extended as long as the weather held, and Christmas and Easter provided further pretexts to get away from the city. Médan had become a kind of refuge: until the end of his life, he was occasionally targeted by threatening demonstrations in the street below his Parisian address. He continued to welcome visitors to his country home. The guest list, however, was significantly different. The literary 'disciples' of the 1880s were no longer part of it. The vast majority of those coming out from Paris for the day, the weekend or longer were those who had been his most active supporters during the Dreyfus Affair.

Céard was one of those no longer welcomed: he had long ago tired of his dual role as go-between in Zola's emotional triangle and as factotum in securing documentation for his novels. An attempt at reconciliation over an awkward lunch in November 1897 had been a failure, as Zola wrote to an unsurprised Alexandrine: 'my residual affection is now dead. He no longer exists for us' (*LA*, 218).

Another previously regular guest who now no longer came was Cézanne. From the date Zola had purchased Médan until 1885, and in spite of Alexandrine's evident distaste for his person, he had made frequent and often extended visits, mainly in order to paint. His *Le Château de Médan* (1880, Burrell Collection, Glasgow), the painter having set up his easel across the river from Zola's property during a five-week stay in 1880, is only one example. For the best part of the last hundred years, there was a consensus that Cézanne had been so hurt by the parallels between himself and Zola's failed fictional artist in *L'Œuvre*, Claude Lantier, that a lifelong friendship had come to a definitive end as a result. That myth has not survived the discovery, in 2013, of an 1887 letter from Cézanne to Zola, the year *after* the publication of *L'Œuvre*.[5] There is no reason to doubt Cézanne's reported distress at the news of Zola's death in September 1902. It remains true that, for the personal reasons outlined in earlier chapters, this was a friendship that was unravelling long before. As important in explaining such a parting of the ways, however, is the fact that during the Dreyfus Affair, Zola and Cézanne were on opposite sides. Zola's involvement, his old friend thought, was further evidence of his pretentious self-importance. Another factor in the distancing between them was Cézanne's related adherence, inseparable from his anti-Dreyfusard positioning, to militant Catholicism. His return to orthodoxy dates from 1891, as Alexis felt bound to report to Zola that year. Given the latter's antipathy to religion, it is not difficult to imagine the painter's reaction to the denunciation in the Catholic press of both *Lourdes* and *Rome*.

The more intimate complications of Zola's private life had been resolved in the sense that, as evidenced by Alexandrine's attitude towards his other family's visits to him during his exile in England, a compromise had been reached. During the two years between Alexandrine's enraged discovery of Zola's liaison and 1893, the possibility of divorce, or at least legal separation, had seemed the only way to bring to a conclusion a succession of marital crises depressing both parties. Jeanne was well aware of this. But Zola had written to her in August 1892 expressing his reluctance to corrode their love with the 'remorse' he would feel if he and Alexandrine were to part (*LR*, 55).

He was not averse in principle to such a denouement. Asked in 1901 about his views on divorce, legalized in France since 1884, Zola was at pains to stress that he believed that marriage was an indissoluble bond only between a couple in undying love and, significantly, who had children. At Médan in the summer of 1893, however, the marital drama had again become unbearable: Alexandrine started to pack her bags, with Zola apparently unconcerned, much to the angry disapproval of Céard, who was also there at the time, berating Zola for his treatment of 'this woman who had shared with him the impoverished years of the past and who, now that he was rich, was being thrown mercilessly out of his house'.[6] The energizing visit to London that autumn had provided only a temporary respite from their mutual anguish. Alexandrine's own official welcome there had brought home to her how much she had to lose were she to forfeit her social identity as 'Madame Zola'. But, for Zola too, a definitive separation would have damaged the much-sought public perception of his respectability. To be officially at his side, as he wrote to Alexandrine on 3 November 1897, was her 'legitimate place . . . testifying to thirty years of tenderness and devotion' (*LA*, 221).

Despite Zola's characteristic discretion, his correspondence can be read between the lines: when, a couple of months after returning from London, he conveyed his best wishes to Alexis' sister, on her marriage, his 'May she be happy! Which is not easy!' (*Corr.*, VIII, 94) is poignantly far from the platitude it might seem. The public mask slipped a lot further in a letter to Jacques van Santen Kolff in March 1894. To the critic to whom Zola had imparted more insights into his writing than to any other, he confessed that he had been so engulfed by a 'long crisis of physical and moral suffering' (*Corr.*, VIII, 125) that he had been unable to reply to his many enquiries about his current literary projects. But even before the visit to London, Edmond de Goncourt's journal entry for 14 May 1893 records Daudet having seen 'a miserable Mme Zola taking out for a walk the two children her husband had had with her chambermaid'.[7] On these excursions in Paris with Zola's (somewhat overawed) offspring, she was often accompanied by their father. However pragmatic a way forward, this did little to reconcile her to her husband's ongoing infidelity.

Zola and his wife Alexandrine (after 1894).

As she reminded Zola in a letter of 7 August 1898, his hopes that her happiness would be restored were in vain: she would never recover from the destruction of it by the discovery of his liaison with Jeanne on 10 November 1891. But this was written to Zola just after he had left for England, and bitterness and regret were balanced by a commitment to support both him and those she loved – which now included Denise and Jacques. His letters to her during his exile can be compared with those to Jeanne: in those to the mother of his children, the Dreyfus Affair is in the background; much of his correspondence with his more politically informed wife, supported in Paris by his friends and associates, reads like a detailed commentary on the progress of the Affair. It was nevertheless punctuated by renewed instances of upsetting interchanges: it needed only oblique confirmation that Jeanne had been present when Zola had met one of his friends for Alexandrine to refer bitterly to what she had suffered as a result of his liaison. But their common focus on the Dreyfus Affair was a balm. It was paradoxically during their enforced separation for most of the months between July 1898 and June 1899 that Zola and Alexandrine's relationship, on a footing of solidarity and mutual respect, was closer than it had been for over a decade.

The boxing and coxing involved in organizing separate visits to his London exile of Alexandrine, on the one hand, and Jeanne and their two children, on the other, provided a template for the years ahead. It would be operative until his death. While Alexandrine had continued to see the children during his absence, the dignified compromise arrived at was that she and Jeanne should inhabit entirely separate spheres: literally, in time and place, but also in the two women never even mentioning the name of the other. And this was extended to Zola's own interactions with them both. Unlike in *Pot-Bouille*, where wife and mistress live knowingly under the same roof, Zola had to ensure that his two 'marital' lives remained compartmentalized. Emblematic, of course, were the public and private dedications of *Le Docteur Pascal* mentioned earlier. But if Alexandrine read this patently autobiographical novel, she would have had no doubt about what Jeanne Rozerot meant to Zola. The elderly doctor of the novel is overcome by an irresistible urge to renew his sexual life. And the descriptions of his and Clotilde's lovemaking are of an unmistakeably lived erotic intensity.

Whether or not the arrangement mitigated hurt and jealousy, its transparency allowed Zola, in his own mind at least, to sustain a measure of self-deception. His letters from England to Jeanne and Alexandrine address both of them as 'my dear wife' although, in those to the former, 'adored' is inserted within the greeting. What they have in common is concern for his two children. They are nevertheless different in tone: to his mistress, there are expressions of longing which must have been closer to the presumably passionate early letters to her which Alexandrine had destroyed; those to his real wife dutifully declare how much he was missing her, together with worries about her health, but are mainly concerned with practical matters: the banal details of his own daily life; minutely elaborated instructions in respect of her travel arrangements and by what precise means she should organize communications to reach him undetected by the French authorities.

Sustaining this double life was only marginally less complicated now that Zola was back in France. At official occasions or in the full glare of publicity, such as his regular visits to the theatre, Alexandrine would accompany him, as she had done on his visits to London, Lourdes and Rome. But when he was less visible, Jeanne could take advantage of such freedom, in the same way as she had joined Zola in Le Havre and Rouen during his research trip for *La Bête humaine* in March 1889, three months after they had become lovers. In Paris, he had set up Jeanne and the children within reach: in 1893, in the rue Taitbout; in 1897, she moved to no. 3, rue du Havre, a shorter walk from the rue de Bruxelles, where Zola and Alexandrine lived. The annual rent of 4,000 francs for rue du Havre seemed to Zola, so he told Alexandrine, who tried to help by sending him from Rome a list of vacancies advertised in *Le Figaro*, to be exorbitant. But he had spent weeks looking for something suitable: he was searching, he told her, for an address which reduced the chances of her unwittingly bumping into his children's mother; he wanted to ensure that Denise and Jacques each had comparable views from their windows. But in telling his wife that he was seeking an apartment with *three* bedrooms, Zola could hardly have been more explicit. During summers in the countryside, Jeanne lived first at Cheverchemont, near Alexis' home in Triel. This was over 4 kilometres (2½ mi.) from Médan, and legend has it that Zola acquired a telescope through which he could espy his family at a distance. From 1892 onwards, he rented for them a substantial house, with a live-in concierge, at Verneuil-sur-Seine, more conveniently close to his own *résidence secondaire*. He secured a maid for Jeanne in Paris and a cook at Verneuil, as well as providing her with a yearly income of 6,000 francs.

He could well afford to finance these responsibilities, even allowing for the expenses incurred by two residences of his own and a staff of four domestic servants (a married couple who acted as valet and cook, a coachman and a chambermaid) in addition to two gardeners. He was a benevolent employer, judging by his reports to Alexandrine detailing

Zola with his family at Verneuil-sur-Seine, 1890s.

extra days off he had allowed so they could visit relatives and treating all of them to an evening at the theatre. But he also regularly gave his wife accounts of the domestic tasks that they had completed to his satisfaction. In 1881 there had been half as many waiting hand and foot on the Zolas. By 1896 he had indeed become the 'respectable bourgeois' he had proclaimed himself to be in the preface to *L'Assommoir*. For Cézanne, this was another reason for their estrangement: 'I no longer felt comfortable . . . with his carpets and surrounded by servants, it was like calling on a government minister.'[8]

Speculation about Zola's revenues from his writing had increased at the same pace as his private wealth. In *Le Figaro* of 8 September 1892, a journalist calculated that the *Rougon-Macquart* alone (including the imminent *Le Docteur Pascal*) would have earnt Zola around 1.5 million francs. His income from all sources in any one year varied depending on sales of a particular novel, serialization and translation rights and his journalistic contracts. There is a consensus that Ernest Vizetelly had it about right when he arrived in 1897 at the estimate of Zola's average annual income as being between 150,000 and 200,000 francs, only meaningful in comparative terms: a doctor at the time would be earning 6,000–15,000 francs a year, while the head of a large commercial or industrial company might secure a salary of 60,000 francs).[9] Zola was not as rich as his detractors insidiously suggested. He had certainly come a long way since the 60 francs a month he was earning while working for the Paris Docks in 1860. Putting behind them the impoverishment of their early years together, however, both Zola and his wife were big spenders: his letters to her are much concerned with bills, whether for coal or domestic repairs, on top of the annual rent of almost 9,000 francs for their Paris home in the rue de Bruxelles.

More difficult to quantify is the emotional cost to all those involved in Zola's double life. What Jeanne felt about the situation can only be inferred from Zola's letters trying to comfort her in her loneliness, out of sight as she was mostly forced to remain. This isolation was not as absolute as he lamented on her behalf: they had been spotted together out walking, and in a note of 24 October 1896, arranging to meet Desmoulin for dinner at the Café de la Paix, Zola alerted him that he would be 'accompanied' (*Corr.*, VIII, 360). He himself was less sanguine than might have been guessed by observers of his daily routine and public life. He wished, he wrote to Jeanne in the summer of 1893, that he could have had his life again, in a loving relationship and as a proper father teaching his children how to build sandcastles on the beach. There is hardly a letter to Jeanne during the last decade or so of Zola's life which does not include such sentiments, and he sometimes inserted an extra note to be read aloud to Denise and Jacques. Even in the midst of his London apotheosis (what he called 'ma gloire'), he was writing to Jeanne to express his regret that the three people he loved the most could not share it with him. From Rome too, in 1894, he had kept her abreast of his latest social triumphs as well as boring moments, both leaving him utterly exhausted.

With the wisdom of hindsight, it is possible to discern the strategies of a double life in admissions of work postponed and apologies for absence in the afternoons; or to decode the elation conveyed to Charpentier on 27 August 1889, coinciding with the final stages of Jeanne's first pregnancy: 'I am in tremendous form, and I feel as I did in my twenties' (*Corr.*, VI, 414). Zola's letters to Jeanne herself over the following years can also be decoded: there is no mistaking the joy inspired by the renewal (or, more likely, the belated discovery) of sexual pleasure. He writes of his impatience to hold his 'darling' in his arms, and frustration that a recent visit had been cut short by Alexis' inopportune, if well-meaning, arrival at their Verneuil love nest. In a letter of 7 May 1899, more than ten years into their relationship, Zola dreams of delicious meals prepared by her cordon bleu cook, partaken together 'like young lovers' (*LR*, 340). He is haunted by nostalgia for their intimate time together in Normandy a decade earlier. He is overwhelmed by the fleeting sight, from his train, of her lighted window at Cheverchemont, and by nervous impatience when not hearing from her. But Zola's letters also suggest the inner turmoil which he occasionally confessed to others: days when he found it impossible to work as a result of the 'situation', and misgivings as to whether it could be sustained. As he wrote to Jeanne on 13 July 1894, 'I am not happy. This sharing, this double life that I am forced to endure will drive me to despair . . . I had dreamt of making everybody around me happy, but I can see that that is impossible' (*LR*, 150).

Notwithstanding the *modus vivendi*, Zola's moral values were inconsistent with such pragmatism. He was deeply troubled by his visits to Jeanne being clandestine. Adultery, as presented in his fiction, is always a subject of opprobrium. In Paris, he would arrive at her apartment towards the end of nearly every afternoon on the pretext of seeing his children. This routine was less fraught during the autumn months: after her visit to Rome with her husband in 1894, Alexandrine had adopted the habit of going to Italy for an annual autumn stay (every year between 1895 and

Zola with Jeanne Rozerot in her garden at Verneuil-sur-Seine, 1890s.

1901, with the exception of the period Zola was in exile in London), often extended until the beginning of December, both to develop friendships there and for the benefit of her chronic bronchitis and rheumatism. Zola was sceptical whether the treatment she received in various spas prior to going on to Rome (initially in Tivoli, but especially the waters of Salsomaggiore, near Parma) was effective. But he was supportive, expressing his pleasure that it was doing her good.

The sentimentality of the private correspondence between Zola and his wife during her absences was enhanced by the two-way enclosure of flower petals, Zola's having been picked by Denise at Verneuil or brought to him in Paris every week from the garden at Médan. These letters reveal a Zola utterly different from his public profile. Nearly every one of them includes a report, inordinately mawkish even for a childless couple, on their little dogs: wagging tails greeting the writer's return; cuddled for warmth; happy or sad; apparently longing for Alexandrine's return; and when one of them died, he told her that he had hastened to see his children in order to overcome his grief. Reports on his own health are as detailed: fatigue, poor sleep, restorative early nights (without specifying where), indigestion. In that last respect, the menu of every meal, either alone or with friends, is subject to critical commentary. And what comes across most forcibly is an anxiety effectively hidden during his external activities but resurgent in introspective brooding: about his wife's own health and that of others afflicted by accident or disease ('everybody seems to be ill at the moment,' he wrote in October 1897 (*LA*, 212)); when not hearing from her when the post was delayed, threatening to lodge an official complaint if the 24-hour service between Rome and Paris was not functioning as it should. Zola's long letters to Alexandrine unfailingly apologize for the lack of interesting news and then proceed to be filled with snippets intended to distract her: progress made in his writing, visits and visitors, the cost of the latest photographic equipment he was tempted to buy, the changing weather. The impression conveyed was of life at home continuing as normal. Given that his wife's absence had removed the constraints of being with Jeanne, Zola's stress on his miserable bachelor-like existence is almost devious. It remains true, however, that his loneliness is a major theme of his private correspondence with *both* Alexandrine and Jeanne, and it cannot be too easily dismissed as either self-pity or duplicitous strategy. His visits to Jeanne notwithstanding, there is a sense in which Zola's isolation in his apartment effectively excluded him from the comforts of 'normal' marital co-habitation, unable to bring his double life into a single domestic and emotional structure.

On the other hand, Alexandrine should not hesitate, he regularly advised, to delay her return if she was enjoying herself. She was in Italy, he stressed, to 'forget your sadness', even though he acknowledged that it was 'incurable' (*LA*, 87, 193). Like those of Jeanne, the substance and tone of Alexandrine's replies to his daily letters can only be deduced from Zola's side of the correspondence. It is clear, however, that every time he alluded to ways in which her Italian stays might be 'consoling' or referred to their life in the past or future ('till death do us part'), the unintended effect was to reawaken her suffering. So as not to reopen 'the wound still within you' (*LA*, 98), Zola promised to avoid raising such sensitive issues, instead filling his letters with news about everything except, of course, his visits to Jeanne herself: these were disguised by details of his excursions with his children on their free Tuesday and Friday afternoons or, less frequently, on public holidays – showing them the splendours of the capital, taking them to the Bois de Boulogne, museums and pantomimes. Reports on their health and educational progress jostled with concern that their secret existence meant they had no playmates; on the few occasions when they had, notably with their cousins (Jeanne's sister's three children of the same age), he forsook his time with them. Much appreciative space was devoted to the thoughtful presents for Denise and Jacques that his wife was engaged in buying in Rome, amid exchanges of views about whether her other many shopping activities were value for money. Equally sincere was Zola's gratitude, in November 1895, for Alexandrine having picked flowers around his parents' tomb in Aix as a souvenir for him, a gesture for which he was 'touched beyond measure' (*LA*, 74).

To further assuage Alexandrine's relapses into misery, he arranged to be with her in the Midi for a few days so that they could return to Paris together at the end of her 1896 stay. But while in Aix with her at the very end of October, the fact that he found a way to write three letters to Jeanne, telling her how he missed her, tells us more about his true feelings. Those in the know remarked how relaxed he suddenly seemed while Alexandrine was away. But his letters might be thought a trifle disingenuous. Writing to his wife on 11 November 1897, his looking forward to her imminent return from Italy and reassurance about her permanent place in his heart are hedged by the admission that 'I don't think I will ever be happy again, because this splitting of my affections is as painful for me as it must be for you in imagining that you've been abandoned' (*LA*, 83).

Apart from these absences of Alexandrine, it was during the summers that Zola's double life was somewhat easier to manage. In setting up Jeanne and the children at Verneuil, he had established alongside Médan a complementary social world. It was one, moreover, which fortuitously filled the gap noted by Edmond de Goncourt, with an insight surprising for a confirmed bachelor, when he had visited Zola's 'absurd' residence outside the capital in 1882: 'a Parisian home doesn't need children, but a country house does.'[10] Habitués of Verneuil after 1897 included, along with their two children, the industrialist Louis Triouleyre (1858–1941) and his wife Hortense (1856–1921), whose joint support for Jeanne was as solid as that of Alexis and his own family. To Zola's dismay, Alexis had been forced by Alexandrine to choose between the two households. She had so insisted on this that when, during her absence in Italy in November 1895, Zola had seen him, he felt it necessary to confess his guilt at having allowed into his home one of 'those people you dislike' (*LA*, 75). Only in 1901, after the deaths of both their parents, would the orphaned Alexis children be exempted from this proscription.

As well as more transient visitors, Médan regularly brought together, sometimes for a week or more, Desmoulin and his wife as well as the Bruneaus, Labordes and Charpentiers. There, fine weather saw them playing boules, boating and swimming or taking long walks along the banks of the Seine. Rainy days confined them to the billiard room or the chessboard. Zola could not be extracted from his study until lunchtime. After his siesta, extended until four o'clock, he would disappear in order to see his family, returning to Médan in time to host his guests at dinner. At Verneuil, he delighted in playing with his children in the house's large garden, teaching them how to ride a bike and taking them out on the river. Detained in Paris in May 1899, Zola's one wish, he wrote to Jeanne, was to be there so that the four of them could hop on their bicycles. With Jeanne herself, his rides through the surrounding countryside are evoked in *Paris*: sharing a 'coup de foudre', the fictional Pierre and Marie take turns to lead the way before ending up rhythmically side by side, 'intoxicated by the joyous speeding taking their breath away' (OC, VII, 1448). For Zola and his lover, such physical 'exercise' *à deux* was clearly mutually satisfying.

Zola's own newfound enthusiasm for cycling made the transit to and from his family that much easier. In *Paris*, the characters articulate his own interest in improvements to initially primitive contraptions. They also celebrate the exciting possibilities of this means of transport, including the emancipation of women from their habitually constraining apparel, setting off in their long shorts 'with the exuberance of schoolchildren let loose to take in the fresh air' (OC, VII, 1417). Zola's support for it had even been the subject of an article in the *Gil Blas* in June 1893. While publicly professing to be a mediocre cyclist, he often rode with Desmoulin in the Bois de Boulogne; he was capable of covering considerable distances, even the 28 kilometres (17½ mi.) from Médan to central Paris, and one of the first things he did on arriving in England in 1898 was to buy a bicycle to allow him to explore his new surroundings.

Cycling was also an activity good for the figure of a man 170 centimetres (5 ft 7 in.) in height who, after the success of *L'Assommoir*, had grown progressively fatter, weighing 96 kilograms (212 lb) by 1887; at the theatre that November, he could hardly squeeze his 114-centimetre (45 in.) girth into his seat. It seems hardly a coincidence that it was just before the start of his relationship with Jeanne that a diet put an end to such ballooning: by 1896 he had reduced his weight to 80 kilograms (176 lb), but not without difficulty. In his diary entry for 4 March 1888, Edmond de Goncourt recorded his amazement at how much weight Zola had lost, so that his face had 'begun to resemble once again his portrait by Manet'; however, barely seven months later, Zola's having (inevitably) put all those kilos back on inspired another entry, in the

Jeanne Rozerot on her bicycle, 1890s.

meeting of a person so unrecognizable that his face no longer 'looks like the one in Manet's portrait which he had momentarily regained'.[11]

Much of the visual evidence of Zola's private life is provided by the other great passion of his later years: photography. It became so all-consuming that he found that it prevented him from getting on with his writing. His interest in it dates from 1888, the year he began his relationship with Jeanne, perhaps reflecting a need to capture her image in the advance knowledge that they would often be apart. It was in 1894–5 that he really devoted much of his time to producing what eventually amounted to a collection of some 7,000 photographs. This was facilitated by the building of a darkroom, in the spring of 1895, in the basement of his house at Médan, as well as organizing similar spaces in Jeanne's house at Verneuil and at his Paris address. He had a dozen cameras, updating them with each successive technical innovation available on the market. His letters are replete with critical comparisons of lenses made by Kodak or Leica, details about photographic plates, the possibilities of enlargement and different kinds of paper used for the optimal development of his negatives. And he scrupulously recorded the exposure times and lighting of each of the last, with a view to subsequent experimentation. Zola was singularly adept in embracing what was then a revolutionary art form. His photographs of Parisian sights, Roman monuments, suburban London streets and the pavilions of the Paris Exposition of 1900 are of professional quality.

The most beautiful of his photographs are now available in a magnificently produced volume. These include not only his urban compositions, but pictures of Alexandrine and life at Médan in the 1890s. Many of them are self-portraits, exploiting the remote button he acquired. But the appropriateness of the volume's subtitle, *Une page d'amour*,[12] resides in Zola's movingly personal photographs of Jeanne and, especially, of his two children. Denise and Jacques are captured at Verneuil in images of unselfconscious curiosity as well as reflective intelligence. Their timid but warm smiles back at the paternal camera lens, patiently enduring

Zola in the 1880s.

necessarily long poses, tell us more than any letter or memoir about Zola's relationship with his children and the intensity of their mutual affection.

Alongside such celebrations of the next generation, these same years after the completion of the *Rougon-Macquart* saw the inevitable passing of members of Zola's own generation or of those who had shaped his career: Flaubert, Manet, Lucas and Littré had all died in the 1880s; Taine died in 1893; on 8 July of that year, two days after Maupassant's death, he gave the funeral oration; in his capacity as president of the Société des gens de lettres, he delivered those for Dumas *fils* in 1895 and for Arsène Houssaye and Edmond de Goncourt in 1896. Van Santen Kolff also died in 1896 and in December 1897, at Daudet's graveside, Zola paid tribute to him both as the writer and as one of his oldest friends. Valabrègue died in July 1900, aged 55; to his widow, Zola granted permission to publish, in a posthumous collection of his verse, fragments of their correspondence in 1864–5. A further reminder of his Aixois years had been news of the death of Cézanne's mother in October 1897, prompting the reflection that 'there's another part of my distant past which has gone' (*LA*, 210).

Zola with his two children, Denise (left) and Jacques, *c.* 1902.

Zola and Paul Alexis at Jeanne's house, Verneuil-sur-Seine (after 1892).

Among this cohort of the deceased, the most mourned was Alexis, Zola's loyal colleague over thirty years but also part of his extended family: Zola was a witness at his wedding in 1888 as Alexis had been at his own in 1870; he was the godfather of Alexis' eldest daughter, Paule-Alexandrine; Alexis and his wife were the godparents, respectively, of Zola's son and daughter, and thus, from the summers of 1889 onwards, they were regularly part of Jeanne's household, sometimes staying with her and Denise and Jacques for weeks on end. When Alexis' wife died in agony on 31 May 1900, as a result of contracting typhoid while caring for Paule-Alexandrine, Zola shared his distress, urging him to find consolation in his two surviving children (another daughter, Marthe, had died in 1890 aged six months). But when Alexis himself died barely a year later, Zola could hardly bring himself to say more than a few words at his burial in the Triel cemetery on 31 July 1901. In acknowledging that Alexis had written relatively little, Zola passed over a long-held view of his indurated laziness. And he made no mention of course of an obsessive womanizing on which the portrait of Trublot in *Pot-Bouille* is based. Instead, he remembered Alexis as one of the last of the companions of Médan in the 1880s: 'Flaubert gone!

Goncourt, Maupassant, Daudet, all dead! It was your turn, Alexis, to depart' (*OC*, XII, 726). Of all of them, he implied, Alexis was closest to his heart. As Zola wrote a week later, in thanking a correspondent who had sent condolences on his loss: 'I am indeed intensely sad, for it's yet another part of my former life which has gone forever. Bit by bit, I am becoming the only remaining member of our literary group' (*Corr.*, X, 301).

Without ascribing a direct correlation between his private and public moods, there is a sense in which their patterning, alternating between optimism and despair, corresponds to that of his fiction. On the one hand, this is true of his personal life: set against his reinvigorating relationship with Jeanne are the tensions of his marriage, and the deaths of friends and colleagues reinforced an isolation reflected in the increasingly anachronistic status of the aesthetic principles underlying the *Rougon-Macquart*. On the other, countering his proselytizing hopes for the new century in *Les Trois Villes* and *Les Quatre Évangiles*, the Dreyfus Affair disappointingly dragging on seemed to him to confirm his foreboding about the symptomatic and terminal degradation evidenced by the *fin de siècle*.

A Life and Work Reframed: The Mirrors of *Vérité*

The novel of the series most obviously indexing the Dreyfus Affair is *Vérité*, the last of *Les Quatre Évangiles* completed before Zola's death. *Justice* was to be its concluding and rousing sequel. In his notes for this final volume, Zola cited from the text of *Vérité*, within a retrospective summary of French history since the Franco-Prussian War which had underpinned, he stressed, the discourse of both *Les Trois Villes* and *Les Quatre Évangiles*. In that sense, the shadow of 1870–71 extends beyond the *Rougon-Macquart*. These notes also testify to Zola's ambition to end this second series by widening his vision: 'Start from the end of *Vérité* – the family regenerated, the *cité* [the ideal social structure] established, the nation reconstituted, and now humanity.' There is a doomsday urgency to the call for the renewal of France's historic mission: its dissemination of the universal Rights of Man heralded by the French Revolution. Zola describes the successive crises of the century as its 'calvaire douloureux', its Calvary of suffering since 1789 prior to national resurrection; it would then be the 'messianic' exemplar for every country on earth. 'For *Justice*,' he wrote, 'reiterate what I've said before: "the France of the Revolution will one day give the world Justice, as it has already given it Liberty"' (*OC*, VIII, 1519).

In the midst of this panegyric dedicated to his country's exceptionality, the clearest echo of *Vérité* is Zola's statement, in thinking about *Justice*, that 'France has been saved from dying by education.' For *Vérité*'s hero, Marc Froment, is a teacher in an elementary school. He personifies Zola's own pedagogic role, throughout his fiction and journalism but nowhere more visible than in his efforts to dispel the ignorance at the heart of the Dreyfus Affair. His aesthetic priority had always been that his novels should be 'true to life'. But, in Zola's interventions in the public sphere, the notion of 'truth' is not limited to that of fictional verisimilitude: it increasingly assumes an ethical dimension. As mentioned earlier, some of the texts generated by his involvement in the Affair would be republished in 1901 under the heading of *La Vérité en marche*. It is a recurrent theme of his writing from 1897 onwards that 'the Truth will out.'

Emblematic of that dimension of his role in the Dreyfus Affair was the painting given to him to commemorate it: *La Vérité sortant du puits* (Truth Emerging from the Well, 1898, Musée de l'Hôtel de Ville d'Amboise) by Édouard Debat-Ponsan (1847–1913). At Zola's funeral, *Le Temps* of 6 October 1902 made a point of reporting that it could be seen in the entrance hall of his Paris residence. Exhibited at the Salon of 1898, the painting was purchased by public subscription and given to Zola, and in his letter of thanks, dated 6 December 1900, Zola used the phrase which posterity would associate with his name: 'La Vérité est en marche et rien ne l'arrêtera' (Truth is on the march and nothing will stop its advance). The very title of the third of the *Quatre Évangiles*, *Vérité*, points to this conviction. That same commitment is echoed in the closing lines of 'J'accuse': 'This action on my part is only a revolutionary means to hasten the explosion of the truth.' This was the only part of the text which President Faure underlined on his own copy of it.

The scope of *Vérité* is far from being limited to the Dreyfus Affair. It also gives fuller vent to the antipathy towards the Catholic Church which characterizes *Lourdes* and *Rome*. Zola had every reason to do so, the Church having reinforced its condemnation of those two novels by inevitably siding with other reactionary anti-Dreyfusard forces. At the same time, however, Marc's profession, and his symbolic act of removing the crucifix from his classroom wall, allow Zola to underline another of his abiding preoccupations: the Church's irreconcilable opposition to the secularization of French schools – statutorily in place since Jules Ferry's Education Act of 1882 – had dealt a major blow to Catholic influence in national life. In the previously cited 1877 article recalling his schooldays,

Édouard Debat-Ponsan, *La Vérité sortant du puits*, 1898, oil on canvas.

its decline – already evident in the 1850s – had been welcomed by Zola. But throughout the second half of the century, the legislative separation of Church and State remained the subject of debate.

At the point Zola was still hesitating over whether to get directly involved in the Dreyfus Affair, he told his wife that the drama was so engaging that 'perhaps one day' it would make a 'splendid work' (*LA*, 252). That *Vérité* ultimately fails to live up to this ambition is the result of its trying to accommodate the very much larger range of contemporary issues mentioned above. As Zola admitted to Alexandrine in a letter of 28 October 1901, he was aware that the first part of the novel was far too long; he hoped to make compensatory cuts as his writing progressed but he was uncomfortably aware of the difficulties posed by the sheer number of its characters and imbricated subplots: 'trying to include so much', he told her, 'requires a huge effort to ensure I don't lose my way' (*LA*, 212).

The plot of *Vérité* revolves around Marc's ultimately successful quest to prove the innocence of his imprisoned colleague, Monsieur Simon, falsely accused of the rape and murder of his nephew. Many of Zola's fellow combatants regretted that the novel's excessively wide purview relegated the place of the Dreyfus Affair to that of a mere analogy. There has been a contrary critical tendency to reduce the entire text to an indirect transposition of it. Less remarked, however, is that even the analogies with the Affair are virtually submerged by a supplementary level of what Zola himself termed its 'complications', as he wrote to a correspondent shortly before starting work on a novel 'complicated to construct because it embraces a whole world. I've never before had to deal with so enormous a subject' (*Corr.*, X, 295).

As far as the novel's historical frame of reference is concerned, the parallels between the plot of *Vérité* and the Dreyfus Affair are mostly transparent. Zola was keen to emphasize that not once in the novel is Alfred Dreyfus named. Unlike in the latter's case, the alleged crime is not that of spying for a foreign power, and the supposed perpetrator is scapegoated by the Church rather than by conservative politicians and the French army. The analogies which can be located within the profusion of themes of *Vérité* nevertheless remain clear-cut, confirmed in Zola's preparatory notes for the novel. Thus some of the minor characters play roles akin to those of the protagonists in the Affair; the fictional David is as determined to prove his younger brother's innocence as Mathieu Dreyfus, likewise having given up his business interests to continue to do so; the figure of Delbos is the target of scurrilous gossip amounting to a 'moral assassination' (*OC*, VIII, 1333), as Dreyfus' and Zola's defence lawyer, Fernand Labori, had been the intended victim of a bullet at the Rennes hearing of August 1899; and various of the novel's colluding priests are based on particular generals implicated in the Affair. The victim of the miscarriage of justice, Simon, is Jewish; he physically resembles the man at the centre of the Affair, not least during his appearance in court; he too cuts a pathetic figure, hollowed out by a brutal captivity which draws on Alfred Dreyfus' own painful reminiscences, brought out in 1901 by Zola's own publisher as *Cinq années de ma vie* (Five Years of My Life) during the year the novelist was writing *Vérité*.

The conspiracy to confirm Simon's guilt is systematically abetted by a hierarchy of officials unscrupulously falsifying evidence and strategically inciting the rage of the local populace. In the novel, that hierarchy is ecclesiastical, from bishops all the way down to the village priest, and when the identity of the real criminal is finally revealed, vindicating Marc's campaign, the Church is as effectively discredited as the military authorities had been in the Dreyfus Affair, itself now terminally confined to the past. That, at least, was Zola's optimistic perception at the moment he sent off the manuscript of *Vérité* to his publishers. The close of the novel celebrates Simon's complete rehabilitation, 'triumphant . . . after so many years of suffering' (*OC*, VIII, 1463). Alfred Dreyfus' own would be postponed until 1906.

Vérité also afforded Zola the opportunity to reflect, two years after his return from England, on his own role in the Dreyfus Affair. He began writing it on 27 July 1901. The distance between the most decisive stages of the Affair and Zola's retrospective thinking was partly closed by moments when he relived it: by recourse to notes he had made three years earlier; his sharing these on 18 October with Joseph Reinach (1856–1921), then engaged on his monumental (six-volume) history of the Affair; and a visit by Dreyfus himself on 31 October. Two days earlier, Alfred's brother had alerted Zola to the possibility that the judges at the Rennes trial (the 'bandits', as Zola termed them in his report to his wife of the conversation (*LA*, 714)) had been privy to the same kind of secret information as had been withheld from defence lawyers at Dreyfus' 1894 court martial. Zola noted that there was no proof of this as yet – nor was there ever. But almost word for word, this interchange is rehearsed in *Vérité*, in the meeting between Marc and David.

As well as having been struck, as Zola had admitted to Alexandrine before actively engaging in it, by the inherently aesthetic and artistically exploitable dimensions of the Dreyfus Affair, there are passages in 'J'accuse' in which its protagonists are conceived in novelistic terms. His penned portrait of Paty de Clam, for example, makes of the senior officer most savagely targeted by Zola a villain straight out of his fiction: this 'woolly minded . . . diabolical agent of the Affair' was 'obsessed by imagined plots . . . stolen documents . . . clandestine meetings . . . mysterious women . . . prey to occultism and communicating with the dead' (*Corr.*, IX, 134–6). In a set of notes not intended for publication, probably written in December 1900, Zola had reflected that only a 'supremely talented dramatist could have invented the Dreyfus Affair's narrative rhythms of suspended expectation and *coups de théâtre*' (OC, XIV, 1548). But apart from the overlaid issues which tend to obscure the unfolding of such a drama in *Vérité*, there is another reason why Zola fails to give the novel such a satisfying structure: his ceding to the temptation to include himself as one of the principal heroes in its story.

It was inevitable that he should do so. Zola's novelistic conception of his experience during the Affair was arrived at long before projecting it in *Vérité*. Even at the time, it was conceived within the story of his life as a 'chapter' in its own right. Its plotting was such that he was himself almost a fictional character in a drama likened to a thriller or detective novel. This is clearest during his exile in England: in his paranoid elaboration of false trails, ludicrously transparent pseudonyms ('Monsieur Pascal' (*LR*, 201)), repeated changes of address to shake off his imagined pursuers and convoluted precautionary instructions to intermediaries to ensure they were not followed when engaged on errands on his behalf. Most revealing is a letter of 11 December 1898: he was so fed up that he only rejected the idea of moving to Italy because 'it would deprive my exile of its significance and aesthetic unity' (*LA*, 390).

As historians of the Affair concur, there were a number of heroes on Dreyfus' side, notably Picquart and Mathieu Dreyfus, both of them sacrificing their personal and professional lives during the Affair. In *Vérité*, mirroring that of Alfred's brother, the figure of David is characterized by his 'heroic tenacity' (OC, VIII, 1142). But this accolade is mainly reserved for Marc. That he functions as Zola's double is evident from the preparatory notes for the novel: Marc's role, like Zola's, was to be the *justicier* (the seeker after justice) (*Ms* 10344, fol. 566). In grappling with an epic subject, 'the greatest injustice of the century' (p. 1104), Marc adopts Zola's own well-tried methodology, 'classifying all the information he had secured' (p. 1033), and the latter is the factual basis of an 'experimental truth' (p. 1033). That is itself ranged against the 'lack of verisimilitude' in the 'fairy tales' (p. 1059) of his antagonists. By contrast, it is through 'logic' (p. 1033) that Marc works through hypotheses in order to elucidate the mystery at the heart of the Simon Affair. As a wordsmith, his pedagogic gifts include transforming the complexities of grammar and mathematics into 'stories' equated with 'masterpieces' (p. 1034). And he has to face the criticism (from official inspectors of his work) of 'substituting your fantasies for the wisdom of your senior colleagues' (p. 1151).

Marc's involvement in the campaign to rectify a 'monstrous' judicial error progresses as Zola's had done: from curiosity to hesitation, and from prudent uncertainty to resolute commitment. In Geneviève's comforting presence while her husband acts upon his conviction, and in her 'marvellous support' for him (p. 1144), Zola pays tribute to both Alexandrine and Jeanne. He also alluded in the novel to Judet's libellous articles on François Zola, displacing the allegations so as to make Delbos the victim of them: 'a shamefully travestied story, from half a century ago, of the lawyer's father ... having been accused of theft' (p. 1333). This unfounded gossip is so ridiculed as to make of this autobiographical parenthesis in *Vérité* an appendix to his letter of 2 October 1898 to Alexandrine:

> to have been attacked in so cowardly a manner through my father ... makes me feel that I am paying too high a price for a victory in which I no longer believe. I've had enough. This disinterment of my poor father's tomb has got to stop. One day, I am going to avenge him. (*LA*, 361)

In due course, in the essays of 1898–1900 devoted to his father with which my Chapter One began, Zola would do just that. But the reasons for doing so, to restore 'the truth' and achieve 'justice' for his father, are couched in this same letter in the very terms thematized in *Vérité*. His 'innocent' father too, in Zola's eyes, had been the victim of the calumny and conspiracy of which Dreyfus was a more public example.

Once committed to his role, Marc is driven by 'his passion for truth', 'forcing' everybody to acknowledge it. Its motivation is the imperative of 'conquest' (p. 1109) akin to that of another of Zola's alter egos, Claude Lantier, in *L'Œuvre*. Such is Zola's identification with Marc that he cannot resist indulging in an idealizing self-portrait of 'power' directed by 'energy and intelligent willpower' (p. 1105): 'a heroic defender of innocence' (p. 1149), 'an apostle of truth' (p. 1347). On the other hand, self-aggrandizement on Zola's part is held in check: Marc does nothing which has the seismic impact of 'J'accuse'; he is also 'a useless hero' (p. 1347) and 'an incompetent revolutionary' (p. 1150).

This ambivalence partly corresponds to Zola's own moods during the Dreyfus Affair, alternating between triumphant self-belief and a gloomy sense of the hopelessness of his endeavours. But it is inseparable from the fact that *Vérité* refracts, rather than simply reflects, Zola's role in his story. Although, like Marc, he imaginatively 'relives the Affair' (p. 1110), the temporal gap between Zola's involvement and its fictional re-enactment in *Vérité* remains significant, for during the three years since 'J'accuse', Zola had lost confidence in the role he had played. His explosive 1898 text in *L'Aurore* was so comprehensive that it had been intended to bring the Dreyfus Affair to an end. The September 1899 verdict at Dreyfus' second court martial made it clear that it had not.

Zola's subsequent repetitions of the arguments of 'J'accuse' imply his awareness of its failure in that respect: in his interviews following its appearance; in his open letter to Prime Minister Henri Brisson (1835–1912) in *L'Aurore* of 16 July 1898; in those also published there, to Dreyfus' wife on 22 September 1899, to the Senate on 29 May 1900, and to Faure's more receptive successor as president, Émile Loubet (1838–1929), on 22 December of that same year. The last two of these are rather desperate efforts, in the face of political developments beyond his control, to reiterate the principles he had championed.

In an attempt to quell the ideological passions tearing the country apart, the government had taken steps to declare a general amnesty in relation to the Dreyfus Affair; this was passed into law on 24 December 1900. During its passage through the two chambers of the National Assembly, Zola was its fierce opponent: in March, he had appeared before a Senate committee to argue against the proposal, and two days before the Senate's confirmatory vote to promulgate the law, his opposition was unchanged, referring to the amnesty, in his letter to President Loubet, as a 'cowardly' means to silence the continuing calls for justice and truth (*OC*, XIV, 995). For the same reason, Zola had been opposed to Dreyfus accepting a presidential pardon on 19 September 1899, following the farcical outcome of his Rennes court martial.

Zola's correspondence between the date of 'J'accuse' and the writing of *Vérité* suggests he was roiled in anxiety about whether his intervention had been worth it or whether, as Cézanne was to claim, he had overreached himself. To Jeanne, in a letter of 2 August 1898, he had been reassuring: 'We are engaged in something very fine for which History will give us credit' (*LR*, 207). But he was excessively reassured himself, while writing *Vérité*, by a Georges Clemenceau article as late as 3 November 1901 praising that same personal 'courage' which Zola ascribes to Marc in the novel. 'J'accuse' had made an enormous impact: in the subsequent so-called 'Manifestes des intellectuels' petitions (14 and 16 January 1898) on Zola's behalf signed by hundreds of writers, philosophers and artists, he found support for his public stand, underlined by letters from all over the world reinforcing his self-image. The fact remains, however, that the publication of 'J'accuse' had, in the short term, made things worse: it was immediately followed by antisemitic violence across France and her overseas colonies, it divided the country as never before and it provoked unprecedented personal attacks on Zola himself. *Vérité* confronts these unwanted consequences of his 'J'accuse', which can be considered each in turn.

Zola had been accused of antisemitism in his portrayal of avaricious Jewish financiers in *L'Argent*. His article in *Le Figaro* of 16 May 1896, headed 'Pour les Juifs' (A Plea for the Jews) was designed to make amends. But, while castigating the caricature of 'usurers' as an 'abomination', Zola so vividly evokes the reasons for the persecution of the Jews down the ages that there is a residual ambiguity in his referencing 'a centuries-old atavism of scorn and vengeance', in reality based on 'physical repugnance' (*OC*, XIX, 779). This is echoed in *Vérité*, in Marc 'disliking Jews as a result of a sort of repugnance and atavistic distrust' (*OC*, VIII, 1019). This is either a startling admission on Zola's own part or, as the novel was to show, integral to a demonstration of prejudice overcome, much as the Pierre of *Rome* had done in relation to the art of antiquity. In none of his texts at the beginning of the Affair had he focused on the antisemitic dimension of the Dreyfus case. And he had been somewhat surprised that warm approval of his 1897 *Figaro* articles had been expressed by representatives of the Jewish community. They had previously kept their heads down for fear of inciting antisemitism by defending Dreyfus too publicly. In addressing the upsurge of precisely that, as an unintended result of 'J'accuse', Zola devotes much space in *Vérité* to refuting the stereotype of the wealthy Jew, presenting the humble and impoverished Simon family as exemplars of positive values enhanced by their loyalty to France.

In a far more explicit way than in *Travail*, *Vérité* is also an extended lament for a country now riven by internecine strife as a result of the Dreyfus Affair: the novel's many plots detail fractures in communities, friendships, families, marriages, generations and professional relationships as irreconcilable as historians, memoirs, films and documentaries have since recorded. In seeking to repair these divisions, the discursive thrust of *Vérité* is as utopian as in any other of Zola's late novels. Marc's personal quest is afforded the amplified status of a mission to save France from its 'fanatical stupidity' (*OC*, VIII, 1297). This is elaborated in endless digressions restating both Marc and Zola's love of their country. Judet had been far from the only polemicist invidiously recalling the writer's Venetian origins, all the more suspect in the context of the Triple Alliance's alignment of Italy and Germany. In its attack on the army, 'J'accuse' was seen as an act as damaging to France as Dreyfus' alleged treason. *Vérité* is an impassioned and very extended counter-declaration of Zola's patriotism.

A week before 'J'accuse', Zola had published a pamphlet headed 'Lettre à la France', begging his countrymen to come to their senses in the interests of national unity. The illusion that he had the authority to speak to, or for, France was quickly shattered. The personal attacks to which he was subject would be sustained not only in the days and months following 'J'accuse' but during the rest of his life. They were of a kind to make those of his hostile literary critics over the decades pale into insignificance. 'Down with Zola!' was the chant of demonstrators on the streets after the publication of 'J'accuse', so threatening that police protection was stationed outside Zola's Parisian home. Nothing could protect him from vilification taken to new extremes. Now juxtaposed were the moral transgression of his novels (especially *Pot-Bouille*) and his equally 'treacherous' political stand. A collection of contemporary caricatures, entitled *Cochon de Zola*, illustrates more graphically than similarly slanted books and newspaper articles the revoltingly cruel lengths to which the writer's enemies were prepared to go.[13]

The problems Zola created for himself in writing *Vérité* stem from his conception of the Dreyfus Affair not only as exemplary of the state of France but as the confirmation of his own vision of the modern world. The novel thus rehearses his entire work's thematic perspectives, inserting scenarios which, by a process of accretion, substantiate that vision: the crime with which the novel begins is ascribed to 'the beast in man'; in the figure of the examining magistrate charged to solve it, the incompetent Denizet of *La Bête humaine* reappears with a different name. In the text's margins, irrelevant to the progress of the narrative, are instances of the moral decadence, financial skulduggery and political venality dramatized throughout the *Rougon-Macquart*; miracle cures are as fallacious as those in *Lourdes*. The emancipation of women, as heralded in the utopian *Travail* and *Paris*, is here considered through another of Zola's familiar concerns: the 'poisonous' nature of convent education. Its corrupting influence is taken to extreme discursive lengths in *Vérité*: the Church 'possesses' female bodies as well as souls. And when Marc protects his daughter from a hypothetically sexually frustrated priest, he conjures up one of the most abiding myths Zola had derived from his reading of Michelet in the 1860s: that a pure young woman would subsequently always belong (as 'la déflorée de ce ministre sacré' (*OC*, VIII, 1239)) to the man who had taken her virginity.

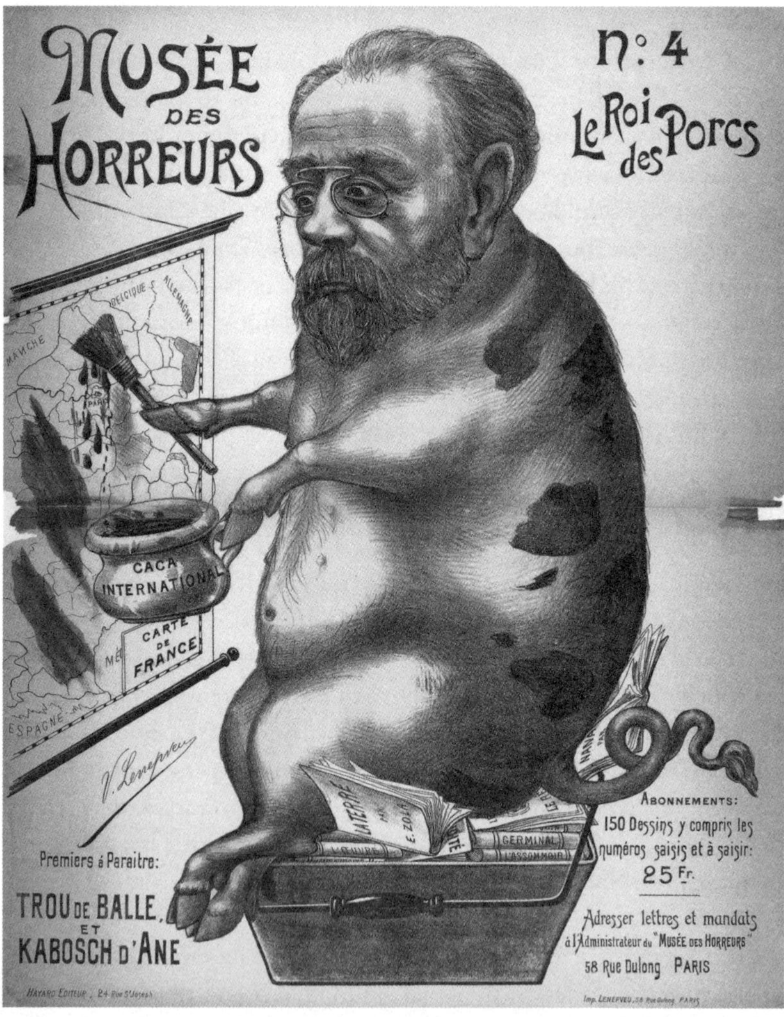

V. Lenepveu, 'The King of Pigs', *Caran d'Ache*, November 1899; *Le Musée des horreurs* (The Freak Show), no. 4, 1899.

A further 'complication' is that *Vérité* overlays on its multiple concerns an autobiographical texture whose tangled threads are not limited to the surrogacy of roles played by Zola and his hero in, respectively, the Dreyfus and Simon 'Affairs'. Without pondering the ramifications of this dimension of the novel, it was alluded to by Zola's daughter Denise: while working on the first edition of Zola's complete works in 1929, she discovered in the work-notes for *Vérité* a reference to 'Denise' (*Ms* 10344, fol. 473) and a pen portrait by her father of Louise Froment, Marc's daughter, obviously based on herself.[14] This was reinforced by the text's reference to Louise 'sharing her adored father's passion for justice' (*OC*, VIII, 1346). Such a mirroring can be extended to the remarkable similarities between Zola's beloved Jeanne and the fictional Louise's mother, Geneviève. Nor are these simply located in their physical resemblance, for Zola has inserted within *Vérité* a love story. And this is exemplary on so many levels that it defies exclusive identification with either of his relationships with Jeanne and Alexandrine while conflating across them intimate concerns.

At a didactic level, the love story between Marc and his wife is elaborated as an object lesson in the power of truth: Geneviève is so in thrall to the pressures exerted by the Church and her own fanatically pious grandmother that her refusal to subscribe to her husband's belief in Simon's innocence separates her from their 'life of mutual adoration'; however, her ultimate conversion to his point of view is signalled by her return to the marital home. This reunited Froment couple and their descendants then live happily ever after. Extracted from this contextualized ideological conflict and its instructive resolution, however, there is another tale: and it is one, moreover, precisely grounded in Zola's personal experience.

Against all his anti-clerical principles, Zola had allowed his own children to be baptized and subsequently, in the case of Denise, to prepare for her first communion in 1900; so too does Marc in relation to Louise, reluctantly giving way to her mother's wishes 'with the weakness of a man in love' (*OC*, VIII, 1198 and 1247). Denise remembered that her father had done likewise 'doubtless to please my mother', including going so far as to hold a small party to celebrate the event. Geneviève herself, whose second child (like Jeanne's) is a boy, is described in much the same terms as the beautiful Clotilde of *Le Docteur Pascal*. And the sexual harmony between her and Marc, even three years after their marriage, is no less euphoric than in Zola's autobiographical novel of 1893: 'She gave herself to him, trembling with desire . . . in the perfection of their loving union' (*OC*, VIII, 1167).

But the differences are illuminating. In their fear of scandal and faced with ancestral disapproval (the Mme Duparque of *Vérité* is as terrifying as the matriarchal Félicité of *Le Docteur Pascal*), Pascal and Clotilde have to keep their relationship secret. Consecrated by marriage, unlike Clotilde (and in spite of Pascal's legitimizing fantasies), Geneviève is the idealized figure of wife *and* mother, the synthesis which the Claude of *L'Œuvre* is unable to enjoy. Zola's parenthetical digression on marriage in general patently looks back to his own: the reason couples split, he underlined, was always 'the end of desire, the permanent break in the carnal bond' (*OC*, VIII, 1238). In *Vérité*, marital fracture is indexed by the couple sleeping apart. Zola's letters to Alexandrine in the aftermath of their own crisis hint as much: in a letter of 2 November 1895, he refers to the servants cleaning 'your bedroom' (*LA*, 70); in booking their hotel in Marseilles for their fraught reunion there exactly a year later, he reassured her that he had taken 'a big room with twin beds' (*LA*, 154). The narrative of their partial reconciliation, even if platonic, progresses from the references to 'our bedroom' in 1897 (*LA*, 210 and 234) to the fact that, on the night of Zola's death five years later, they were side by side in the huge four-poster bed which Edmond de Goncourt had once unkindly described as being akin to that of an 'archbishop in a downmarket play'.[15]

A number of other scenarios are also suggestive of personal preoccupations. These contribute to the justification for considering *Vérité*, at least in part, as an autobiographical novel to set alongside some of Zola's early fiction as well as *L'Œuvre* and *Le Docteur Pascal*. Marc is struck by 'the fragility of human happiness' in learning of a character called François 'in love with his wife' who suddenly goes off with an attractive young woman. Zola's commentary on what is an anecdote unrelated to the novel's plotting refers to 'the madness of desire which devastates a man', virtually the identical formulation he had applied to his father's Algerian love affair. The betrayed wife in *Vérité* rejects the idea of separation; instead, and 'by tacit agreement' with him, 'gives back his freedom to a husband who no longer loved her' (*OC*, VIII, 1470–71). That the unfaithful man bears Zola's father's name is as intriguing as his apologetic return to the marital home once he has come to his senses. In the deathbed scene of the prematurely widowed Mme Berthereau, in which she says her final goodbyes to her daughter, there is another version of Zola's own mother, so devoted to her late husband that she had never remarried, 'with her pale face still coloured by the warmth of a love briefly experienced which she had mourned for ever' (*OC*, VIII, 1364).

Only in retrospect could Zola reframe in *Vérité* his Dreyfus Affair experience and relate it to his life and work: his values; his determination; his understanding of the modern world; his personal affections; his perseverance and doubts; and, perhaps above all, his endurance, across much of his career, of the hostility of authorities both political and cultural. Marc, as another of his authorial surrogates, identifies with Simon, the victim of injustice, in a way that Zola had probably not done in the case of Dreyfus himself. Marc is as isolated and insulted in his microcosmic provincial world as Simon had been. He takes the place in the distant village school vacated by his double. And on Marc returning from this exile, the destiny imagined for Simon is also Zola's. Or so he hoped. The rehabilitation of Simon at the end of *Vérité* is an optimistic dream: in relation to Dreyfus' future in the real world, Zola wrote to Alexandrine on 29 October 1901, 'I am under no illusion, knowing perfectly well that I shall be dead before the final victory ' (*LA*, 715). It was all too accurate a premonition. *Vérité*, the last and just about the longest (751 pages) of Zola's novels, was published posthumously in volume form on 20 February 1903, its cover edged in black. In confronting the denunciation of his writing, both before and after the Dreyfus Affair, *Vérité* makes the case for his own rehabilitation, ultimately confirmed only by posterity.

Zola's Death

On 27 September 1902, as his daughter poignantly remembered, his family saw Zola alive for the last time: he had come over to Verneuil while his two households were packing up for their return to Paris after the summer. On the Sunday afternoon, the 28th, he and his wife (shortly due to depart for Italy again) were driven to the Paris townhouse at 21b rue de Bruxelles, in the 9th arrondissement, where they had rented since 1889 the ground-floor service facilities and the living quarters above it. They had been preceded by one of their servants, Jules Delahalle, charged with preparations for their arrival. He noticed that debris in the bedroom fireplace seemed to prevent the smoke going up the chimney, but he contented himself with opening the windows to let it out. Not fully aware of the fumes from the smouldering *boulets* (pellets of smokeless fuel) which had been placed in the grate, Zola died during that night from carbon monoxide poisoning, as the autopsy would confirm. The door to

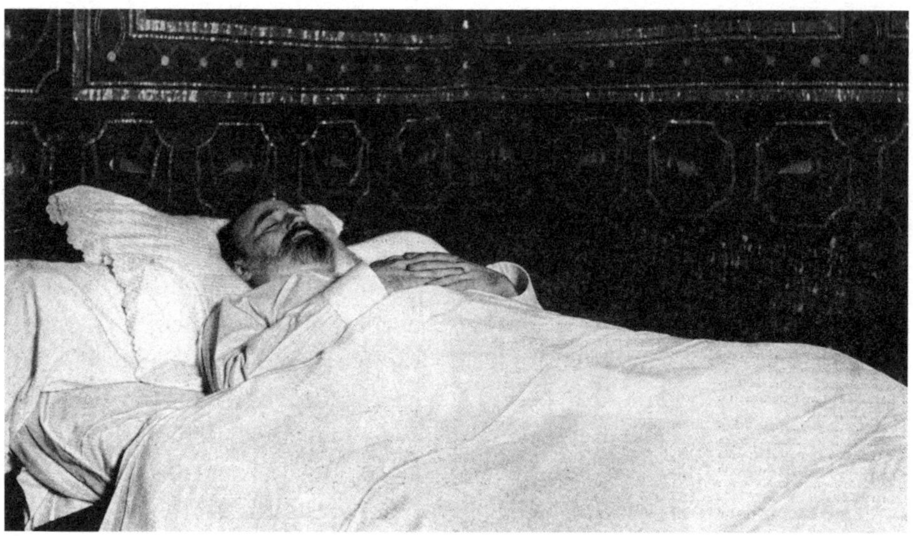

Zola's deathbed, 1–4 October 1902.

their private apartment on the first floor was forced open at nine o'clock on the Monday morning. Alexandrine was still breathing and rushed to a clinic in Neuilly, where she regained consciousness in the early evening, but Zola's lifeless body was found on the floor, still warm enough for the summoned doctor to certify that he had died in the hours before. It seemed like a death more banal than any Zola had invented for his fictional characters. A judicial enquiry was opened on the day of his death, securing supporting evidence from toxologists and specialists in chimney design: its official report in December concluded that Zola had indeed died as the result of an accident. That, however (as my final pages in the Epilogue, will explain), was not the end of the story.

Zola's shockingly premature death, at the age of 62, made worldwide headlines, many of them reprinted in the Parisian press. For days and weeks afterwards, the newspapers were filled with tributes and reminiscences. More immediately, they devoted many column inches to his secular funeral. Because Alexandrine's doctors were concerned about the progress of her recovery, this was postponed until Sunday, 5 October. Prior to it, Zola's body was laid out on the divan in his study. The week-long wake brought his closest associates together there, taking turns in pairs to watch over it. Desmoulin had been given responsibility for having Zola's corpse embalmed, while leaving his face untouched, recognizable for all those come to pay their respects. On seeing her husband for the first time after being discharged from hospital, Alexandrine

Zola's funeral, 5 October 1902.

collapsed in distress and remained so to the extent that she was ultimately unable to attend the funeral itself. Some 2,000 people gathered in the rue de Bruxelles, watching as a long queue of dignitaries and others with special passes registered their condolences in the hour before the procession of three carriages set off from this quiet backstreet and into the main thoroughfare of the boulevard de Clichy. It did so to the slow beat of muffled drums while being saluted by troops presenting arms.

When the coffin emerged from the house, it was lifted onto a hearse draped in black with Zola's name in gold lettering. The eight pall-bearers included representatives of many aspects of his life and work: Duret, who had recruited him to *La Tribune* back in 1868 and who had been so continually involved in Zola's art criticism that he had even checked the proofs of his prefatory essay for the great Manet retrospective of 1884; Mirbeau, one of the organizers of the 1877 dinner in honour of Zola, Flaubert and Edmond de Goncourt, later distancing himself from Naturalism but not at the expense of a personal friendship; his two publishers, Fasquelle and Charpentier; Bruneau, the composer with whom Zola had collaborated in the 1890s; and Abel Hermant (1862–1950), one of his successors as president of the Société des gens de lettres who, in that capacity, would give an oration at the Montmartre Cemetery. The procession's short journey there, in the autumn sunshine, attracted a crowd of at least 50,000 onlookers, hushed save for the occasional cry of 'Long live Zola.' Some press reports calculated that by the time it arrived at the cemetery gates, the crowd had swelled to twice as many. The right-wing papers' denigrating estimates of a few hundred were erroneously par for the course. At the cemetery itself, 45 bouquets of flowers were laid on the makeshift tomb as delegation after delegation passed it with heads bowed. Many of these represented working-class, socialist and educational associations. The finest of the floral tributes, so it was reported, was one from the French community in San Francisco, and Alfred Dreyfus' personal one bore the inscription of his everlasting gratitude.

Alexandrine had wanted the occasion to be politics-free. She implored Anatole France, who had decided at the last minute to return from Bordeaux to give one of the funeral orations, to be 'tactful' in respect of mentioning the Dreyfus Affair. Only when such reservations were overcome did he confirm his willingness to make his speech. For the same reason, she had also secured Dreyfus' agreement to absent himself from the funeral on the Sunday, but he had paid her a visit the day before and persuaded her to change her mind. He was one of those watching over

Zola's body that evening. His presence at the head of the mourners was significant enough for detailed reports of those in attendance to single him out, while noting that he was virtually hidden from view. Not without a certain irony, the other individual identified among the mourners was the bailiff who had been sent to sequester some of Zola's effects on three occasions during his exile; this intrusion had been authorized in order to meet the accumulated debt of 30,000 francs that he had incurred in punitive fines at his trials (in the event the process was halted when his friends bid for the requisitioned objects intended for auction).

To focus on both Dreyfus himself and the bailiff was a reminder, in the charged political context of Zola's funeral, of what was at stake. The left-wing press celebrated a supremely 'republican occasion' bringing together government ministers and ordinary folk. Its ideological antagonists continued to refer to Zola as 'France's greatest enemy', even going so far as to describe the accident of his death as 'divine retribution'. In anticipation of possible trouble, there were barriers reinforced by a huge police presence. The day before the funeral, the civic authorities had announced unprecedented security measures. In the event, there were only minor scuffles and a small number of arrests as Dreyfusards and diehard nationalists confronted each other in the place de Clichy. But even the reported scale of such disruption varied according to the polemical colour of conservative and radical newspapers, alternatively congratulating the forces of law and order or warning of the continuing threat to the nation. A telling epilogue to the funeral was the reception of the officer commanding the troops: on his return to barracks, he was assaulted by his military colleagues for his complicity in the celebration of the army's arch-enemy.

Alexandrine's wishes were in any case incompatible with Zola's public profile. His hearse was accompanied not just by his closest friends and colleagues but also by all the leading figures supporting his stand in the Dreyfus Affair. Zola's reputation extended further back, as the 'magnificent' and 'grandiose' spectacle reported in the press underlined: a 'picturesque' delegation of miners from the Denain region in which his great novel of 1885 had been set filed behind Zola's coffin to the cry of 'Germinal, Germinal' echoing through the streets; one of them came in working garb, complete with clogs and holding a pit lamp and coal bucket; two others came dressed, respectively, as a peasant and a blacksmith, in homage to the author's immortalization of the working poor in *La Terre* and *L'Assommoir*.

At the cemetery, the last of the three graveside orations has remained the most memorable. It was indeed given by Anatole France, the future recipient of the Nobel Prize in Literature (1921). He has long since been consigned to critical obscurity. But that he was the speaker chosen to conclude proceedings fortuitously reflected the contradictions both of his own intellectual stance and of the period. On the one hand, he was hostile or indifferent to innovative directions: as journalists at the funeral reminded their readers, he had been one of Naturalism's most outspoken critics, and he had been repeatedly cited by Zola himself as the representative of trends at odds with his own aesthetic. On the other, with his own abiding concern for justice and truth, he had been at Zola's side during the Dreyfus Affair. The tribute he fashioned was nevertheless devoid of ambiguity: generous in its evocation of Zola's personality ('a good man . . . with the greatness of simple souls');[16] wholehearted in the recognition of his massive literary achievements, comparing him to Tolstoy; in praise of Zola's lifelong denunciation of social evils; and in the admiration for the balancing of the pessimism of much of his writing with a faith in the future, characteristic of Anatole France's own ambivalence. There was no need to remind this particular audience of the role Zola had played in the Dreyfus Affair. It was sufficient to refer to the fact that no patriot had ever been subjected to the kind of malevolence which Zola had endured. Nor was the writer's honour limited to that which would be posthumously bestowed merely by his own country. Giving to the funeral ceremony what would be a universalizing echo down the years to come, Anatole France's encomium closed with the judgement of posterity: 'he was a moment in the history of the human conscience.'

Epilogue

Six months after Zola's sudden death, his personal effects were auctioned at Drouot, the Parisian equivalent of Sotheby's. The sale took place over the two days of 9 and 10 March 1903. Alerting its readers to the standard private and public viewing during the weekend preceding the auction opening on the following Monday, *Le Figaro* of 7 March stressed 'the good taste of the great writer'. On the 10th, *Le Siècle* reported that the first auction sessions, initially devoted to Zola's library, had attracted an enormous crowd of bibliophiles and admirers of 'le maître'; on the same day, *Le Matin* and *Le Temps* listed those present at the sale, including not just art dealers who would buy the most significant paintings and various prominent social and political figures, but also intimates mentioned earlier in this book, including Mirbeau, Hennique, Duret and Zola's publishers. A number of those mentioned, as well as others such as Roux and Bruneau, subsequently bid successfully for various artefacts and items of furniture (even those listed as being 'distressed'), doubtless motivated by nostalgia rather than acquisitiveness.

As well as by mourning friends and colleagues, this retrospective occasion was also peopled by some of Zola's implacable enemies. Seldom indeed can a posthumous sale have provoked vituperative commentary of the kind exemplified by the polemicist Henri Rochefort. His hatred of Zola had been registered ten years earlier: in *Le Figaro* of 25 November 1893, he had been one of the first to dismiss *Fécondité* as yet another example of the depths to which its author had sunk in order to advance his efforts to be elected to the Académie Française. His 'Saint Zola, priez pour nous', published in *L'Intransigeant* of 2 March 1903, based on advance sight of the catalogue of items owned by Zola, attacked his 'bewilderingly impressionist modern landscapes' as well as his personal 'museum of religious knick-knacks'. In his column the following day, Rochefort ironically juxtaposed these comments with the novelist's well-known atheistic views and the fact that Zola 'had nevertheless filled his house with ultra-religious leftovers'. The last of these derogatory remarks was aimed at the heterogeneous collection of statuary and miniatures which had so surprised journalists granted access to Zola's house at Médan. This jibe was rehearsed elsewhere in the press. A notable exception was the *Journal des débats* on 11 March, whose correspondent exploited the timing of the sale to direct attention to the imminent opening of Durand-Ruel's latest exhibition of Impressionist paintings.

It was precisely, however, such paintings that inspired Rochefort's most outrageous article. In 'L'Amour du laid' (The Love of Ugliness), in *L'Intransigeant* of 3 March, he referred contemptuously to Monet and Pissarro – Zola owning pictures by both of them – as 'confetti painters'. But by comparison with Cézanne, he added, they were wonderful. Struck by the dozen or so Cézannes up for auction, Rochefort suggested that the catalogue description of them as 'very early works' was designed to apologize for their bizarre renderings. Artistic value was not, of course, his real concern. What Rochefort's malicious perspective underlined was the unresolved fractures of the Dreyfus Affair. At the public preview on Sunday, 8 March, he had come across, in his words, 'all the intellectuals . . . and all the Dreyfusard snobs', an acid reminder that, in respect of those present, it was Bruneau, Charpentier and Desmoulin who had protectively escorted Zola to his trial for criminal libel in February 1898 and had been subjected to violent abuse as he had made his way to court, captured in Henri de Groux's (1866–1930) rendering of the scene in a painting which Zola retained at Médan. In a ludicrously uninformed conflation of childhood friendship and political allegiance, Rochefort singled out Cézanne as an 'ultra-impressionist' Dreyfusard:

> I've always said that there were Dreyfusards long before the Dreyfus Affair . . . and if one subscribes to the kind of representation of reality practised by Zola and his undistinguished painter friends, it's but a logical step to consider it patriotic and honourable for a military officer to hand over to the enemy the plans for the defence of our country.[1]

Henri de Groux, *Zola aux outrages*, 1898, pastel on canvas.

The relatively modest prices achieved at the auction, though to the immediate advantage of art-market insiders, may reflect the negative publicity engendered by Rochefort and others.

Memorializing Zola in the shape of a monument did not go smoothly either. The idea surfaced as early as his funeral. The Belgian sculptor Constantin Meunier (1831–1905), much admired by Zola himself, was commissioned to create a statue, but died before completing the constellation of figures (imaging Fecundity) at its base. The project was taken over by Alexandre Charpentier (1856–1909), but so delayed that, in the interim, a copy of the bust of Zola (which graced his Paris home) by one of his oldest Aixois friends, Philippe Solari (and the model for Mahoudeau, the fictional sculptor in *L'Œuvre*), was placed on his tomb in the Montmartre Cemetery in 1904. After being stored for years in the Grand Palais, the bronze statue itself was finally erected in 1924 in the avenue Émile Zola in the 15th arrondissement (the previous rue Frémicourt having been rebaptized in his honour by the new left-wing municipal council in 1907), only for this tribute to the defender of Alfred Dreyfus to be demolished under the Occupation in 1942. The square where it had once stood assumed Dreyfus' name in 2000. In the context of renewed antisemitism in France, the association of Zola and his defence of the Jewish officer was further underlined by his restored country house having been designated since 2021 as the Maison Zola–Musée Dreyfus.

The conflation of art and politics had bedevilled the idea of a memorial from the start: Rodin had been the obvious choice when it came to commissioning the Zola monument; their names were intertwined in the public mind as a consequence of the Balzac project initiated by Zola in 1891 – the progress of which, or lack of it, had been continually monitored in the press. Such were the resulting tensions that by 1895, on a personal level, according to his biographer, 'as everybody knew, Rodin could no longer even stand to be in the same room' as Zola.[2] More to the point was that his anti-Dreyfusard leanings were thought to make it inappropriate for him to be involved. This was much to the regret of many, including Monet, who wrote in a letter of January 1903 that he was 'profoundly sorry' that Rodin would not be entrusted with the Zola monument 'since this concerns a question of art, the homage of a great sculptor to a great man, and in such cases the question of politics should not arise'.[3]

Politics, however, would continue to play its part in commemorative tributes to Zola's life and work. His friends had been frustrated in their hopes, much against Alexandrine's wishes, that he might be accorded a state funeral on the model of Victor Hugo's in 1885. Amends were made by the government in its decision that Zola's remains should be exhumed and transferred from the Montmartre Cemetery to the Panthéon. There is still no higher honour in France than to be laid to final rest there among the greatest non-military figures in its history. In its crypt, Zola's remains lie next to Hugo's – appropriately enough, given Zola's awareness of partly writing in his poetic shadow. At the time, two other writers had preceded him: Voltaire, in 1791 and Rousseau, in 1794. Only after more than half a century, in 1966, did André Malraux become the next writer after Zola to have his reputation thus consecrated.

Had it not been for the Dreyfus Affair, however, it is not certain his literary achievements alone would have elevated Zola to such heights. The proposal in July 1906 to bestow the honour on him had been linked more generally to 'repairing the injustices' of the Affair. The year 1906 was a key one, and that July a key month, in its epilogue. In response to now unassailable doubts about his original conviction, Dreyfus himself had been brought back from Devil's Island in 1899 to face a second court martial in Rennes; to widespread disbelief, on 9 September he was again found guilty, but with 'extenuating circumstances'. Although pardoned shortly afterwards, it was not until 12 July 1906, after three years of petitions and 'investigations', that the Rennes verdict was overturned by the Supreme Court of Appeal. On the 13th, in the very same session of the Chamber of Deputies formally reinstating Dreyfus in the army, a bill was passed (by an underwhelming majority) setting in motion the process to transfer Zola's remains to the Panthéon.

Originally built as the Church of Sainte-Geneviève, the Panthéon's story reflected much of the history of nineteenth-century France which Zola had lived through: six times its symbolic function had been redefined since the Revolution of 1789, alternating between Catholic restoration and national necropolis; its last reconsecration had been during the Second Empire. As the transfer of Hugo's remains to the Panthéon was symptomatic of the definitive establishment of the Republic, so Zola's own posthumous journey to this secular hall of fame marked his own triumph over the reactionary forces to which his life and work had been opposed.

The date of 2 April originally chosen for the occasion to memorialize his name was Zola's birthday. It was postponed until 4 June 1908 because the proposal's tortuous and contested way through parliament since July 1906 had not yet arrived at formal approval of its financing. The ceremony itself was dignified by the leading role of the president of the Republic, Armand Fallières (1841–1931), intended to further the impression of a renewed national unity. The only speech was given by the Minister of Education, who recalled Zola's campaign on behalf of Dreyfus. Patriotism, solemnity and triumph were signalled by music both suitably traditional and personally resonant: the national anthem, 'La Marseillaise'; the prelude to Zola and Bruneau's *Messidor*, premiered in 1897 in the presence of President Félix Faure (1841–1899); the funeral march from Beethoven's Seventh Symphony; and the choral finale of his Ninth.

Zola's funeral had passed off with relatively little trouble. By contrast, fears for the safety of those involved in this second, and even more public, ceremony were confirmed. Zola's opponents had had plenty of time over the previous two years to get organized; on arrival at the Panthéon, the procession was met by some 5,000 nationalist demonstrators who had to be forced into adjoining streets by the forces, some of them horse-mounted, of law and order. When Zola's hearse came into view, this raucous mob threatened again to get out of control, with some forty arrests being made. That was not the end of it: as the massed troops prepared for their valedictory presidential inspection and as the recessional music began, two shots rang out, one of them slightly wounding Dreyfus in the arm. Eight years after the attempt during the Rennes court martial to assassinate Fernand Labori, the lawyer who had defended both Zola and Dreyfus, it was a reminder of the alarming legacy of the Affair. So was the fact that the clearly identified assailant on this occasion, Louis Grégori, was acquitted at the end of his trial in September in a feat of legal escapology. It was argued in court that this former soldier and military correspondent of *Le Gaulois* did not hold a grudge against Dreyfus himself but was motivated by the continuing denigration of the French army by the left-wing movement which had appropriated his cause. Faced with the irreconcilable contradiction between attempted homicide and 'heroic violence', the jury took only twenty minutes to conclude that no good would be served by reigniting the passions of the Affair.

Dreyfus' exoneration was not met with the unalloyed elation which Zola had prematurely lent to the innocent victim of *Vérité*. His presidential 'pardon' in 1899 had been viewed by both the novelist and the Dreyfusards as a travesty. The award to Dreyfus of the Légion d'honneur for 'services to the nation', at the same time as his military reintegration, was no less subject to commentary – varying between nationalist outrage and accusations of government hypocrisy. On 26 June 1907, emotionally exhausted by almost a decade and a half of controversy and physically impaired by his imprisonment, Dreyfus asked to retire from the army. He was to serve in it again: approaching his fifty-fifth birthday at the outbreak of the First World War, he was posted as an artillery officer in the fortified zone north of Paris. Only in uniform and in the service of the *revanche* against the hated Germans, he confessed, would his rehabilitation be complete. He was in due course promoted from captain to lieutenant colonel and upgraded to *Chevalier* in the Légion d'honneur. He died on 12 July 1935. On both sides of the Affair, those with long memories remained unrepentant: aged Dreyfusards attributed his death to the medical consequences of his 'martyrdom' in French Guyana; opponents continued to use his name in right-wing and antisemitic diatribes. As late as 1945, one of the most prominent anti-Dreyfusards, Charles Maurras (1868–1952), on hearing the verdict of a life sentence for his role in the Occupation, famously shouted out in court that it was 'the revenge of Dreyfus'. But neither had Zola been forgotten in that context: a few months later, at the trial of Marshal Philippe Pétain (1856–1951) for his Vichy government's collaboration with the enemy, one of his Resistance accusers adopted the pseudonym of 'Germinal'.

After her husband's death, Alexandrine moved to smaller premises at 62 rue de Rome. The extensive property at Médan had always been Zola's fiefdom rather than her home, and in 1903 she sold most of the estate (outhouses, farm buildings and so on), together with the house's furniture; in February 1905 she gifted the house itself to the Social Services' charitable organization that cared for sick children. This was in effect an orphanage and Alexandrine's gesture may have been in remembrance of the sad fate of her own baby. That generosity was compounded by a spirit of forgiveness towards Jeanne Rozerot. It was Alexandrine who insisted that Fasquelle and Desmoulin should immediately break the painful news of Zola's death to his other family, and, three days later, Jeanne and her children were invited to the rue de Bruxelles apartment to view Zola one last time before his funeral.

In response to Jeanne's concern for her children, their 'elderly' father had promised, in a letter of 16 August 1892 (*LR*, 55), that he would put in place secure financial arrangements for their future. Zola had been equally worried when renting a new apartment for the family in 1897: as he wrote to Alexandrine at the time, 'if I were to die, which at my age could happen any day', they would be in great difficulty; 'it terrifies me in thinking about it. I want to live long enough to see them grown up' (*LA*, 266). Legally Alexandrine was the writer's only heir. But she arranged that Jeanne should receive a comfortable annual income from Zola's legacy. She helped her with her own move to a new address. Now with Jeanne often alongside her, she continued to see Denise and Jacques on a regular basis. In September 1903 the three of them accompanied her to the inaugural literary pilgrimage to Médan, which has remained ever since an annual occasion, now traditionally on the first Sunday of October, at which Zola's descendants and admirers gather to pay tribute to his memory This is not, however, a merely cultural event any more than Zola's reputation as a novelist can be disassociated from that of the defender of Dreyfus. As stressed in the Introduction, the latter was at least partly responsible for the refusal, at least in France, to recognize his greatness as a writer. In the 1920s and '30s, guest speakers at the Médan pilgrimage included some of the most prominent left-wing intellectuals of the day, thereby implicitly testifying to their opposition to the exclusion of Zola from the literary canon. More recently, the ideological resonance of his life and work has been celebrated at the occasion by four (either future or serving) French presidents signalling their enlightened political credentials: François

Mitterrand (1976), Jacques Chirac (2002), François Hollande (2016) and Emmanuel Macron (2021).

The personal dimension of Zola's legacy is nowhere more durable than in Alexandrine implementing, with remarkable generosity, one of her late husband's dearest wishes: in a letter to Jeanne from London in September 1893, he had written of his hope that one day the paternity of their two children would be officially recognized (*LR*, 136). In November 1906 Alexandrine initiated the legal process, completed the following May, entitling them to bear the family name, hyphenated for them to become Denise and Jacques Émile-Zola, and thus able to pass it to their descendants. In her will, dated 30 March 1919, Alexandrine left half of Zola's future royalties to them. She also stipulated that, at her death, she should be placed next to her husband's now empty tomb in the Montmartre Cemetery and that, should they wish it, Denise and Jacques should be laid to rest beside her. She took a particular interest in Denise, whom she saw twice a week during her schooldays. Shortly after the transfer of Zola's remains to the Panthéon, she attended her wedding in October 1908, having introduced her to her future husband.

In Zola's memory, Alexandrine sustained at first a weekly gathering of his closest friends and associates. Of Zola's paintings, she retained those by Baille and Guillemet, with whom she stayed in contact and whose deaths, both in 1918, affected her badly. She also kept Berthe Morisot's *Femme et fillette au bord de la plage* (*c.* 1877, current location unknown), as she herself had acquired it: a letter from her, dated 5 March 1877, thanks Morisot 'for the delightful painting you've been so kind to give me', adding an apologetic note for employing Manet as an intermediary to secure 'a canvas by an artist whose refined and delicate talent we've loved for so long'.[4] Besides Baille and Guillemet, the other one of Zola's friends with whom she shared a nostalgia for the past was Georges Charpentier: he remained as loyal to Alexandrine as he had been to Zola himself over more than thirty years; in her early widowhood, she received much personal support from him and his wife; and after the latter's death in 1904 and his the next year, their extended family remained in close contact with Alexandrine until the end of her days.

In 1907–8 Alexandrine oversaw the publication of Zola's early correspondence in two volumes. Much of it was with Cézanne, who, shortly before his own death and overcome by emotion throughout the ceremony, attended her unveiling of the copy of Solari's bust of Zola for the Méjanes library in Aix; she had given the library the manuscripts and notes for *Les Trois Villes*, complementing the much larger gift of his papers to the Bibliothèque nationale in Paris in 1904. She endowed a prize in Zola's name to be awarded by the Société des gens de lettres over which he had presided. Less visibly, she multiplied the trips to Italy which had so conveniently enthused her over the years since her long stay in Rome in 1894. In contrast to Zola's relative indifference towards his Italian relatives, Alexandrine developed such family ties as well as establishing a circle of genuine friends to whom she remained devoted. To those who had known her all her adult life, she seemed transformed, her energy and happiness restored. As she got older, her movements inevitably became more restricted, particularly from 1917 onwards. The First World War saw her knitting clothes for the troops and helping tend the wounded. Her last trip to Italy had taken place in 1913. By 1924 the symptoms of a terminal condition were such that she was unable to attend the unveiling of the memorial statue of Zola. On 24 April 1925, Alexandrine suffered a cerebral haemorrhage; she died two days later. She was 86.

When her own effects were sold at Drouot in November, the political resonance surrounding the auction of Zola's, more than two decades earlier, had somewhat dissipated. Instead, alongside respect for the deceased, what the newspapers underlined was the generosity of Alexandrine's gift to the Louvre of the three Manets that Zola had owned but which had been retained with a life interest after she formalized the bequest in 1918. Within a month of her death, *Le Petit Journal* had announced this legacy, highlighting that of Manet's 1868 portrait of her husband. The heading 'Zola au Louvre', in *Le Rappel* of 9 August 1925, provides a celebratory conclusion to any account of the paintings he owned. Zola's pioneering critical prediction that Manet would one day enter the pantheon of French art had been given, thanks to Alexandrine, who had witnessed at first hand his early writing on the visual arts, an appropriately personal dimension.

Zola's beloved Jeanne had died in May 1914, following a gynaecological operation. She was only 47. The daughter Zola had had by her, Denise, kept his flame alive by publishing fond memories of her father in a number of essays which formed the basis of her *Émile Zola raconté par sa fille* (1931). After Alexandrine's death, Denise took over responsibility for the annual literary pilgrimage to Médan. She married Maurice Le Blond (1877–1944) on 14 October 1908. Zola's letters to him in 1900–1901 suggest that he knew him principally as one of his admirers, greeting Le Blond's review of *Travail* with effusive thanks: 'in the midst of my profound distress as regards the present, the only thing which consoles me is your faith in a better future' (*Corr.*, X, 285). Denise's marriage to Le Blond also did much to ensure that Zola's work was not forgotten: notably Le Blond's publication in 1927–9, in collaboration with his wife, of the first edition of Zola's complete works, in fifty volumes. Denise died in 1942.

Her brother Jacques had been even more deeply affected by his father's sudden death. He had celebrated his eleventh birthday only four days earlier. In *Le Gaulois* of 6 October 1902, the reporter identifying various individuals in the funeral procession noticed in it a distressed small boy, his hand held by a bemedalled gentleman, and wondered whether he was Zola's son. It seems unlikely: other witnesses of the occasion noted that Jeanne Rozerot and her two children were in the crowd outside the rue de Bruxelles; Denise remembered that they were comforted there by the Triouleyre couple. Zola's letters to Jeanne from England never failed to convey his thanks to this couple for the support they gave her during his exile, and they figure in his photographs in the summer of 1899. But even the journalist's question confirms that Zola's double life was no longer a secret. If Denise's role in sustaining her father's memory was important, even more significant and enduring was that of Jacques as the keeper of an enormous family archive, to which he added Zola's letters and manuscripts collected throughout his life. By giving modern scholars access to it in the years immediately prior to his death in 1963, Jacques Émile-Zola was as instrumental in the renewal of interest in his father's work as in his co-founding in 1955 of the specialist academic journal *Les Cahiers naturalistes*. During the Second World War, he was a decorated member of the Resistance. Appropriately enough, the son of the author of *Le Docteur Pascal* and *La Bête humaine* had spent his career as a doctor: employed successively by a provincial railway company and the SNCF. In due course, his own son (Zola's grandson, François) would also become a doctor.

This book began by alluding to the fact that the revival of interest in Zola's life and work, to which his son had contributed behind the scenes, coincided with the 1952 anniversary of his death. It was also the moment when that death was itself the subject of renewed investigation. It was partly prompted by speculation about what Zola might have gone on to do had he not died at the age of 62, given that the autopsy had revealed that his general health was such that he should have had many years still ahead of him. This had been raised as early as in an article in *Le Temps* of 1 October 1902 commenting on Zola's 'stupid death'. The ensuing inquest, while apparently conclusive, had left unresolved a number of questions: most baffling was the fact that several simulations of the circumstances had, on one occasion only, asphyxiated two of the birds placed in the smoke-filled room, but had never produced sufficient carbon monoxide to be fatal for the guinea pigs also used in the experiment, let alone for a human being. Inspection of the chimney, swept annually, revealed the same quantity of soot as had failed to block it when a fire had been lit in mid-June, before Zola and his wife had left for Médan.

Nationalist and antisemitic newspapers like Drumont's *Libre Parole* suggested that, on account of his guilt at having 'harmed France' during the Dreyfus Affair, Zola had committed suicide. This left unexplained, of course, Alexandrine's falling unconscious too, let alone that the small dog on the end of the couple's high four-poster bed had visibly been taken unwell. She and the dog had been saved by virtue of their distance from the floor to which Zola himself had fallen. The less invidious hypothesis very tentatively put forward by some of the experts contracted for the inquest was that the chimney must have become obstructed at some stage during the Zolas' absence from their Paris address. Eyewitness accounts, but after the fact, spoke of men working on the roof of an adjacent property at the time. Added to these uncertainties was another troubling dimension for those no longer content to subscribe to the inquest's conclusion that Zola's death had been an accident: the examining magistrate leading it had arrived at such a conclusion with unseemly haste, perhaps as a result of external pressure; in the simmering aftermath of the Dreyfus Affair, the last thing the government needed was any other version of what had happened to Zola.

Exploiting all the above, Jean Bedel (1911–2005) published in 1953 the results of his own investigations under the sensational heading of 'Zola a-t-il été assassiné?' (Was Zola Murdered?). Bedel was at the start of a career which would see him becoming one of the most prominent contemporary French journalists. The question mark at this stage suggested doubts short of an assertion. More might be levelled at the fact that Bedel's pointing the finger at right-wing fanatics was consistent with the anti-establishment demonology of *Libération*, the daily in which, between 29 September and 2 October, he produced his evidence for their probable criminality. It could not, however, be lightly dismissed. It was based on a 1928 (not the year before as it was originally misremembered) confession made to a friend by a fitter of heating appliances, a month before his death from a heart attack, that he had blocked up the Zolas' chimney shortly before their return to Paris on 28 September 1902 and removed the obstruction the next day.

The reliability of the friend in question, Pierre Hacquin, was an obvious potential problem: but that he was a serious professional journalist and aspiring provincial politician was the unambiguous impression left on all Zola's biographers who interviewed him between 1953 and his death in 1970. They stressed that he was in full command of his faculties. This does not quite fit with Hemmings's characterization of Hacquin as 'a 68-year-old correspondent of [*Libération*] who chose this way of unburdening himself of certain confidences'. A less pejorative residual scepticism lay in the pertinent question Hemmings asked (in the 1966 revised edition of his classic study of the novelist), as to how any perpetrator could have known that the chimney in question came from the bedroom and in which smokeless (and thus invisible) fuel had been laid; a decade later, Hemmings remained judiciously uncertain: 'Though there is nothing inherently improbable in this version of events, the degree of uncorroborated testimony and unverifiable assertion' left it open to doubt.[5]

The version of the confession to which Hacquin had allegedly been party, transcribed in the 1 October 1953 issue of *Libération*, was given added credibility, however, by Bedel's subsequent revelation, in 1978, that the name of the presumed assassin was Henri Buronfosse (1874–1928). The archives identified him as belonging to the Ligue des patriotes, a working-class association of anti-Dreyfusard militants; its guiding light was Paul Déroulède (1846–1914), who had led an abortive nationalist uprising in February 1899. Such were his prejudices that it was he who had shouted out during Zola's 1898 trial 'Go back to Venice.' Research confirmed that, although not always resident in the capital itself, Buronfosse was plying his trade in Paris between 1900 and the First World War. But those trawling through the extant official files were also struck by the fact that members of his immediate family, living with him, suffered from the kind of psychological condition (prone to delusion and paranoia) which could possibly have coloured his confession – a 'deathbed' one perhaps made in the knowledge that his diagnosed cardiac problems meant he had not long to live; or the confession may have been motivated by pretensions of self-importance in imagining he had played a crucial role in an event as historic as Zola's death. There was also the curious discovery that, only after 1902, Buronfosse had intermittently, but unaccountably, inserted 'Émile' in registering his forenames on bureaucratic paperwork. That too, however, could be interpreted in various ways: as a sign of mental instability; as an admission of another sort of guilt, related to professional incompetence; or as a bit of tomfoolery gone wrong.

At first sight, Bedel's hypothesis remains plausible: during the Dreyfus Affair, Zola had received so many death threats that he required police protection; during his 1898 trials, the more extreme members of the nationalist press went as far as suggesting how he might be physically attacked on emerging from the courtroom into the less protected street; on 31 July 1901, a home-made explosive device, easily defused, had been placed in the entrance to his Paris residence. He would not live to see, of course, the wounding of Dreyfus at the Panthéon ceremony, let alone the 1914 assassination by right-wing extremists of Jean Jaurès, one of the most high-profile of his allies during the Affair (who, in 1924, would himself be interred beside Zola in the Panthéon). But the bullet fired into Labori's back in Rennes in August 1899 had left Zola and his family under no illusion about the violent lengths to which the anti-Dreyfusards were prepared to go. Faced with Bedel's conspiracy theories, Zola's son needed no further persuasion, recalling (in an interview published in *Le Monde* of 6 October 1953) that his mother, on being told of Zola's death, instantly concluded that he had been murdered. Denise's 1931 memoirs, referred to above, were equally specific.

Over the decades since this sinister version of Zola's death hit the headlines, his admirers have tended to lend credence to the evidence, thereby overlaying on his heroic life and writing a sanctification over and above that afforded by the Panthéon: that of martyrdom on the altar of Justice and Truth. By the time he published *Zola assassiné* in 2002, coinciding opportunely with the centenary of Zola's death, Bedel's own question mark half a century earlier had been eliminated. He died in 2005, six weeks short of his 95th birthday. With participants in his story now much longer dead, the most scrupulous reconstruction, published in 2002, of the facts and hypotheses surrounding the writer's death could go no further, however, than referring to the events of the night of 28 September 1902 as an 'enigma'.[6]

The 2014 publication of Zola's letters to his wife is only potentially more enlightening. They do reveal that, from 1896 onwards, he was intermittently worried by the chimneys and roof of their Paris apartment. In October 1899 Zola was again having problems with its heating system: he reported to Alexandrine (in Italy at the time) that it was not working properly; a man had just fixed it, but so late in the day that he had arranged to have a fire lit in his study instead in order to provide a warm welcome for his guests. On that chilly evening of 12 October, however, this room had so filled with noxious fumes that the assembled dinner party had had to escape into the street, staying there until 10 p.m. while the smoke billowing from the opened windows had led neighbours to think that the townhouse itself was on fire. Zola told Alexandrine that it was a mystery how this had occurred but would get hold of a chimney sweep first thing next morning. Her awareness of these repeated instances of their fireplaces not drawing efficiently, as also reported in *Le Constitutionnel* of 2 October 1902, may explain why Alexandrine, at least, never doubted the inquest's conclusion – nor wanted to, given the risk that any further inquiries would delay her regaining a semblance of peace of mind. The conversation that evening, Zola told her, had inevitably focused on the 'never-ending Affair'. And he added that, after it was safe to go back inside, one of his guests, Desmoulin, had claimed that 'anti-Dreyfusards had climbed on to the roof to block up our chimneys' (*LA*, 530). On the one hand, this was eerily prophetic. On the other, what is unknowable is both the tone of the original remark and that of Zola's reporting of it: whether in jest on Desmoulin's part, to lighten the atmosphere after the little domestic drama, and, on Zola's, to reassure his wife, or, more ominously, to be taken seriously.

That still leaves the 'enigma' unresolved. But, in retrospect, such uncertainty perhaps provides an appropriate conclusion to this book. Zola was either the victim of chance, subject to a set of arbitrary circumstances so inexplicable as to personalize insights in his fiction at odds with deterministic principles; or, as was his life, his death too was indirectly determined by the social and political forces of his times.

REFERENCES

Introduction

1 Hemmings obituary, David Baguley, *The Independent*, 21 May 1997.
2 There have been of course a number of biographies of Zola during the last fifty years: notably by Joanna Richardson (London, 1978), Philip Walker (London and Boston, MA, 1985) and Frederick Brown (New York, 1995). See also Gillian Tindall, 'On Zola's Lives', *Encounter*, LXIX/5 (1987), pp. 71–7, prompted by the appearance of Alan Schom's *Emile Zola: A Bourgeois Rebel* (London, 1987), a book dismissed by F.W.J. Hemmings (in the *TLS*, 9–15 September 1988) as both 'ludicrous' and so 'misleading' that 'the wonder is that it should ever have found a publisher'; it was nevertheless reissued in paperback in February 2021! Hemmings's own *The Life and Times of Emile Zola* (London, 1977), aimed at the general reader, justifies its claim to be complementary to his classic study (*Émile Zola*, Oxford, 2nd edn, 1966) mainly by virtue of its splendid illustrations. By far the most authoritative and admiring (in the French tradition) *summa* is Henri Mitterand's encyclopedic, three-volume (and 3,000-page) *Zola* (Paris, 1999–2002).
3 Édouard Toulouse, *Enquête médico-psychologique sur la supériorité intellectuelle. Émile Zola* (Paris, 1896), pp. 250–52.
4 John Lapp, *Zola before the 'Rougon-Macquart'* (Toronto, 1964), p. 4.
5 Edmond and Jules de Goncourt, *Journal. Mémoires de la vie littéraire*, 3 vols, ed. Robert Ricatte (Paris, 1956), vol. II, p. 1337 (entry for 5 April 1886).
6 Paul Alexis, *Émile Zola: notes d'un ami* (Paris, 1882), p. 39.
7 Goncourt, *Journal*, vol. II, p. 925.
8 Letter to Zola of 19 November 1865; in Colette Becker, 'Un ami de jeunesse d'Émile Zola: Georges Pajot. Lettres inédites', *Les Cahiers naturalistes*, 53 (1979), pp. 95–123 (p. 118).
9 See Evelyne Bloch-Dano, *Madame Zola* (Paris, 1997), pp. 11–20.
10 Marie-Ange Voisin-Fougère, *L'Ironie naturaliste: Zola et les paradoxes du sérieux* (Paris, 2001); and Voisin-Fougère, ed., *Zola et le rire* (Dijon, 2003).
11 Sharon Marcus, *Apartment Stories* (Berkeley, CA, 1999), p. 194 (facing a reproduction of the caricature).
12 Henry James, *The House of Fiction* (London, 1957), p. 224.
13 Hemmings, *Émile Zola*, p. 51.

1 Origins

1 In the preface to Jacques Dhur, *Le Père d'Émile Zola. Les prétendues lettres Combe(s): lettre à M. le Procureur de la République* (Paris, 1899), p. i.
2 Alain Pagès and Owen Morgan, *Guide Émile Zola* (Paris, 2002), p. 8.
3 Fernand Xau, *Émile Zola* (Paris, 1880), pp. 15–17.
4 Renée Baligand, 'Lettres inédites d'Antoine Guillemet à Émile Zola (1866–70)', *Les Cahiers naturalistes*, 52 (1978), p. 182.
5 Paul Alexis, in his authorized biography and thus with Zola's approval, was explicit in this respect; see his *Émile Zola: notes d'un ami* (Paris, 1882), p. 13.
6 F.W.J. Hemmings, *Émile Zola*, 2nd edn (Oxford, 1966), p. 6.
7 Denise Le Blond-Zola, *Émile Zola raconté par sa fille* (Paris, 1931), p. 12.
8 Henri Mitterand, *Zola*, 3 vols (Paris, 1999–2002), vol. I, pp. 17–19; and Mitterand, *Zola: la mort du père* (Paris, 2021).
9 *RM*, II, p. 1253; and Alexis, *Émile Zola*, p. 18.
10 Jean Borie, *Zola et les mythes; Ou, de la nausée au salut* (Paris, 1971), pp. 79–80.
11 Hemmings, *Émile Zola*, pp. 6–9.
12 Angus Wilson, *Emile Zola: An Introductory Study of His Novels* (London, 1952; revised edn 1964), p. 11.
13 Le Blond-Zola, *Émile Zola*, p. 69.
14 Alexis, *Émile Zola*, p. 105.
15 See Olivier Lumbroso, *Les Manuscrits et les dessins de Zola: l'invention des lieux* (Paris, 2002).
16 Edmond and Jules de Goncourt, *Journal. Mémoires de la vie littéraire*, 3 vols, ed. Robert Ricatte (Paris, 1956), vol. II, p. 187 (entry for 14 December 1868).
17 Le Blond-Zola, *Émile Zola*, pp. 130–31.
18 Alexis, *Émile Zola*, p. 190.
19 Goncourt, *Journal*, vol. II, p. 928 (entry for 6 March 1882).
20 See David Baguley, 'L'Indicible de la sexualité dans l'œuvre de Zola', *Nineteenth-Century French Studies*, 27 (1998–9), pp. 108–16.
21 Remarks originally recorded in *La Revue blanche* of 1 March 1902, reprinted in 'Émile Zola: Tolstoï et la question sexuelle', *Les Cahiers naturalistes*, 20 (1962), pp. 171–3.
22 Robert Nye, *Masculinity and Male Codes of Honor in Modern France* (New York, 1993), pp. 120–21.
23 'À la mémoire d'Émile Zola', in the 1907 edn of Saint-Paul's *Archives d'anthropologie criminelle*, pp. 825–41. The annotation for Zola's letter of 25 June 1895 (*OC*, XII, 753–4) provides details of the parts of Saint-Paul's study into which the novelist's contribution is inserted.
24 See Anne E. Linton, *Unmaking Sex: The Gender Outlaws of Nineteenth-Century France* (Cambridge, 2022), pp. 137–69.
25 Goncourt, *Journal*, vol. II, p. 1134 (entry for 5 May 1876).
26 Mitterand, *Zola*, vol. I, p. 93; Joanna Richardson, *Zola* (London, 1978), p. 5. The most penetrating analysis of the incident's ramifications is Hannah Thompson, *Taboo: Corporeal Secrets in Nineteenth-Century France* (London, 2013), pp. 125–39.

27 See the inventory of such incidents compiled by Shoshana-Rose Marzel, 'Abus sexuels sur mineurs dans *Les Rougon-Macquart* et *Vérité*', *Les Cahiers naturalistes*, 97 (2023), pp. 199–212. While Zola only changed the victim's gender in *Vérité* to meet the imperatives of verisimilitude (on account of the rapist not having access to the separate space for girls in the segregated school in which he works), the description of the crime is specifically focused on the young male body.
28 Richardson, *Zola*, p. 57.
29 Goncourt, *Journal*, vol. III, p. 350 (entry for 21 November 1889).
30 Ibid., vol. II, p. 699 (entry for 5 May 1876).
31 Ibid., vol. III, p. 219 (entry for 22 January 1889).
32 Naomi Schor, *Zola's Crowds* (Baltimore, MD, 1978), p. xi.

2 Apprenticeships

1 F.W.J. Hemmings, *The Life and Times of Emile Zola* (London, 1977), p. 13.
2 'In the Days of My Youth', *The Bookman* (December 1901).
3 Ibid., p. 343.
4 See Émile Zola, *Carnets d'enquêtes: une ethnographie inédite de la France*, ed. Henri Mitterand (Paris, 1986).
5 This suggestion is made in her documented study of the firm during Zola's years working for it: Colette Becker, 'Zola à la librairie Hachette (1862–1866)', *Revue de l'université d'Ottawa/University of Ottawa Quarterly*, XLVIII/4 (1978), pp. 287–309. Some other sections of the present chapter are also inevitably indebted to Becker's synoptic account: Becker, *Les Apprentissages de Zola* (Paris, 1993).
6 In this respect, the comprehensive analysis of Zola's literary criticism across the whole of his career is François Mourad's *Zola critique littéraire* (Paris, 2003).
7 Nicholas Hewitt, *Wicked City: The Many Cultures of Marseille* (London, 2019), p. 32. Hewitt provides the most precise comparison ever undertaken between the real and fictional geographies of the novel (pp. 29–35).
8 F.W.J. Hemmings, *Émile Zola*, 2nd edn (Oxford, 1966), p. 4; Hewitt (*Wicked City*, p. 30) describes it as a 'literary curiosity'.
9 These letters are cited by J. C. Lapp in his 'Taine et Zola: autour d'une correspondance', *Revue des sciences humaines*, 87 (1957), pp. 319–26.
10 Martin Kanes, 'Zola, Pelletan and *La Tribune*', *PMLA*, 79 (1964), pp. 473–83 (p. 479).
11 Paul Alexis, *Émile Zola: notes d'un ami* (Paris, 1882), pp. 202–3.
12 Angus Wilson, *Emile Zola: An Introductory Study of His Novels* (London, 1952; revised edn 1964), p. 117.
13 For a less abbreviated account, see my *Zola's Painters* (Cambridge, 2022).
14 Léon Laurent-Pichat, in *Le Phare de la Loire*, 16 June 1868.
15 Edmond and Jules de Goncourt, *Journal. Mémoires de la vie littéraire*, 3 vols, ed. Robert Ricatte (Paris, 1956), vol. II, pp. 186–7 (entry for 14 December 1868).
16 Armand Silvestre, *Au pays des souvenirs* (Paris, 1892), p. 159.
17 For example, Henri Mitterand, 'Un jeune homme de province à Paris: Émile Zola de 1858 à 1861', *Les Cahiers naturalistes*, 11 (1958), pp. 444–53.

3 Writing the *Rougon-Macquart* I: From Planning to Realization

1 See Rachel Chrastil, *Bismarck's War: The Franco-Prussian War and the Making of Modern Europe* (London, 2023).
2 In *La Marseillaise*, reprinted in *Le Messager de Provence*, 25–6 October 1870. Cited by Roger Ripoll, 'Quelques articles retrouvés de *La Marseillaise*', *Les Cahiers naturalistes*, 34 (1967), p. 163.
3 Quoted by Ernest Vizetelly in his preface to *The Downfall* (London, 1899), p. vi, recording Zola's interview with Robert H. Sherard, editor of the *Weekly Times and Echo*, in which the translation of *La Débâcle* had originally been serialized.
4 Henry James, 'Letter from Paris: *Son Excellence Eugène Rougon*', *New York Tribune*, 13 May 1876.
5 Cited by Roger Ripoll, 'Zola et les Communards', *Europe*, 468–9 (1968), p. 19.
6 Ibid., p. 17 (*Le Sémaphore de Marseille*, 3 June 1871).
7 Reproduced by David Baguley in the appendices to his critical edition of *La Fortune des Rougon* (Paris, 2015), pp. 495–6.
8 David Charles has argued otherwise, detecting in Zola's 1871 revisions to the serial text a hardening, in the light of his hostility to the Commune, of his depiction of the novel's revolutionary crowd; see his 'La Révision de *La Fortune des Rougon*', in Charles, *Émile Zola et la Commune de Paris* (Paris, 2017), pp. 25–71. Baguley (see above, note 7), on the other hand, concludes that all the revisions are essentially stylistic.
9 Fernand Xau, *Émile Zola* (Paris, 1880), p. 51.
10 See Colette Wilson, *Paris and the Commune, 1871–1878: The Politics of Forgetting* (Manchester, 2007), pp. 144–57; and Wilson, '*Une page d'amour*: un panorama politique', *Les Cahiers naturalistes*, 76 (2002), pp. 177–91.
11 Jann Matlock, 'Everyday Ghosts: *La Curée* in the Shadow of the Commune', *Romanic Review*, CII/3–4 (2011), pp. 321–47.
12 Letter of 20 April 1875; cited by John Lapp, 'Taine et Zola: autour d'une correspondance', *Revue des sciences humaines*, 87 (1957), pp. 319–26 (p. 324).
13 Letter to Zola of 15 February 1880; in Gustave Flaubert, *Correspondance*, 5 vols, ed. Jean Bruneau and Yvan Leclerc (Paris, 1973–2013), vol. V, pp. 883–4.
14 Letter of 28 October 1870; ibid., vol. IV, pp. 253–4.
15 Letter to Zola towards the end of April 1878; ibid., vol. V, p. 378. The emphasis (the erotic *excité* in the original French) is Flaubert's own.
16 Edmond and Jules de Goncourt, *Journal. Mémoires de la vie littéraire*, 3 vols, ed. Robert Ricatte (Paris, 1956), vol. II, p. 739 (entry for 5 May 1877).
17 As Peter Brooks puts it in his *Henry James Goes to Paris* (Princeton, NJ, 2007), p. 36.

4 Writing the *Rougon-Macquart* II: Naturalism and Beyond

1 Jackie Wullschläger, *Monet: The Restless Vision* (London, 2023), p. xix.
2 Edmond and Jules de Goncourt, *Journal. Mémoires de la vie littéraire*, 3 vols, ed. Robert Ricatte (Paris, 1956), vol. II, pp. 728–9.
3 *La Vérité est en marche et rien ne l'arrêtera*, catalogue for Maison Zola–Musée Dreyfus (Médan, 2023).
4 Kate Griffiths, '*La Terre* and the Art of Inheritance', in Griffiths, *Emile Zola and the Artistry of Adaptation* (London, 2009), pp. 12–36.
5 Goncourt, *Journal*, vol. II, pp. 777–8 (entry for 6 May 1878).
6 Naomi Schor, *Zola's Crowds* (Baltimore, MD, 1978), p. 77.
7 Paul Alexis, *Émile Zola: notes d'un ami* (Paris, 1882), p. 125.
8 Michel Serres, *Feux et signaux de brume*: *Zola* (Paris, 1975), pp. 24–7.
9 Goncourt, *Journal*, vol. III, p. 414 (entry for 17 April 1890).
10 Martin Kanes, *Zola's 'La Bête humaine': A Study in Literary Creation* (Berkeley, CA, 1962).
11 Cited by Alain Pagès, *Zola et le groupe de Médan. Histoire d'un cercle littéraire* (Paris, 2014), p. 373.
12 Cited in Micheline Hanotelle, 'Léo Gausson et Zola: réflexions relatives à une lettre du peintre Léo Gausson à Émile Zola et réponse inédite du romancier', *Les Cahiers naturalistes*, 63 (1989), pp. 193–203.
13 Goncourt, *Journal*, vol. II, p. 949 (entry for 6 July 1882).
14 Jules Huret, *Enquête sur l'évolution littéraire* (Paris, 1891), p. 169.

5 The Last Chapters of a Writing Life

1 Cited from Zola's 'Notes sur Londres', edited by Colin Burns within his comprehensive study of Zola's visit: 'Le Voyage de Zola à Londres en 1893', *Les Cahiers naturalistes*, 60 (1986), pp. 41–75 (p. 65).
2 So Goncourt recorded in his diary entry for 6 March 1892; Edmond and Jules de Goncourt, *Journal. Mémoires de la vie littéraire*, 3 vols, ed. Robert Ricatte (Paris, 1956), vol. III, p. 675.
3 *Le Journal*, 15 September 1897; cited by Alain Pagès and Owen Morgan in their *Guide Émile Zola* (Paris, 2002), p. 318.
4 Henri Mitterand, 'La Révolte et l'utopie: de *Germinal* à *Travail*', in Mitterand, *Le Discours du roman* (Paris, 1980), pp. 150–63 (p. 163).

6 Public and Private Lives

1 Alain Pagès, *Émile Zola, un intellectuel dans l'Affaire Dreyfus* (Paris, 1991).
2 Bernard-Lazare, *Une erreur judiciaire: la vérité sur l'Affaire Dreyfus* (94 pp.) (Paris, 1896); *Une erreur judiciaire: l'Affaire Dreyfus (deuxième mémoire avec des expertises d'écritures)* (304 pp.) (Paris, 1897); *Comment on condamne un innocent: l'acte d'accusation contre le capitaine Dreyfus* (23 pp.) (Paris, 1898).
3 Ruth Harris, *The Man on Devil's Island: Alfred Dreyfus and the Affair that Divided France* (London, 2010), p. 109.
4 Ibid., p. 110.

5 On the publication details of this letter, see my 'The End of the Affair: Zola and Cézanne', *French Studies Bulletin*, 133 (2014), pp. 95–9.
6 Edmond and Jules de Goncourt, *Journal. Mémoires de la vie littéraire*, 3 vols, ed. Robert Ricatte (Paris, 1956), vol. III, p. 826 (entry for 14 May 1893).
7 Ibid., vol. III, p. 825.
8 As reported by Ambroise Vollard, *En écoutant Cézanne, Degas, Renoir* (Paris, 2003), pp. 115–16.
9 Ernest Vizetelly, *Émile Zola, Novelist and Reformer: An Account of His Life and Work* (London, 1904), p. 489; cited in Alain Pagès and Owen Morgan, *Guide Émile Zola* (Paris, 2002), p. 142, from where figures for comparative incomes are drawn.
10 Goncourt, *Journal*, vol. II, p. 949 (entry for 6 July 1882).
11 Ibid., vol. III, pp. 105 and 173–4.
12 *Émile Zola et la photographie: une page d'amour* (Paris, 2023).
13 Bertrand Tillier, *Cochon de Zola; ou, Les infortunes caricaturales d'un écrivain engagé* (Paris, 1998).
14 Denise Le Blond-Zola, *Émile Zola raconté par sa fille* (Paris, 1931), p. 267.
15 Goncourt, *Journal*, vol. II, p. 990 (entry for 20 February 1883).
16 Anatole France, *Vers les temps meilleurs* (Paris, 1949), pp. 117–20. The full text of each of the funeral orations was reprinted in most newspapers covering the occasion.

Epilogue

1 Henri Rochefort, 'L'Amour du laid', *L'Intransigeant*, 3 March 1903.
2 Ruth Butler, *Rodin: The Shape of Genius* (New Haven, CT, and London, 1993), p. 345.
3 Cited by Gustave Geffroy, *Claude Monet: sa vie et son œuvre* (Paris, 1980), p. 358.
4 Cited by Anne Higonnet, *Berthe Morisot's Images of Women* (London, 1992), p. 25.
5 F.W.J. Hemmings, *Émile Zola*, 2nd edn (Oxford, 1966), pp. 303–4; Hemmings, *The Life and Times of Emile Zola* (London, 1977), p. 183.
6 Alain Pagès and Owen Morgan, 'Une énigme: la mort', in Pagès and Morgan, *Guide Émile Zola* (Paris, 2002), pp. 163–80.

SELECT BIBLIOGRAPHY

Works in French

There are innumerable paperback editions of Zola's works available in the original French. I have translated the quotations cited in this book from the following scholarly editions:

Les Rougon-Macquart, ed. Henri Mitterand, 5 vols (Paris, 1960–67)
Œuvres complètes, ed. Henri Mitterand, 15 vols (Paris, 1966–70)
Correspondance, ed. Bard Bakker et al., 10 vols (Montreal and Paris, 1978–95)
Écrits sur l'art, ed. Robert Lethbridge (Paris, 2021)

Translations into English

The Attack on the Mill and Other Stories, trans. and ed. Douglas Parmée (Oxford, 1984)
The Dreyfus Affair: 'J'Accuse' and Other Writings, trans. Eleanor Levieux, ed. Alain Pagès (New Haven, CT, and London, 1996)
Thérèse Raquin, trans. and ed. Andrew Rothwell (Oxford, 2008)
The *Rougon-Macquart* (listed below in order of the date of their original publication in French). These have all been published by Oxford University Press in their 'Oxford World's Classics' series:

The Fortune of the Rougons (*La Fortune des Rougon*, 1871), trans. and ed. Brian Nelson (2012)
The Kill (*La Curée*, 1872), trans. and ed. Brian Nelson (2008)
The Belly of Paris (*Le Ventre de Paris*, 1873), trans. and ed. Brian Nelson (2009)
The Conquest of Plassans (*La Conquête de Plassans*, 1874), trans. Helen Constantine, ed. Patrick McGuinness (2014)
The Sin of Abbé Mouret (*La Faute de l'Abbé Mouret*, 1875), trans. and ed. Valerie Minogue (2017)
His Excellency Eugène Rougon (*Son Excellence Eugène Rougon*, 1876), trans. and ed. Brian Nelson (2018)
The Assommoir (*L'Assommoir*, 1877), trans. Brian Nelson, ed. Robert Lethbridge (2021)

A Love Story (*Une page d'amour*, 1878), trans. Helen Constantine, ed. Brian Nelson (2017)
Nana (*Nana*, 1880), trans. Helen Constantine, ed. Brian Nelson (2020)
Pot Luck (*Pot-Bouille*, 1882), trans. and ed. Brian Nelson (2009)
The Ladies' Paradise (*Au bonheur des dames*, 1883), trans. and ed. Brian Nelson (2008)
The Bright Side of Life (*La Joie de vivre*, 1884), trans. and ed. Andrew Rothwell (2018)
Germinal (*Germinal*, 1885), trans. Peter Collier, ed. Robert Lethbridge (2008)
The Masterpiece (*L'Œuvre*, 1886), trans. Thomas Walton, ed. Roger Pearson (2008)
Earth (*La Terre*, 1887), trans. Julie Rose, ed. Brian Nelson (2016)
The Dream (*Le Rêve*, 1888), trans. and ed. Paul Gibbard (2018)
La Bête humaine (*La Bête humaine*, 1890), trans. Thomas Walton, ed. Roger Pearson (2009)
Money (*L'Argent*, 1891), trans. and ed. Valerie Minogue (2014)
La Débâcle (*La Débâcle*, 1892), trans. Elinor Dorday, ed. Robert Lethbridge (2017)
Doctor Pascal (*Le Docteur Pascal*, 1893), trans. Julie Rose, ed. Brian Nelson (2020)

Bibliographies of critical studies on Zola and Naturalism

Bibliographie de la critique sur Emile Zola, ed. David Baguley: vol. I (1864–1970); vol. II (1970–80) (Toronto, 1976, 1982)
Les Cahiers naturalistes publishes an annual bibliography on this specialist journal's website: www.cahiers-naturalistes.com

Other material related to Zola can be found on www.archives-zoliennes.fr

Book-length studies of Zola and Naturalism in English

Baguley, David, *Naturalist Fiction: The Entropic Vision* (Cambridge, 1990)
—, *Emile Zola: 'L'Assommoir'* (Cambridge, 1992)
Berg, William J., *The Visual Novel: Emile Zola and the Art of His Times* (Philadelphia, PA, 1992)
Brown, Frederick, *Zola: A Life* (London, 1995)
Butler, Ronnie, *Zola: 'La Terre'* (London, 1984)
Clark, Roger, *Zola: 'Nana'* (London, 2004)
Cousins, Russell, *Zola: 'Thérèse Raquin'* (London, 1992)
Grant, Richard B., *Zola's 'Son Excellence Eugène Rougon'* (Durham, NC, 1960)
Griffiths, Kate, *Emile Zola and the Artistry of Adaptation* (London, 2009)
Harrow, Susan, *Zola: The Body Modern* (Oxford, 2010)
Hemmings, F.W.J., *Émile Zola*, 2nd edn (Oxford, 1966)
—, *The Life and Times of Emile Zola* (London, 1977)
Kanes, Martin, *Zola's 'La Bête humaine': A Study in Literary Creation* (Berkeley, CA, 1962)
Lapp, John C., *Zola before the 'Rougon-Macquart'* (Toronto, 1964)

Lethbridge, Robert, *Zola's Painters* (Cambridge, 2022)
—, and Terry Keefe, eds, *Zola and the Craft of Fiction* (Leicester, 1990)
Minogue, Valerie, *Zola: 'L'Assommoir'* (London, 1991)
Mitterand, Henri, *Émile Zola: Fiction and Modernity*, trans. and ed. Monica Lebron and David Baguley (London, 2000)
Nelson, Brian, *Zola and the Bourgeoisie* (London, 1983)
—, *Émile Zola: A Very Short Introduction* (Oxford, 2020)
—, ed., *The Cambridge Companion to Zola* (Cambridge, 2007)
Niess, Robert J., *Zola and Cézanne: A Study of 'L'Œuvre'* (Ann Arbor, MI, 1968)
Richardson, Joanna, *Zola* (London, 1978)
Schor, Naomi, *Zola's Crowds* (Baltimore, MD, 1978)
Smethurst, Colin, *Zola: 'Germinal'* (London, 1974)
Thompson, Hannah, *Naturalism Redressed: Identity and Clothing in the Novels of Emile Zola* (Oxford, 2004)
Wilson, Angus, *Emile Zola: An Introductory Study of His Novels* [1952] (London, 1964)

ACKNOWLEDGEMENTS

My most recent debt is to Anne Green, who kindly read every page of this book in draft. Her invaluable insights were subsequently reinforced by advice from Vivian Constantinopoulos, notably in the reorganization of what were once two indigestibly extended chapters. She and her team at Reaktion have been enormously helpful, not least the work put in on the illustrations by Susannah Jayes. In sourcing a number of these, thanks are also due to Jean-Sébastien Macke at the Zola Research Centre in Paris; Bruno Martin of the French Ministry of Culture; and Martine Le Blond-Zola, Zola's great-granddaughter, who generously made accessible material archived in the Maison Zola–Musée Dreyfus at Médan. Alain Pagès, the leading Zola scholar of this generation, has provided information, often corrective, throughout the writing of this book. A more long-standing debt is to the late Henri Mitterand, the *doyen* of Zola studies over the past half-century, whose friendship and encouragement have inspired my own work on the writer during the whole of that same period.

PHOTO ACKNOWLEDGEMENTS

The author and publishers wish to express their thanks to the below sources of illustrative material and/or permission to reproduce it:

Author's collection: p. 46; Collection Association du Musée Emile Zola: p. 68; Collection Maison Zola–Musée Dreyfus: pp. 26, 29; *Illustrated London News*: p. 265; Library of Congress, Washington, DC: p. 39; © Ministère de la Culture, France: p. 40; Wikimedia Commons (All Public Domain): pp. 8 (Ancienne collection François Émile-Zola/artcurial.com), 17 (Museum of Photographic Arts), 18 (André Gill/Bnf Gallica), 31 (Amgueddfa Cymru – Museum Wales), 34 (unknown author/cleaned by Malost), 47 (*Une page d'amour*, Gallica/Emile Zola), 73 (Zeno Fotografie), 81 (Hathi Trust), 85 (Félix Nadar), 86 (https://expositions.bnf.fr), 98 (Musée d'Orsay/Google Art Project), 102 (National Gallery of Art, Washington, DC/Collection of Mr and Mrs Paul Mellon), 104 (Art Institute of Chicago), 105 (Private Collection/The Yorck Project, 2002), 108 (Musée d'Orsay/The Yorck Project, 2002), 122 (São Paulo Museum of Art), 158 (Zeno Fotografie), 168 (Félix Nadar/Gallica Digital Library), 198 (Félix Nadar), 230 (scan of *L'Aurore*, 1898), 232 (Zeno Fotografie), 237 (Zeno Fotografie), 239 (unknown), 242 (Zeno Fotografie), 246 (Ancienne collection François Émile-Zola/artcurial.com), 247 (Félix Nadar/ *Contemporary French Novelists* by René Doumic (from https://archive.org), 248 (unknown), 249 (Zeno Fotografie), 252 (Musée de l'Hôtel de Ville, Amboise), 260 (*Caran d'Ache, Le Musée des horreurs*, no. 4, 1899), 264 (*Ilustracya Polska*, no. 41, 1902), 271 (https://expositions.bnf.fr).

INDEX

Page numbers in *italics* refer to illustrations